NATIONAL UNIVERSITY
LIBRARY

THE
Knowledge
Executive

047311

BY HARLAN CLEVELAND

Next Step in Asia (1949) with John K. Fairbank, Edwin O. Reischauer, and William L. Holland

The Overseas Americans (1960) with Gerard J. Mangone and John Clarke Adams

The Obligations of Power (1966)

NATO: The Transatlantic Bargain (1970)

The Future Executive: A Guide for Tomorrow's Managers (1972)

China Diary (1976)

The Third Try at World Order: U.S. Policy for an Interdependent World (1977)

Humangrowth: An Essay on Growth, Values and the Quality of Life (1978) with Thomas W. Wilson, Jr.

EDITED BY HARLAN CLEVELAND

The Art of Overseasmanship (1957) with Gerard J. Mangone

The Promise of World Tensions (1961)

The Ethic of Power: The Interplay of Religion, Philosophy and Politics (1962) with Harold D. Lasswell

Ethics and Bigness: Scientific, Academic, Religious, Political and Military (1962) with Harold D. Lasswell

Energy Futures of Developing Countries: The Neglected Victims of the Energy Crisis (1980)

Bioresources for Development: The Renewable Way of Life (1980) with Alexander King and Guy Streatfeild.

The Management of Sustainable Growth (1981)

HARLAN CLEVELAND

THE
Knowledge
Executive

LEADERSHIP IN AN INFORMATION
SOCIETY

NORTH COUNTY

T·T TRUMAN TALLEY BOOKS / E. P. DUTTON / NEW YORK

Grateful acknowledgment is made for permission to reprint copyright material:

From "Choruses from the Rock" in Collected Poems: 1909–1962 by T. S. Eliot, copyright 1936 by Harcourt Brace Jovanovich, Inc.; copyright © 1963, 1964 by T. S. Eliot. Reprinted by permission of the publisher.
From Russell Baker, "The Ship of Followers," The New York Times, November 13, 1979. Copyright © 1979 by The New York Times Company. Reprinted by permission.

Copyright © 1985 by Harlan Cleveland

All rights reserved. Printed in the U.S.A.

No part of this publication may be reproduced or transmitted in any form or by any means, electronic or mechanical, including photocopy, recording or any information storage and retrieval system now known or to be invented, without permission in writing from the publisher, except by a reviewer who wishes to quote brief passages in connection with a review written for inclusion in a magazine, newspaper or broadcast.

Published in the United States by
Truman Talley Books · E. P. Dutton,
2 Park Avenue, New York, N.Y. 10016

Library of Congress Cataloging in Publication Data

Cleveland, Harlan.
The knowledge executive.

"A Truman Talley Book."
Bibliography: p.
Includes index.
1. Leadership. 2. Executive ability. 3. Information science—Social aspects. 4. Information services— Management. I. Title.
HM141.C55 1985   303.3'4   85-4442

ISBN: 0-525-24307-0

Published simultaneously in Canada
by Fitzhenry & Whiteside Limited, Toronto

COBE

10 9 8 7 6 5 4 3 2 1
First Edition

for Amiko and Reggie Pell

Contents

CONTENTS

Foreword

People in every generation think they are living in a time of transition, and of course they are quite right. It's hard to achieve perspective on one's own era. The past is still too much with us; and it's tempting to think up futures that don't require getting there from here. That's why we must now make the effort to develop a perspective on the present.

When I was a university president, trying to deal with campus protests against the war in Vietnam, building a law school and a medical school and three community colleges, handling several budget crises a year, serving as a defendant in twenty lawsuits at a time, and even having to worry about three assassination threats, it was a condition of survival to take the longer and the wider view. On one particularly noisy day a kind and perceptive friend handed me a letter sent by an American college girl to her parents.

Dear Mom and Dad:

I'm sorry to be so long in writing again, but all my writing paper was lost the night the dormitory was burned down by the demonstrators. I'm out of the hospital now, and the doctor says my eyesight should be back to normal sooner or later.

The wonderful boy, Bill, who rescued me from the fire kindly offered to share his little apartment with me until the dorm is rebuilt. He comes from a good family, so you won't be too surprised when I tell you we are going to get married. In fact, you always wanted a grandchild, so you will be glad to know that you will be grandparents next month.

Please disregard the above practice in English composition. There was no fire, I haven't been in the hospital, I'm not pregnant, and I don't even have a boyfriend. But I did get a "D" in French and an "F" in chemistry, and I wanted to be sure you received this news in proper perspective.

Love,
Mary

Using a similar sense of "proper perspective," things could be a lot worse in the United States and the world. We could be trying to cope with plague, pestilence, famine, and flood on a biblical scale. We could already be living, or dying, in the predicted "nuclear winter." We could be striving for survival rather than merely for fairness, security, prosperity, and lower interest rates.

Yet, in this less than apocalyptic age, I think we can still claim to be living at the confluence of more historic transitions at once than any of our ancestors. That's partly because of the looming danger of 50,000 nuclear weapons—a destructive capacity beyond human experience. It's also because our potentials are greater: We live in a time when it is technologically possible to meet the basic human needs of everyone in the world, though we are appallingly short of the moral imperatives, the social systems, the political will, and the administrative apparatus to make this happen. But our lifetime is also special because the rate of change is without precedent, and the number of significant changes occurring all at once, all over the world, is unexampled.

These comprise changing population patterns, changing technologies, and changing concepts about security, about growth, and about equity (or fairness). Somewhere near the center of the picture is what (adapting a French phrase) I will call *the informatization of society,* greatly accelerated in the 1980s by the marriage of computers and telecommunications, hastening the destiny forecast in an E. B. White story in *The New Yorker* half a century ago.

"I predict a bright future for complexity in this country," says one character, and goes on to ask the question that is still bothering us in the mid-1980s: "Have you ever considered how complicated things can get, what with one thing always leading to another?"

America's most readable philosophers have long been its humorists. In capsule words and cartoon pictures, they often capture a public mood before it *is* a public mood—forecasting, the best of them accurately, what is *about* to make us all frightened or frustrated, bored or belligerent. The two best humorists of my youth, E. B. White and James Thurber, were both obsessed with the social complexity that now obsesses us all, but no longer seems so laughable today. White was apprehensive about it, treated it with gingerly restraint as if it might bite if roughly handled. Thurber reveled in complexity, wading into it like a small child into a large puddle.

Thurber, for example, narrated an impressive profusion of accidents resulting from an impression in the family that the bed upstairs had fallen on Father, which it had not. More unnecessary trouble ensued that night, from that small piece of misinformation, than any reader would ever be likely to experience in a single evening, but not so much more that the reader missed the implied prediction.

As Americans zeroed in on complexity as the villain of their lives and labors, the practitioners of comedy helped find the words to complain about it, for what people laugh at is always a serviceable index to what troubles them most deeply. Resistance to parental rule revived that pungent line from a Ring Lardner story: " 'Shut up,' my father explained." And the Vietnam-induced yen to avoid involvement in an anarchic and dangerous world enabled Bob Hope to score with his legendary two-word commencement speech to a crowd of seniors at Georgetown University, about to go out into the world: "Don't go."

Personal reactions to social complexity seem to fall into two molds: sardonic acceptance and belligerent rejection. Belligerent rejection is obviously more fun and, during the 1960s and 1970s, it was increasingly in evidence in the more "developed" societies. Our reaction to complexity was to vent a generalized anger on the nearest symbol of authority.

Angry students blamed the draft and the Vietnam War on the college of their choice. Angry parents blamed the schools for not keeping their children under better control than they did at home. Sudden converts to ecology blamed the government and the corporations for pollution. (But as manager of a university system, I was often struck with the amount of litter left behind by students demonstrating for more sensitivity to the environment.)

Urban congestion accounted for so much frustration that piquant examples of belligerent rejection became daily newspaper fare. For a time I collected clippings on this subject. The most outlandish case was recorded in Rome, which routinely has the world's worst traffic congestion. Two drivers almost collided, then emerged from their cars to argue in the presence of a growing—and, as always in Italy, participatory—audience. One driver with exaggerated politeness asked the other to go ahead. The other, adopting a similar stance of mock courtesy, said, "No, no, after you!" For five minutes they disputed, this Alphonse and this Gaston, which one of them would persuade the other to pass. Finally one of the men went back to his car, extracted a revolver, and shot his adversary for *not* going first.

It is in fact a world where belligerent rejection of complications over which nobody seems to have control spills over into direct action; the people in whose name the action is taken often get hurt, and sometimes killed. Small wonder that an applicant for federal employment, faced with the standard question, "Do you favor the overthrow of the government by force, subversion, or violence?," thought that it was multiple-choice, and answered "Violence."

As the complications became more ubiquitous and menacing, they seemed harder and harder to accept, even with a sardonic twist to the acceptance. Instead of Thurber we got Norman Mailer. He too reveled in complexity and wrote compellingly about it. But in Mailer's case, it was not so much the society he observed around him that produced his frustrations, but rather the other way around: His frustrations produced the observations he reported as the world around him. And with a sure sense of his market, he was not nearly as funny as Thurber. Most of us are no longer in a mood to regard complexity as comic.

It is easy to locate the "knowledge executive" in the midst of what Shakespeare would have called our "most admired disorder": he and she are in the middle of it. Picture, if you will, a large traffic intersection where a dozen streets come together, each carrying traffic both ways. In our physical world the nearest analogue might be the Étoile in Paris, where all day and half the night, in a massive, slow-moving complexity, Parisians weave and shout and play "chicken" as they circle the great triumphal arch and disturb the unknown dead with their Klaxons.

Place the generalist executive out in the middle of this purposeful anarchy, with the assignment to analyze it and keep things moving: pointing directions, negotiating priorities, allocating scarcities, settling arguments, and calming tempers.

Until very recently the executive stood, if not on a pedestal, at least on a traffic island—protected from the bumpers, shielded from the headlights, raised a little above the honking and hollering. Now the central traffic island has been swept away, and the executive weaves and dodges among his or her constituencies, persuading, cajoling, lobbying, budgeting, arbitrating, bargaining, fund raising, trying to keep cool in the management of contradiction.

The human brain delights in the balance of contrasting thoughts. The most effective rhetoric often exploits an apparent paradox ("Let us never negotiate out of fear but let us never fear to negotiate"). Truth often seems to come wrapped in small paradoxical packages. I have come to believe that the art of executive leadership is above all a taste for paradox, a talent for ambiguity, the capacity to hold contradictory propositions comfortably in a mind that relishes complexity.

The executive function is to bring people together in organizations to make something different happen. Its central paradox is all too clear. Some years ago Sir Isaiah Berlin, a philosopher interested in how people govern themselves, described it in one of his *Conversations with Henry Brandon:*

> As knowledge [becomes] more and more specialized, the fewer are the persons who know enough . . . about everything to be wholly in charge. . . . One of the paradoxical consequences is therefore the dependence of a large number of human beings upon a collection of ill-coordinated experts, each of whom sooner or later becomes oppressed and irritated by being unable to step out of his box and survey the relationship of his particular activity to the whole. The experts cannot know enough. The coordinators always did move in the dark, but now they are aware of it. And the more honest and intelligent ones are rightly frightened by the fact that their responsibility increases in direct ratio to their ignorance of an ever-expanding field.

Once again, with feeling: Your responsibility increases in direct ratio to your ignorance. If you turn the thought around it is equally valid: Your ignorance increases in direct ratio to your responsibility. What you need to know in order to act knowingly expands much faster than does your ability to absorb new knowledge. The obvious escape from this dilemma is not to learn more about the details of whatever-it-is but to learn more about its *context.*

Of course none of us is trained for the scary assignment of managing more while understanding less. No university in the world yet offers a Ph.D. in Getting It All Together. I do not claim that reading this book is the moral equivalent of such a course of study; but my purpose in writing it is precisely to serve, and also to celebrate, the "get-it-all-together profession."

It is not easy, I find, to discuss the get-it-all-together role in society without appearing to put down experts. So I must hasten to testify that some of my best friends are experts.

I shall argue in this book that the indispensable quality of executive leadership—the get-it-all-together function in complex systems—is breadth. But a person who is willing without embarrassment to be styled a generalist is constantly impressed with the importance of *somebody* getting to the bottom of specialized questions. To focus on the generalist role is emphatically not to say that specialization and disciplinary expertness are passé. A world of coordinators would be as much of a mess as a world of specialists. The need is to stir them together in the stew of social theory and action, which means that both kinds of people have to learn to live with each other in a symbiosis of mutual respect and mutual dependence.

In that synergistic alliance the front line of attack on the world's problems and the problems of each community has to be led by the generalists, the integrators. It is the generalists, for better or worse, who box the compass, chart the course, and say where we shall go together, and when and why.

The premise of this book is that the pushy progress of science and technology and especially the explosive fusion of computers and telecommunications are changing the options and opportunities for the generalist leaders and especially for those who lead by getting things done—the executives.

We begin by reviewing, in Chapter 1, what seems to be generic about the generalist role and the changes in that role that were evident even before computers and telecommunications got married. Aristocracies of birth, rank, and wealth were already giving way to aristocracies of achievement. The achievers found that, with no one in general charge, they each became partly responsible for the general outcome of their efforts. Each of them had to graduate from the mind-set of an expert to organize his or her mind for the analysis and projection of breadth.

I then invite you, in Chapters 2 through 7, to survey the kaleidoscope of changes in prospect, advances in technology that make imperative the widening of our perspective if we the people are going to channel and control the new technologies instead of the other way around.

Information (organized data, the raw material for specialized knowledge and generalist wisdom) is now our most important, and pervasive, resource. Information workers now compose more than half the U.S. labor force. But this newly dominant resource is quite unlike the tangible resources we have heretofore thought of as valuable. The differences help explain why we get into so much trouble trying to use for the management of *information* concepts that worked all right in understanding the management of *things*—concepts such as control, secrecy, ownership, privilege, and geopolitics.

Because the old pyramids of influence and control were based on just these ideas, they are now crumbling. Their weakening is not always obvious, just as a wooden structure may look solid when you can't see what termites have done to its insides. Whether this "crumble effect" will result in a fairer shake for the world's disadvantaged majority is not yet clear. But there is ample evidence that those who learn how to achieve access to the bath of knowledge that already envelops the world will be the future's aristocrats of achievement, and that they will be far more numerous than any aristocracy in history.

Most executives are involved, one way or another, in harnessing technologies to human purposes. Chapters 8 and 9 gather some promising evidence, partly from my own experience, to suggest that it is possible, after all, for human organizations to make technology work for society instead of society's being driven by the "inner logic" of technological change.

What does it take to be a get-it-all-together person? In the shadows cast by the twilight of hierarchy, I suggest in Chapter 10 the qualities that seem especially useful for those who navigate the participatory perils of the new knowledge environment.

Equipping minds for generalist leadership should be one important task for every part of our educational system. It mostly isn't, not yet. In Chapter 11 we find that the mismatch requires a new kind of "core" for general education, a new emphasis on education for leadership in midcareer, and a newly global perspective in formal education from kindergarten to the Ph.D. and beyond.

Until recently my awareness of aging as a topic for study was minimal. What I am now beginning to see in my shaving mirror has engaged my interest. Chapter 12 is a brief for nonretirement: to take fuller advantage of much pent-up wisdom, to maintain the mental health of senior citizens, and also to maintain the fiscal health of "entitlement" systems that will otherwise impoverish both young and old.

An Afterword brings together fourteen "aphorisms for executives," whose métier is the management of conflict and cooperation. You may find them useful to test what you are learning in action against what I have learned in action. This is a test with no "correct" answers.

We can learn much from inherited wisdom about the generalist role in society and the art of leadership. But most of the intuition and wisdom required for executive leadership can be learned only on the hoof, by trial and, especially, error, learning by doing what (we may later discover) was long since practiced by other leaders and preached by philosophers in centuries or even millennia past.

I shall confess right now that my own writings on leadership and management and diplomacy lean much more heavily on what I have learned in action than what I have learned by reading. If I nevertheless hope that you will profit from what I have written, that is because I think it may stimulate your own powers of observation, your own capacity to derive from your study and experience some personal guidelines for life and work in the new knowledge environment.

HARLAN CLEVELAND

Minneapolis, Minnesota
February 15, 1985

THE
Knowledge
Executive

Everybody gets so much information all day long that they lose their common sense.

GERTRUDE STEIN
(1874–1946)
Reflections on the Atomic Bomb

1

The
Get-It-All-Together
Profession

There was a time, celebrated in song and story, when leadership was entrusted to "leaders." Their numbers were tiny, their information scarce, their expertise primitive, the range of their options narrow, the reach of their power marginal, the scale of their actions limited. But they were at least in charge.

In those days it was possible to believe that policy was actually made by people whom others called policymakers. The policy-making few made broad decisions, it was said (and even taught in schools); a much larger group of unsung experts and civil servants converted these principles into practices; and the job of the masses was to comply with the regulations, pay their taxes, and reelect the policymakers or acquiesce in their seizure of power by divine right, coup d'état, or both.

In Aristotle's Athens, Confucius's China, Cicero's Rome, Charlemagne's Europe, and Jefferson's Virginia, the educated and affluent few did the social planning and made the destiny decisions that drew the distinctions between war and peace, poverty and prosperity, individual freedom and collective coercion, minority rights and majority rule. The uneducated "lower orders" of slaves, servants, peasants, workers, and tradesmen were not expected (and did not expect) to join in the elegant conversations about policy. In their vertical, presystem societies, dogma, doctrine, and dictation were the natural style of leadership.

Somewhere along the way, in the colorful story of people getting things done, the processes we now call modernization made the vertical society obsolete. Man-as-manager had to learn how to manage the complexity that man-as-scientist-and-engineer and man-as-educator were making possible. In a world of intercontinental conflict, gigantic cities, congested living, and large and fragile systems of all kinds, the traditional modes of leadership, featuring "recommendations up, orders down," simply did not work very well. Nobody could be fully in charge of anything, and the horizontal society was born.

The key to the management of complexity was the division of labor and the training of specialists: The benefits of "modernization" were available only to societies that educated most of their people to function as specialists in a division-of-labor economy. Thus there came to pass, late in the second millennium A.D., slaveless societies that responded to a technological imperative by giving citizenship to all their people and legislating education as an entitlement for all their citizens. Jefferson foresaw this macrotrend as early as 1813. "An insurrection has . . . begun," he wrote to John Adams, "of science, talents, and courage, against rank and birth, which have fallen into contempt." He was spending his postpresidential years building the University of Virginia and promoting education and scholarship from his Monticello home.

When every man, and now every woman too, is entitled to earn through education an admission ticket to active citizenship, when leadership is not the province of a few hundred noblemen or a few thousand landholders but is spread among an aristocracy of achievement measured in the hundreds of thousands, decision making is done not by a club but by a crowd. The core issues of executive leadership are puzzles of participation. "How do you get everybody in on the act and still get some action?" (The dilemma is sharpened in Chapter 4, when we come to "the costs and benefits of openness.")

If the get-it-all-together people used to be born to rank and wealth, now they are mostly made, and self-made, by competition and competence. This is true not only in the United States. Today, in all but a rapidly dwindling number of still-traditional societies, men and women become executive leaders by what they *do*. The nations still owned by extended families (Saudi Arabia, for example, and some of the Emirates in the Persian Gulf) are greatly outnumbered by the nations ruled by self-appointed tyrants who got where they are by elbowing their way to power (often by coup d'état), and sometimes to personal prosperity as well. The closest thing to a "ruling class" is to be found these days in the Soviet Union and other totalitarian societies; in each of them, a small group of people who have fought their way up the bureaucratic ladder maneuver for power and preferment, and achieve a precarious lifetime tenure when they get to the top.

In the United States and the other industrial democracies in the Atlantic Community and the Pacific Basin, the aristocracy of achievement is numerous and pervasive. These people are usually leaders because they want to be, but sometimes because they are selected, promoted, or adopted as protégés by earlier achievers. (No one, of course, is a leader in everything she or he touches; all of us are followers in most of our life and work.) They may be leaders in "public" or "private" employ, but that distinction, as we shall see, is increasingly indistinct in our "mixed economy." They may be leaders in politics or business or agriculture or labor or law or education or journalism or religion or affirmative action or community housing, or any policy issue from abortion to the municipal zoo. They may be in the establishment or the antiestablishment. Their writ may run to community affairs, to national decisions or global issues, to a whole multinational industry or profession or to a narrower but deeper slice of life and work: a single firm, a local agency, a neighborhood.

Some years ago, because I was publisher of a magazine I wanted them all to read, I tried to estimate the number of "opinion leaders" in the United States, and came up with 555,000 of them. Extrapolating that 1955 guess sixteen years later, my guess in 1971 was that at least one million Americans could be classified as opinion leaders.

Seven out of ten opinion leaders were what I then called *public executives*—"policymakers in public, philanthropic, voluntary and large-scale 'private' enterprise." A later guess, in 1980, put the number of these executive leaders at about a million: 1 American out of 220, counting men, women, and children. By 1985 our aristocracy of achievement will have multiplied even further. A nice round figure would now be 1 out of every 200 Americans.

Even that guess, well over one million Americans in the get-it-all-together profession, probably understates our pervasive requirement for leadership. Consider, for a start, that there are some 83,000 governmental units in the United States, and about 175,000 corporations doing more than $1 million worth of business a year. The galloping rate of growth of complexity means that a growth curve of the requirement for leaders (if anyone were clever enough to construct such an index) would show a steeper climb than any other growth rate in our political economy.

Every person who seeks or assumes the role of executive leadership in an information-rich society must develop the aptitudes and attitudes of the generalist. For reasons developed in the rest of this book, the generalist has to be skeptical of inherited assumptions (because some of them are being knocked into a cocked hat by *the informatization of society*); curious about science-based technology (because those who would control it must first understand, not how it works, but what it can do for us and to us); broad in their perspective (to take account of the disappearing distinctions between "public" and "private" and between "domestic" and "foreign"); eager to pull people and ideas together (rather than split them apart); really interested in issues of fairness (because the people to be pulled together are); and self-confident enough to work, not in a back room, but riskily out on a limb in our increasingly open society.

You will find in this book more emphasis on attitudes than on skills. Attitudes are the steepest part of the generalist's learning curve. Survival and growth in the get-it-all-together profession, perhaps the world's toughest occupation, requires a mind-set that is, by and large, neglected in our education. I tried to define this mind-set before a convention of city managers, who certainly do some of the world's toughest and least rewarded work. The characterization is not complete, and I will be enriching it in the pages that follow; but it may help you understand where, as my children would say, I am "coming from." These attitudes, I told the urban executives, are indispensable to the management of complexity:

- •The notion that crises are normal, tensions can be promising, and complexity is fun;

- •a realization that paranoia and self-pity are reserved for people who don't want to be executives;

- •the conviction that there must be some more upbeat outcome than would result from adding together the available expert advice; and

- •a sense of personal responsibility for the situation as a whole.

The generalists may start as scientists or MBAs or lawyers or doctors or union organizers or civil servants or mobilizers of feminists or ethnic groups, or citizen-advocates of a particular cause. They may be managers who (as a committee of the International City Management Association puts it) know how to "lead while being led." They may even be judges who know that the law has to be molded to reflect both technological change and the election returns. They are, by and large, men and women who are not preoccupied with formal power or getting their names in the newspapers, people whose concern exceeds their confusion and may even preempt their egos, because they are busy (and having fun) doing something that hasn't been done before. But what makes them the shock troops of the get-it-all-together profession is, above all, their overriding concern for the *general* outcome of their efforts.

Some generalists are legislators and editorialists and other situation-as-a-whole people whose administrative responsibilities are comparatively light. But most of them are executives in business, in government, and in the independent sector.

We who practice as executive leaders come in all sizes and shapes, pursue a wide variety of goals and purposes, and operate in many modes—in federal, state, and local bureaus, in big corporations, in small businesses, in academic settings, in nonprofit agencies ranging from the EXXON Education Foundation to Alcoholics Anonymous. But each of us is ultimately responsible, for his or her behavior and decisions, to people-in-general.

The buck doesn't stop with any of those intermediate bodies from which we derive our mandates: legislatures, stockholders, boards of directors, or trustees. What Harry Truman said of the U.S. presidency is true for each of us who presumes to bring people together to make something happen: "the buck stops here."

The skills and aptitudes of generalists who have graduated beyond their initial calling as experts were well described almost a century ago by Woodrow Wilson while he was a professor, before he became the twenty-eighth president of the United States. He was trying to capture in words the skills a president would need to sniff out the people's policy and convert it to action. Read it now as a description of the integrative talent needed by executive leaders in very large numbers.

A great nation is not led by a man who simply repeats the talk of the street-corners or the opinions of the newspaper. A nation is led by a man who hears more than those things; or who, rather, hearing those things understands them better, unites them, puts them into a common meaning; speaks, not the rumors of the street, but a new principle for a new age; a man [to whom] the voices of the nation . . . unite in a single meaning

6

and reveal to him a single vision, so that he can speak what no man else knows, the common meaning of the common voice. Such is the man who leads a great, free, democratic nation.

I can hear the reader mutter: If such a man, or woman, were elected to the presidency, we would be uncommonly lucky. Yet I am saying, quite seriously, that we now need in our leadership several hundred thousand such people. The search for unifying themes in the plural voices of the general public is precisely the mission of generalists in our society.

Commenting on this passage in his great book on the presidency, Sidney Hyman called the executive role "a sublime madness . . . half historian and half prophet." He thought it was best exemplified by the Abraham Lincoln of the Gettysburg Address and the Second Inaugural, depending "less on his intellect—brilliant men can ruin a country—and more on the quality of his passions, his will and his imaginative faculties."

The executive imagination is shown in the leader's

capacity to foretell the course of events; in the problem he chooses to bring to the center of national attention, the time when he does it, the degree of gravity he attaches to the problem, the sense of lassitude or urgency he creates when he defines alternative solutions to it. It is shown in the degree to which he is "the great asker and patient hearer of the truth about those things" into which he ought to inquire. It is shown in the way he creates his own luck, or builds safety nets against misfortune. It is shown in how he stretches old forms to cover new functions, without exciting those of us who are suspicious of any change until we have had experience with it.

The gender is male: Both Wilson and the historian were writing about U.S. presidents, and women were not yet running for president —or even voting in Wilson's time. But the sentiment applies to women as well as men, numbered, I repeat, in the hundreds of thousands. (I will later suggest that it is no accident that women are streaming into leadership positions at just the moment when the knowledge revolution is reinforcing the consensual mode of decision making.) Wilson thought the president was in some sense in charge of the nation, or at least in charge of providing its vision of the future. But in a nobody-in-charge society it falls to each generalist leader *both* to sniff at the street corners (as Mao would have recommended if he had been talking about an urban scene) and *also* to integrate (as Woodrow Wilson proposes) what he or she hears to produce a "common meaning" and a policy that can be put into action. And the description applies not only to matters on a national or international scale, but to the policies we all make by living through each working day.

If you now regard yourself as a generalist or have aspirations in that direction, I can with some confidence trace or predict your double career.

First you pick a specialty: legal services or health care, engineering or economics, accounting or planning, production management or consumer advocacy, weaving or welding, brainwork or manual skill or some combination of the two. As you rise in your chosen field (we used to say "rise like cream in a milk bottle," but homogenized milk in an opaque carton has spiked that metaphor), you find yourself drawn into broader supervisory, managerial assignments, and then into the generalist role, either in your own right or (more likely at first) as staff assistant to a leader whose preoccupation with the whole you are expected to share.

You may be (to adapt some words of John Gardner) a clarifier, definer, critic, or teacher. Or you may be an implementer, manager, problem solver who will "redesign existing institutions or invent new ones, create coalitions and fight off the people who don't want the problem solved." Or again, you may be counted among the "mobilizers" who "catalyze the social morale, help people know what they can be at their best, and nurture a workable level of unity." You may even come to be effective in all three roles; a good many people do.

This broader role requires intellectual tools you didn't learn in school, "people skills" that may not have been needed for you to excel as an expert, attitudes that differ in fundamental ways from those that made you a rising young specialist. Graduation from successful specialist to generalist leader is a wrenching, demanding, sometimes traumatic change of life.

As you shift gears, you will already have had a good deal of practice getting around in, and getting around, large-scale bureaucracies: foiling the personnel classification system, outwitting the budgeters, hoodwinking the organization analysts, avoiding the auditors, and securing a bigger office with a private phone, a personal computer, and above all a carpet. You will also have learned, if you are considered a promising "comer," that despite those pyramidal organization charts the real world of work consists mostly of horizontal relationships. Most of the people you see from day to day don't work for you, and you don't work for them. You work together, even if that isn't the way it looks on the chart.

You will thus already have explored in action the leadership of equals and tried to get things done in consensual systems—learning, for example, that overt confrontation is more likely to produce resistance than results. This environment will already have required you to cultivate the suasive arts, the soft voice and the low key, the constructive uses of ambiguity, the self-restraint not to cross bridges before you come to them, and such conventions of committee work as introducing your personal views with one of two phrases: either "I agree with everything that's been said, but . . . ," or "What I hear you all saying is . . . "

The geometry and gimmickry of bureaucratic behavior are sometimes taught as "business management," or "public administration," or even "advanced management." They are, indeed, essential survival skills in societies full of public and private bureaucracies. The bird that never learns to get around in its environment, that is, to fly, will never go far. But the critical dimension of leadership, and the centerpiece of education for leadership, is not the technology of office work and committee sitting. That's the easy part. The hard part is organizing your mind for the analysis and projection of breadth.

Breadth is a quality of mind, the capacity to relate disparate facts to a coherent theory, to fashion tactics that are part of a strategy, to act today in ways that are consistent with a studied view of the future.

No one person can know enough to send a team of people to the moon, in the sense that Grandpa and Grandma could know just about everything about managing their corner grocery store. (The best of the old grocers virtually kept the inventory in their heads, as many merchants in Mideast bazaars, West African "mammy-wagons," and Oriental jewel markets still do today. Imagine trying to keep in your head even the list of spare parts for your refrigerator or automobile, let alone for the space shuttle.) So different kinds of people, with differing knowledge and skills and personalities and networks of friends and acquaintances, have to be brought together in organizations designed to transmute their separate expertnesses and their collective insights into wise day-to-day decisions about what to do next, *together*.

Breadth is therefore not a contradiction of depth, but its complement. Everything really is related to everything else; therefore, the person who plumbs the depths of his or her own specialty finds more and more connections with every other specialty. The astronomers who reach far back in time to postulate a big bang must in scholarly honesty ask the humanistic next questions: Why the bang? Who set it off? What does it mean? And so the experts come, by the circuitous route of pure reason, to speculations that can only be explorations of faith.

The Scientific Revolution, and its younger sibling the Industrial Revolution, were made possible by our capacity to divide into separable disciplines the proven methods of inquiry, and to retrieve from bins of manageable size and complication the knowledge we accumulated by observing, experimenting, and theorizing. But in the latter part of the twentieth century, we came to realize that most of our troubles stem from neglecting the interconnectedness of knowledge and the interdisciplinary character of all real-world problems.

Isaac Stern, who is not only a musician but a philosopher of music education, was once asked in a public forum at the Aspen Institute why all professional musicians seemed to be able to play the same notes in the same order, yet some sounded wonderful and many did not. The world's best violinist paused and scratched his head. "But it isn't the *notes* that are important," he objected. "It's the intervals *between* the notes." A wise comment, not only about music but about other forms of knowledge. It's not mainly our capacity to dig out the facts, but rather the educated intuition and practical experience to arrange them in meaningful patterns, that make the human brain something more than a data-collecting machine.

Just the same, the executive leader is very likely to be unsuccessful unless he or she has, earlier in life, been a first-rate specialist; it doesn't really matter in what field. In the words of poet Charles Olson,

> Best thing to do is *to dig one thing or place or man* until you yourself know more about that than is possible to any other man. It doesn't matter whether it's Barbed Wire or Pemmican or Paterson or Iowa. But *exhaust* it. Saturate it. Beat it. And then U KNOW everything else very fast: one saturation job (it might take 14 years). And you're in, forever.

The get-it-all-together person needs above all to be good at judging whether the experts who stream through the executive office, creating a chronic condition of information entropy on the executive's desk, are functioning as competent experts. If the executive has never had personal experience with specialized research and analysis, he or she won't know what competent expertise feels like. Liu Shao, a Chinese Machiavelli of the third century A.D., wrote it 1,700 years ago: "You cannot recognize in another a quality you do not have yourself."

Who are these generalists, these integrators, these paragons of getting it all together? Are they concepts or flesh-and-blood human beings?

Each of us has known some people who would pass the tests implied in what I have written about the generalist role, about integrative thinking, about making things happen. Indeed, in any successful organized effort, from a Boy Scout encampment to a television show to a corporate merger to a peacetime alliance, you will find working generalists near the center of things. They are the people who furnish the glue that holds people together and the executive imagination around which people mobilize. Most of them might even object at first if you were to call them generalists; they describe themselves, and their peers describe them, as scoutmasters, artists, businesspeople, or diplomats. But their talisman is *their concern for the general outcome* and their capacity to do something about their concerns.

I shall answer your unspoken question by mentioning four of my own generalist role models: two executive leaders, a legislator, and a journalist. All of them—Paul Hoffman, Jean Monnet, Hubert Humphrey, and Barbara Ward—have departed this life, leaving an indelible mark on their time and on those of us who happened to work with them.

Each of them, in their differing ways, illustrates the upbeat, can-do spirit of generalist leadership, an attribute to which we will return in a later chapter. They were all people who in their time asked not only "Why?" but "Why not?" They all learned enough about enough subjects to use expertise without being mesmerized by the experts. They all acted as if everything were related to everything else. They all played out by instinct the ethic of ecology expressed so well when Alfred North Whitehead wrote of "that appreciation of the structure of ideas which requires an eye for the whole chessboard, the bearing of one set of ideas upon another."

Paul Hoffman, who was president of Studebaker before he ran the Marshall Plan for European Recovery, started his working life running a filling station. Like most of the best people I have known, he never forgot the things he learned in the earlier parts of his life, and he was able to relate them to the later parts.

While I was working with him (you didn't feel that you were working *for* Paul Hoffman) early in the Marshall Plan, he came into a staff meeting and said: "Listen. We all really ought to answer every letter the day it comes in." Now to a group of Washington bureaucrats, that was a rather stirring comment; it stirred a lot of resistance.

He explained: "When I worked in a filling station, I found that if somebody came and sat at the pump for three or four minutes and nobody paid any attention to him, he would go away and never come back. But if you gave him a big hello and said, 'There are a few people ahead of you, but I'll get to you just as soon as I can,' he'd sit there perfectly happily for a quarter of an hour." Hoffman's point was that we didn't have to give a substantive answer; we could answer the letter and just say: "We got your letter and we're working on it." It would at least give the people an idea that we were there. It's an even more important lesson now that people who write letters to big organizations suspect that computers, not people, are reading the incoming mail.

Perhaps because he had been a major executive and a business statesman before he was asked to carry the Marshall Plan into action, Paul Hoffman had a well-developed sense of personal confidence. More than that, he had a feeling that whatever was wrong in the organization of the U.S. government, or in Europe, it was always his turn to do something about it. It was never the moment for him to sit down and wait for somebody else to do something. He always felt that somehow he should be taking the initiative.

But it was not always his turn to take the credit for his initiatives —in fact, it almost never was. One of the most extraordinary lessons in human relations I have witnessed in my life was watching Hoffman work with Averell Harriman as his nominal subordinate. (Harriman, a multimillionaire, later became governor of New York and American ambassador to Moscow.) Harriman was responsible for carrying out the European end of the Marshall Plan, and the publicity from our European headquarters in Paris kept describing Harriman as in charge of the Marshall Plan. Hoffman, his boss, never called him on it; it never even seemed to bother him. His ego was invested in getting the job done, not in telling the world who was doing it. When President Eisenhower later said that there's no limit to what you can accomplish if you don't want the credit for it, he might have been thinking of Paul Hoffman.

I watched Dean Rusk work in a similar way as secretary of state when Adlai Stevenson was the ambassador to the United Nations.

For most countries, the foreign minister goes to New York to make an opening speech at the UN General Assembly. I knew that Stevenson, who thought he should have been secretary of state, would want to make that speech himself, so I raised the question with Secretary Rusk, wondering whether (as the assistant secretary of state responsible for relations with the UN) I would find myself on a one-track railway line with two cabinet-level locomotives approaching from opposite directions. Dean Rusk got my meaning so fast that the same question must have been on his mind too. "We have one of the world's greatest public speakers as our ambassador to the United Nations," he said with a smile. "There's no point in my going up there and elbowing him aside." So each year when the General Assembly opened, Ambassador Stevenson would make the leadoff speech for the United States. The next day, his boss, the secretary of state, would slip into town for a couple of weeks of quiet bilateral diplomacy with the dozens of other foreign ministers visiting New York at that season.

But getting back to Paul Hoffman: Most of all, I was struck with the fact that there was no veneer, no wax exterior, no dissembling. It was not a case of one thing going on inside and something different going on outside—what you might call the Richard Nixon syndrome. It is very difficult always to say what you mean, and mean what you say. So when I once heard somebody comment that Hoffman was made of the same stuff inside and out, I always thought that was the nicest thing that could be said of anybody.

Jean Monnet, too, was made of the same stuff all the way through, but he is on my list of role models because he decided what he wanted to see happen—a United States of Europe—and kept at it till he died. I could equally have cited Mahatma Gandhi, who single-mindedly devoted himself to ending British colonial rule in the Indian subcontinent; or Chaim Weizmann, who single-mindedly drove toward a Jewish homeland and of whom Isaiah Berlin wrote: "He was a man who made the improbable happen."

Monnet's case should be particularly interesting to executives both public and private, because he made a deliberate choice in middle life to stay *out* of government so he could push the integration of Western Europe. He didn't get as far as he had hoped, but he achieved more than most of us dared hope—because he had a vision, a strategy, and a masterly sense of tactics and timing that moved "Europe" from an abstract idea to a working Community. If you want to see the very model of an integrative man in action, read Jean Monnet's *Memoirs,* certainly one of the great books about leadership written in this century.

Hubert Humphrey could qualify for a list of public-service role models on any of several counts. History may remember him as Lyndon Johnson's vice-president, who blew his chance to be president by an excess of loyalty to a failed president. Others will remember him as an astute political entrepreneur and the greatest platform orator of his time. He had the courage to innovate, like Anwar Sadat; like Paul Hoffman, he was content to get his policies adopted even if it meant slipping his innovative bills to other senators to "author"; he was a man of integrative thought and action, like Jean Monnet. "One thing marked him out," former Prime Minister James Callaghan said of him in a lecture on leadership at the Hubert H. Humphrey Institute of Public Affairs. "He was never content to just denounce. 'There are times,' he said, 'when it's better to lose than to be partially successful. But to make a habit of losing in the name of moral principles or liberal convictions is to fail to govern and to demonstrate incapacity to persuade and convince and to develop a majority.' "

But for me, Humphrey was a very special public-service role model because he was literally interested in everything. He was blessed with an intellectual curiosity that embraced the world, spanned the oceans, and extended into outer space. As a situation-as-a-whole person, he felt a personal responsibility for growing more food, making useful goods, distributing wealth fairly, creating better jobs, combating inflation, managing government, and ensuring international peace. When any situation demanded action, he always thought it was up to him to organize the action.

Barbara Ward, the British editor and journalist, is on my list of role models because she was queen of the upbeat. For some forty years she was the voice of vision in international affairs, and particularly in North-South relations. During the time she wrote for *The Economist,* the authors of individual articles were not usually identified. But Barbara Ward's eloquence and passion, combined with good research and leavened by a sunny sense of humor, came through so strongly that a regular reader of that excellent weekly could pick out her prose in the first few sentences of an article. She was also my world-favorite public speaker, a first-rate mind attached to a vibrant personality, able to let light and air into the sometimes soporific complexities of environment and development or the international monetary system. Here is a sample of her inspirational style, still fresh after a decade and a half in print:

> . . . the two worlds of man, the biosphere of his inheritance and the technosphere of his creation, are out of balance, indeed, potentially in deep conflict. And man is in the middle. This is the hinge of history at which we stand. The door of the future opening onto a crisis more sudden, more global, more inescapable, more bewildering than any ever encountered by the human species. And one which will take decisive shape within the life span of children who are already born. No problem is insoluble in the creation of a balanced and conserving planet, save humanity itself. Can it reach in time the vision of joint survival? Can its inescapable physical interdependence, the chief new insight of our century, induce that vision? We do not know. We have the duty to hope.

That duty—to hope and to do something about it—is the mandate for the generalists of the next generation. For reasons we will consider in Chapter 7, the "general outcome" is now world-scale.

Paradoxically, the generalists who listen most attentively to what our Declaration of Independence calls "the general opinion of mankind" may seem (to their peers, the establishment, the media, and even members of the general public for whom they purport to act and speak) to be uttering heretical thoughts, diagnosing unauthorized diseases, proposing bizarre solutions—because others have not exercised the wider curiosity or done the integrative thinking that are the hallmark of the generalist.

It can be an exciting profession, but also a vulnerable one. The resistance to what has never been done before may remind them of Peter Ustinov's claim that one of his grade-school teachers wrote on his report card, "Peter shows great originality, which must be curbed at all costs." The first birds off the telephone wire (the image is John Gardner's) need the spunk and persistence of that courageous, original woman who was arrested on a one-way street for going the other way. "Officer," she asked, "has it occurred to you that that arrow may be pointing the wrong way?"

Each of us who presumes to the kind of leadership that welcomes innovation while it is still new has to try hard to think about what the Club of Rome calls the *problématique,* the constantly changing general context. I mean this quite literally. None of us can expect to *act* on more than a tiny corner of the great complexity. But in our interrelated society, itself part of an uncompromisingly interdependent world, we have to *think* about the whole complexity in order to act relevantly on any part of it. A 1980 convention of futurists summarized the generalist mandate in four words: "Think Globally, Act Locally.'

The message comes through, loud and clear, from the most prophetic of our contemporary public philosophers. In one of his many lucid and useful books, *Managing in Turbulent Times,* Peter Drucker poses the puzzle of pluralism: "Each institution pursues its own specific goal. But who then takes care of the common weal?" His answer (and mine) is: the specialized professional who graduates into general leadership. "He does not cease to be a 'professional'; he must not cease to be one. But he acquires an additional dimension of understanding, additional vision, and the sense of responsibility for the survival and performance of the whole that distinguishes the manager from the subordinate and the citizen from the subject."

Scary as it is to be a citizen-manager so defined, we have to agree with John Gardner's exhortation (in a pithy little piece called "The War of the Parts Against the Whole"). "This is a moment," he writes,

17

when the innumerable interests, organizations and groups that make up our national life must keep their part of the bargain with the society that gives them freedom, by working toward the common good. Right now. In this time of trouble. Their chances for long-term enjoyment of pluralism will be enhanced by a commitment to the common good as we go through this difficult passage. At least for now, a little less *pluribus,* a lot more *unum.*

It's a tough assignment. But don't blame the messenger who brings the news, blame the complexities and dynamics of a society in rapid transition. And be assured, by one who has been there, that the exhilaration usually exceeds the exhaustion.

2

The Knowledge Dynamic

It was a big day. On Friday, January 8, 1982, the explosive fusion of computers and telecommunications went critical. The U.S. Department of Justice, in two separate moves that cannot have been coincidental, unleashed those two great postindustrial lions, AT&T and IBM, to wrestle in a common arena, the information society.

The revolutions that began with Charles Babbage's "analytical engine" (less than 150 years ago) and Guglielmo Marconi's wireless telegraphy (not yet a century old) started on quite different tracks. But a quarter of a century ago, computers and telecommunications began to converge to produce a combined complexity, one interlocked industry that is transforming our personal lives, our national politics, and our international relations. Courts and antitrust lawyers and Congress naturally got left behind.

In the spirit of the small boy who couldn't see the emperor's clothes, the Reagan administration, by its actions if not its words, declared what is now obvious: It's all one industry, the information industry; its parts might as well compete with each other, and devil take the hindmost. The devil may have slim pickings: both IBM and AT&T are already adapting with gusto to the newly permissive rules of the game.

Postindustrial is the term that Harvard sociologist Daniel Bell proposed to describe the coming complexity. I have never been comfortable with it. Can't we find a term for the future that goes beyond saying it comes after the past? Surely *postindustrial* is too reductionist a tag for so different and exciting a prospect, and too economic a name for a period in which the discoveries of science, the innovations of technology, and integrative thinking about politics, culture, and psychology will be at least as important as economic analysis to an understanding of what's going on. And an understanding of what's going on right now is the beginning of wisdom about the future. One remembers the reaction of the pope in Rome when he heard that Martin Luther had hurled an inkwell at a bishop. The pontiff, undisturbed, airily dismissed the event: "Just another heretical monk."

The industrial era was characterized by the influence of humankind over *things,* including Nature as well as the artifacts of Man. The information era features a sudden increase in humanity's power to think, and therefore to organize.

The information society does not replace, it overlaps, the growing, extracting, processing, manufacturing, recycling, distribution, and consumption of tangible things. Agriculture and industry continue to progress by doing more with less through better knowledge, leaving plenty of room for a knowledge economy that now accounts for more than half of our work force, our national product, and our global reach.

As information moves to center stage in the advanced economies, it comes to be regarded as a resource *in itself.* This is new. Until the early 1970s information (science, technology, values, social authority, and organization) was seen as the handmaiden of "real resources": the tangible things that lay in the ground, swam in the water, or grew in the soil, and latterly the air and water that once were regarded as free goods. In this context, information was merely what enabled people to use the real resources for good or ill, sustenance or deprivation, peace or war. As late as 1972, the widely debated report on *The Limits to Growth* did not treat information as one of the resources whose depletion, the authors believed, could bring us to the edge of catastrophe.

But information is now commonly held to be the primary basis for social cooperation (what people know or believe about each other, true or not, defines their relations with each other), for human rights (knowledge of one's entitlements is the precondition for seeking their fulfillment), for military strategy (deterrence is an uncertainty-based information game), and for international politics (the relations of the richer North with the poorer South can be seen as an information bombardment).

In a remarkably short span of years—the 1970s and the early 1980s —the once prescient notion that industrial society was being transformed into a postindustrial, "information," or "knowledge" society has become a cliché.

We are already past the jaw-dropping, gee-whiz stage of technological wonder, and have internalized, even if most of us do not really understand, the prospect of trillions of transactions performed in tiny fractions of time, circling the globe at the speed of light. But we are not yet very far along in learning how to think about the implications of the technical wizardry, and especially the spreading linkage of computers and telecommunications, for the way we live, work, and play.

This subject appeared so recently on the agenda that it is important, without being pedantic about it, to get our vocabulary clear. You can use the key words any way you want, of course; but just now you are reading mine, so I had better define what I mean by them. The key words are *data, information, knowledge,* and *wisdom.*

I find the hierarchy suggested long ago by T. S. Eliot (in *The Rock*) a useful starting point: "Where is the wisdom we have lost in knowledge? Where is the knowledge we have lost in information?" And, he might have added, where is the information we have lost in data?

In my lexicon, *data* are undigested observations, unvarnished facts. If you could imagine yourself noticing that the ground underfoot is green and soft, without having the context to infer that you are walking on the grass, those would be data. A newborn baby has lots of (somewhat blurry) data, lots of sights and sounds and smells and tactile sensations, without context. But having been provided with learning capacities by the information in its genes, the baby quickly catches on—learns, for example, that making a loud noise usually produces some action, and that it's usually the same blurry shape who acts in the baby's perceived interest and is warm and comfortable to snuggle against.

In its narrower sense *information* is organized data—organized by others, not by me. The pile of back issues of *The New York Times* that I haven't yet dipped into is information; the data have certainly been organized by somebody, but they are doing me no good. All the masses of information collected by the New York Stock Exchange or The Library of Congress are not useful to an Australian aborigine, or indeed to most of the world's people; they haven't learned to use that information so there is always the danger that those who have learned will use it against them.

When Cassio, in *Julius Caesar,* says "It's Greek to me," he is drawing the line between information and knowledge. For *knowledge* is organized information, internalized by me, integrated with everything else I know from experience or study or intuition, and therefore useful in guiding my life and work. Nothing you learn is ever wasted, my mother used to say; and over the years I have so frequently found myself applying some insight or deriving some metaphor from intellectual raw materials I had previously thought of as interesting but useless that I know now what she meant.

I find it helpful to think of *data* as the ore, the sum total of all the undifferentiated observations—facts—that are available to be organized by somebody at a given moment in time. *Information,* then, is the result of somebody's applying the refiner's fire to that ore, selecting and organizing what is useful to somebody. But it isn't *knowledge* until I have put some part of that semifinished product to use in my own mind.

Most knowledge is expertise—in a field, a subject, a science, a technology, a system of values, a form of social organization and authority. *Wisdom* is integrated knowledge, information made super-useful by theory, which relates bits and fields of knowledge to each other, which in turn enables me to use the knowledge to do some-thing. That's why wisdom is bound to cross the disciplinary barriers we set up to make the fields of knowledge manageable by the use of scientific method.

A colleague at the University of Minnesota, geographer Yi-fu Tuan, presents the T. S. Eliot hierarchy in a fashion I find congenial:

The difference is one of order of complexity. Information is horizontal, knowledge is structured and hierarchical, wisdom is organismic and flexible. Any diligent student can, with the help of a computerized system, acquire vast amounts of information; for instance, the population of every township in the United States. But the data are pretty useless because they are stretched out at one level. (Information is horizontal.) For the data to be useful—come to life, as it were—they have to be linked to another rung or category of data. The result is knowledge. (Knowledge is structured and hierarchical.) Every teacher knows how difficult it is to pass knowledge, as distinct from information, to students; hence, we give objective tests to deter-mine how much information, rather than knowledge, they have acquired. As for imparting wisdom, it . . . has to do with personal chemistry and slow osmosis.

There are plenty of other ways of using these key words. Daniel Bell, the granddaddy of much creative thinking about the postindustrial society, defined information as "data processing in the broadest sense" and knowledge as "an organized set of statements of facts or ideas . . . communicated to others." Scholars who have come to the subject from thinking about communications theory have been much influenced by the work of Claude Shannon and Warren Weaver (1949), who saw information as the difference between two states of uncertainty, the uncertainty before and after receiving a "message." (Hence, the expression *information entropy* crept into the language.) A 1984 paper by Klaus Krippendorff of the University of Pennsylvania's Annenberg School of Communication finds this theory "not powerful enough," and suggests instead that information should be seen as "the organizational work a message enables its receiver to perform."

Kenneth Boulding of the University of Colorado, who has one of the most original minds of our time, theorized about the *noösphere* (the envelope of knowledge around the globe, which Pierre Teilhard de Chardin added to the natural *biosphere* and the manufactured *technosphere* created by humans, to make a complete picture). Boulding defined the noösphere as "the totality of the cognitive content [and] values, of all human nervous systems, plus the prosthetic devices by which this system is extended and integrated in the form of libraries, computers, telephones, post offices and so on."

In previous societies, says Krippendorff,

the noösphere was more limited than it is today, not just by the properties of the inquiring mind and by its capacity to premeditate, to invent and to create new ideas, but particularly by the availability of storage facilities to preserve, and of communication media to transmit, the collectively created potential. It is this potential that information technology now transforms in ways unprecedented in human history.

The extraordinary increases in our human capacity to handle information, he suggests, "redirect social attention from tradition, from how things were done in the past and what was good about them, to the future, to what is conceivable or can be done. . . . The idea of historical determinism [the root of Karl Marx's thinking] can certainly no longer be left unquestioned."

From what I can understand of the scholarly writings (they speak much of messages, but some of them have trouble getting their own messages across in plain words), three seminal ideas strike me as containing the most nourishment for our purpose, which is to think about what the new information environment means for leadership and the executive function.

One is that information (in its generic sense) is not *like* other resources; neither, as some would have it, is it merely another form of energy. It is not subject to the laws of thermodynamics, and efforts to explain the new information environment by using metaphors from physics will just get in our way.

A second idea I find nourishing is that the ultimate effect of all knowledge is to organize things or people, arrange them in ways that make them different from the way they were before. This is true of rearranging the genes in a chromosome, and it is equally true of rearranging people's ideas to create a movement. There is no such thing as useless knowledge, only people who haven't yet learned how to use it. This was the powerful message carried in a 1979 article in *Science* by Lewis Branscomb, chief scientist of IBM. He wrote that information is so far from being scarce that it is in "chronic surplus." There is still plenty for scientists to find out, but "the yawning chasm is between what is already known by some but not yet put to use by others."

A third insight, from the late British communications theorist Colin Cherry, is the distinction between the information ("message") itself and the service of delivering it. Think of the distinction this way. You may own the book you hold in your hand: the delivery service. But you don't own the contents: the message itself. Neither, now that I have written them down, do I. (Cherry and others make another distinction too, between the message itself and

NORTH COUNTY

its meaning, which depends on the receiver as well as the sender.)

However they use the key words, those who have thought most deeply about the macrotransition we are in seem to agree that something terribly important is going on right under our noses, and that the most "practical" thing we can do is to think hard about it. Note that, in my own effort to do this in the pages that follow, I will be using the word *information* generically, to include the whole hierarchy from raw data to integrated wisdom and the organized systems ("bundles of relations") that the human processing of information into knowledge and wisdom makes possible.

We can probably take as common ground the size and scope of the transition we are in. The French call it *l'informatisation de la société*, the *informatization* of society. (The new word still rolls off the tongue more readily in French than in English.) Both the size and scope are impressive, if partly impressionistic.

In 1920, fewer than 10 percent of American workers were doing information work. In the United States, still the most postindustrial country, more than half of all work, as defined by the Census Bureau's employment categories, is now information work—not only writing and calculating but what executives, salespeople, advertisers, lawyers, accountants, secretaries, programmers, consultants, and hundreds of other kinds of workers do.

The Census Bureau doesn't admit it, but it seems likely that the ratio of brainwork to drudgery keeps rising in nearly every job. Many tasks are still *comparatively* routine, of course; but any routine that can be taken over by a machine will be lost to the labor force. A machine is a slave, and free people won't indefinitely opt to compete with slaves for their jobs.

In this picture the actual production, extraction, and growing of *things* now soaks up less than a quarter of our human resources. Of all the rest, which used to be lumped together as "services," more than two-thirds are information workers. By the end of the century, something like two-thirds of the whole labor force will be information workers.

Here is the sweep of change—historical numbers and estimates pulled together from varied sources by G. Molitor of Public Policy Forecasting, Inc.:

U.S. WORK FORCE DISTRIBUTION					
	1880	1920	1955	1975	2000 (est.)
Agriculture & extractive	50%	28%	14%	4%	2%
Manufacturing, commerce, industry	36	53	37	29	22
Other services	12	10	20	17	10
Information, knowledge, education	2	9	29	50	66

The existence of these trends is regularly reinforced now by a variety of attempts to figure out what's happening. A recent study at MIT, for example, found that of the 19 million new jobs created in the United States in the 1970s, only 5 percent were in manufacturing, 6 percent were in services in the goods-producing sector, and 89 percent were outside the goods-producing sector. A good guess would be that some two-thirds of the non-goods-producing jobs were information work of one kind or another.

Not only in the United States has the informatization of society proceeded so far so fast. A recent study by the Organization for Economic Cooperation and Development (the club of richer nations, with headquarters in Paris) puts the average information labor force of several of its member countries at more than one-third of the total during the early to mid-1970s. That same study showed that the information component of the labor force increased its share of the total by 2.8 percent during each five-year period since World War II.

Having fewer workers in production and more in services is not new. What's new is the pace of change made possible by computers and telecommunications, and the degree to which people in what used to be called "service" jobs are now recognized to be processing and producing information. When Peter Drucker, a much-read philosopher of business administration, started to call knowledge "the central capital, the cost center, and the crucial resource of the economy," nonphilosophers responsible for the managing of organizations had to sit up and take notice.

My University of Minnesota colleague G. Edward Schuh, an agricultural economist, confirms that farming, too, is becoming more and more of an information game. Indeed, agriculture may be further ahead in the embedding of information in physical processes than any other industry. "All of the increase in agricultural output from the mid-1920s through the mid-1970s (a fifty-year period!) came about with no increase in the capital stock of physical resources. It was all due to increases in productivity, with most of that due to new knowledge or information. That makes clear the extent to which knowledge is an input or resource."

What's also new is a theory crisis, a sudden sense of having run out of basic assumptions. We have carried over into our thinking about information (which is to say *symbols*) concepts developed for the management of *things*—concepts such as property, depletion, depreciation, monopoly, market economics, the class struggle, and top-down leadership.

The assumptions we have inherited are not producing satisfactory growth with acceptable equity in either the capitalist West or the socialist East. As Simon Nora and Alain Minc said in their landmark report to the president of France: "The liberal and Marxist approaches, contemporaries of the production-based society, are rendered questionable by its demise." Maybe it would help if we stopped treating information as just another *thing,* a commodity with pseudophysical properties, and looked hard instead at what makes it so special.

Compared to "natural resources," information (refined into knowledge and wisdom) is a mighty peculiar resource. The resources I learned about in school were tangible: minerals, fuel, fibers, and food. During my career in the U.S. government, I helped buy and sell resources for the Board of Economic Warfare, transferred resources to other countries through the Marshall Plan and the early foreign-aid programs, argued about "sovereignty over national resources" in UN committees, and helped mobilize resources for defense in NATO. In these and other assignments I brought people ("human resources") together in organizations to manage things and to manage ideas about things. We never said "to manage information."

We have grown up thinking of business as built on resources-as-things. But the physical component of most business now is a small base for an inverted pyramid of organized information. Most people in business now work on ideas, procedures, marketing, advertising, administration, and trying to stay out of trouble with the consumers, the regulators, the public, and the law.

By the same token, the American labor movement was built by and for people who worked with things; its main power base is still in automobiles, steel, freight transportation, metalworking and other crafts. But thing-oriented work is now the province of a dwindling minority of the U.S. labor force. More and more of the organized workers, and the great bulk of the unorganized, are working in services, and most of the service employees are in information work, which means they are "producing," too, only their output is not things but symbols.

If information (through being refined into knowledge and wisdom) is now our "crucial resource," what does that portend for the future? Thinking about the inherent characteristics of information provides some clues to the vigorous rethinking that lies ahead for all of us, and especially for those of us who would like to play the generalist role:

1. Information is expandable. In 1972, the same year *The Limits to Growth* was published, John McHale came out with a book called *The Changing Information Environment,* which argued that information expands as it is used. That idea has won reluctant but widening acceptance ever since. Some information for some purposes is certainly depletive over time. A tip on the fourth race at Belmont might be valuable at lunchtime and valueless by dinnertime. Yesterday's weather forecast is of merely historical interest tomorrow. But for the most part, as Anne Wells Branscomb says, information is "a synergistic resource . . . the more we have the more we use and the more useful it becomes."

Whole industries have grown up to exploit this characteristic of information: scientific research, technology transfer, computer software (which already makes a contribution to the U.S. economy that is three times the contribution of computer hardware), and agencies for publishing, advertising, public relations, and government propaganda to spread the word (and thus to enhance the word's value).

Information is consequently not scarce. Because it is expandable without any obvious limits, the facts are never all in—and facts are available in such profusion that uncertainty becomes the most important planning factor. The further a society moves toward making its living from the manipulation of information, the more its citizens will be caught up in a continual struggle to reduce the information overload on their desks and in their lives in order to reduce the uncertainty about what to *do*.

In the information society, we trade glut for scarcity, flood for drought. To find that our "crucial resource" is not scarce does not mean that life will be easier. "Information-rich" does not mean affluent; it is quite as likely to mean swamped. The ecologists have taught us that, in nature, too much is often as troublesome as too little; scarcity can be either drought or flood. All of us, and the leaders among us most of all, have to learn how to deal with information entropy.

The ultimate "limits to growth" of knowledge and wisdom are *time* (available to human minds for reflecting, analyzing, and integrating the information that will be "brought to life" by being used) and the *capacity* of people—individually and in groups—to analyze and think integratively. There are obvious limits to the time each of us can devote to the production and refinement of knowledge and wisdom. But the capacity of humanity to integrate its collective experience through relevant individual thinking is certainly expandable, not without limits, to be sure, but within limits we cannot now measure or imagine.

2. Information is compressible. Paradoxically, this infinitely expandable resource can be concentrated, integrated, summarized—miniaturized, if you will—for easier handling. We can store many complex cases in a single theorem, squeeze insights from masses of data into a single formula, capture many lessons learned from practical experience in a manual of procedure.

Information can also be compressed physically, and in consequence *the information society is not resource-hungry.* Compared to the processes of the steel-and-automobile economy, the production and distribution of information are remarkably sparing in their requirements for energy and other physical and biological resources.

Every new breakthrough (miniaturization of computers, fiber optics for telecommunication, genetic engineering for the information systems called plants, animals, and our own bodies) seems to decrease the resource-hungriness of the "advanced" economies. Investments, price policies, and power relationships that assume that the more-developed countries will gobble up disproportionate shares of "real" resources are overdue for wholesale revision.

3. Information is substitutable. It can and increasingly does replace land, labor, and capital. People who use computers hooked up to telecommunications don't need much real estate to be efficient. Robotics and automation in factories and offices are displacing workers and thus requiring a transformation of the labor force. Many workers who have previously helped grow or extract or make things, or who have been in the noninformation services, are learning to become information workers, or getting used to being unemployed. This transformation may affect as many as 40 million workers between 1985 and the year 2000.

The substitution of organized data for capital goods and physical materials is not quite as obvious but is also proceeding apace. Any machine that can be accessed by computerized telecommunications doesn't have to be in your own inventory. And Dieter Altenpohl, an executive of Alusuisse, has calculations and charts to prove that, as he says, "The smarter the metal, the less it weighs."

4. Information is transportable—at the speed of light and, perhaps, through telepathy, faster than that. In less than a century, we have been witness to a major dimensional change in both the speed and volume of human activity, a change in transportability of resources greater than the multimillennial shift from foot travel to supersonic jets.

As a result, remoteness is now more choice than geography. You can sit anywhere there is a workable telephone service and play the New York stock markets in real time, though in some time zones you might have to keep rather peculiar hours. And the same is true, without the big time gaps in time zones, of people in any rural hamlet in the United States. Indeed, there is no real reason for the New York Stock Exchange to be in New York City at all. Citicorp has already located its whole credit-card operation in a place in South Dakota that is "remote" only by preelectronic standards. Concurrently with editing this book on an IBM PC in Punalu'u, on the Big Island of Hawaii, in order to "get away from it all," I am conducting a computer teleconference on leadership with three dozen executives and a few other participants, scattered from Miami to Seattle in the United States, and one of them participating from London. Since each of us comes "on line" at times of his or her own choosing, the time zones that separate us suddenly become irrelevant. In the world of information-richness, you will be able to be remote if you want to, but you'll have to work at it.

5. Information is diffusive. It tends to leak; the more it leaks the more we have and the more of us have it. Information is aggressive, even imperialistic, in striving to break out of the unnatural bonds of secrecy in which thing-minded people try to imprison it. Like a virus (itself a tiny information system), information tries to affect the organisms around it, whether by over-the-fence gossip or satellite broadcasting. The straitjackets of public secrecy, intellectual property rights, and confidentiality of all kinds fit very loosely on this restless resource.

It is not the inherent tendency of natural resources to leak. Jewels may be stolen; a lump or two of coal may fall off the coal car on its way from Montana; there is an occasional spillage of oil in the ocean. But the leakage of information is wholesale, pervasive, and continuous. And the technologies of the leak are gaining fast on the pitiful efforts to bottle up information: that great pirate ship, the

Xerox machine, led the way, followed by the advancing forces of high-resolution photography, parabolic listening devices, remote sensing, electronic computation, satellite communication, and, closer to home, universal education combined with the human urge to pass a secret along.

It probably goes too far to say what one army general was quoted in *The Christian Science Monitor* as having said at a congressional hearing: "There are no secrets." But in the era of the institutionalized leak, monopolizing information is very nearly a contradiction in terms; that can be done only in more and more specialized fields, for shorter and shorter periods of time.

6. Information is shareable. The great communications theorist, Professor Colin Cherry of the University of London, has been insisting for many years that information by nature cannot give rise to exchange transactions, only to *sharing* transactions. Things are exchanged: if I give you a flower or sell you my automobile, you have it and I don't. But if I sell you an idea, we both have it. And if I give you a fact or tell you a story, it's like a good kiss: sharing the thrill enhances it. Conversely, if the kiss carries a disease (information harmful to your mental health), the sharing transaction could be infectious.

An information-rich environment is thus a sharing environment. That needn't mean an environment without standards, rules, conventions, or ethical codes. It does mean the standards, rules, conventions, and codes are going to be different from those created to manage the zero-sum bargains of market economics and traditional international relations.

The information resource, in short, is different in kind from other resources. And that's important because information has become our key resource. Information now plays so prominent a role in postindustrial society that we are tempted to treat it as a new subject or field, or even a separate discipline. It's something like the early reaction to the drama of space exploration. When the Mercury and Apollo programs were planned, it seemed at first that outer space might become a new principle of organization, maybe even requiring a new kind of academic department. But it soon dawned on us that space was not a new subject but a new *place* where all the old subjects —physics, biochemistry, medicine, military science, law, economics, politics, even art and philosophy and religion—took on interesting new dimensions.

In a similar way, the convergence of computers and telecommunications doesn't resolve any of the ancient puzzles about human rights and responsibilities, man and nature, liberty and authority, productivity and fairness, pursuit of the common good in a world full of individuals, and protection of the global commons in a world full of nation-states.

But the informatization of society does change the *context* in which these durable dilemmas present themselves in the 1980s and 1990s. Out there in the marketplace of ideas, this expandable, compressible, substitutable, transportable, leaky, shareable resource is creating a lot of confusion as it undermines our inherited knowledge and wisdom.

A society in which information is the key resource is not necessarily "better" or "worse," fairer or more exploitative, cleaner or dirtier, happier or unhappier than agricultural or industrial societies in which physical, tangible resources are dominant. The quality, relevance, and usefulness of information are not givens. They depend on who uses the dominant resource, how astutely, and for what purposes. What is different now is that information is, in all sorts of ways, far more *accessible* than the world's key resources have ever been at any previous time in history.

The first task for leaders and potential leaders, then, is to look much more sharply at our heritage of assumptions. The most troublesome concepts are those which were created to deal with the main problems presented by the management of things—problems such as their scarcity, their bulk, their limited substitutability for each other, the expense and trouble in transporting them, and the fact that, being tangible, they could often be hidden or at least hoarded. It was in the nature of things that the few had access to resources and the many did not.

Thus, the inherent characteristics of physical resources (natural and man-made) made possible the development of hierarchies of *power based on control* (of new weapons, of energy sources, of trade routes, of markets, and especially of knowledge), hierarchies of *influence based on secrecy,* hierarchies of *class based on ownership,* hierarchies of *privilege based on early access* to valuable resources, and hierarchies of *politics based on geography.*

Each of these five bases for hierarchy and discrimination is crumbling today—because the old means of control are of dwindling efficacy, secrets are harder and harder to keep, and ownership, early arrival, and geography are of dwindling significance in getting access to the knowledge and wisdom that are the really valuable legal tender of our time.

Out of dozens of assumptions requiring a newly skeptical stare in the new knowledge environment, these five seem to me to bear most directly on executive leadership because they are likely to affect most profoundly the ways in which, and the purposes for which, people will in future be brought together in organizations to make something different happen.

The next chapter focuses on the erosion of power based on control. Chapter 4 considers the erosion of secrecy and asks how much openness is enough. Chapters 5, 6, and 7 examine how, in the changing information environment, the old advantages of ownership, privileged access, and geography are wearing thin.

3

Control:
The Twilight
of Hierarchy

Some people collect coins or stamps or snuffboxes or forgeries of Salvador Dali paintings. I have taken to collecting Canutes—instances of behavior reminiscent of the legendary Danish monarch who stood on an English beach and commanded the tides to stand still as proof of his power. King Canute was not stupid. According to the Viking historians, he intended the waters to give him a wetting, as an object lesson in humility for his courtiers, who believed him to be all-powerful. But Canute's name has gone down in myth as a metaphor for attempts to avoid the unavoidable, and it is in this sense that we evoke his memory here.

The information environment created by the fusion of computers and telecommunications is full of examples of contemporary Canutish behavior. The trouble seems to be that we have adopted uncritically for the management of *information* concepts that have proven useful during the centuries when *things* were the dominant resources and the prime objects of commerce, politics, power, and prestige. When we do this, our inherited wisdom is somehow transmuted into folly. Nowhere is this truer than in the exercise of power in management, administration, and politics.

Knowledge is power, as Francis Bacon wrote in 1597. So the wider the spread of knowledge, the more power gets diffused. For the most part individuals and corporations and governments don't have a choice about this; it is the ineluctable consequence of creating, through education, societies with millions of knowledgeable people.

We see the results all around us, and around the world. More and more work gets done by horizontal process, or it doesn't get done. More and more decisions are made with wider and wider consultation, or they don't "stick." The Japanese call it *consensus.* The Indonesians call it *mushyawara.* The communists call it *collective leadership.* We call it *teamwork,* or *committee work.* If the Census Bureau counted each year the number of committees per thousand population, we would have a rough quantitative measure of the bundle of changes called the information society.

In the new knowledge environment we have to rethink the very nature of rule, power, and authority. A revolution in the technology of organization—the twilight of hierarchy—is already well under way.

Information has always been the basis of human organization, of course. Those with better or more recent information (Moses with his tablets, generals with their fast couriers, kings with their spies and ambassadors, speculators with their quick access to markets for gold, diamonds, or ownership shares, security forces with their sources of rumor and gossip) held sway over the rest of humankind.

But once information could be spread fast and wide—rapidly collected and analyzed, instantly communicated, readily understood by millions—the power monopolies that closely held knowledge made possible were subject to accelerating erosion. Strangely, both the monopolies and their victims have often been slow to perceive the trend.

Even among the well informed, of course, the best or most recently informed still have an edge. A vignette stored in memory may help make the point.

During the Congo crisis in the early 1960s, the United Nations had a five-thousand-man brigade of peacekeeping troops chasing the local gendarmerie around the copper-rich province of Katanga. The UN force was well led by a gung-ho Indian commander, who tended to advance on his own instinct rather than on instructions from UN headquarters in New York. This was easy for the commander to do as long as Ralph Bunche (an American winner of the Nobel Peace Prize who, as undersecretary general, was responsible for UN peacekeeping operations) didn't get direct reports of his forces' action in the field until twenty-four hours or more after the fact. I was the person in Washington responsible for worrying about this state of affairs. Fortunately we had an air attaché in our embassy (to the newly independent country then known as Congo, now called Zaire), whose airplane was stuffed full of state-of-the-art communications equipment. He flew around the Katanga, keeping close track of the shifting positions of the UN force. My colleagues and I would talk to him once or twice a day on his single sideband radio, from a room within two minutes' walk from my State Department office. From time to time, I would phone Ralph Bunche in New York to tell him where his troops were, long before he knew himself. There is no doubt that our timelier access to useful knowledge at that critical juncture enhanced U.S. influence on UN peacekeeping policy, then and later.

In the old days when only a few people were well educated and "in the know," leadership of the uninformed was likely to be organized in vertical structures of command and control. Leadership of the informed is different: it results in the necessary action only if exercised mainly by persuasion, bringing into consultation those who are going to have to do something to make the decision work. Where people are educated and are *not* treated this way, they either balk at the decisions made or have to be dragooned by organized misinformation backed by brute force. Recent examples of both results have been on display in Poland.

This is the origin of Chester Barnard's seminal theory of the executive function: authority is *delegated upward.* As director of an organization, you have no power that is not granted to you by your subordinates. Eliciting their continual (and if possible cheerful) cooperation is your main job as director; without it, you cannot get the most routine tasks (for which others are holding you, not your staff, responsible) accomplished. Indeed, nowadays in many offices orders that used to be routinely accepted are now resisted or refused. In the modern American office, if you want a cup of coffee you don't take that co-worker, the secretary, off her or his own work to get it for you.

In this environment the King Canute prize for 1981 was easily won by Secretary of State Alexander Haig. Shortly after the attempted assassination of President Reagan, Haig announced on television from the White House that "I am in control here. . . . " That produced neither reassurance nor anger from the American people but nervous laughter, as in watching theater of the absurd. We the people know by instinct that in our pluralistic democracy no one is, can be, or is even supposed to be "in control." By constitutional design reinforced by the information-rich conditions of work, we live in a nobody-in-charge society.

We all know other Canutes and courtiers whose absurdities don't get on national television: executives who give orders when they should be asking questions, managers who think of their co-workers as superiors or subordinates, impatient doers who don't have time for lateral consultation—in sum, the builders of bureaucratic pyramids who haven't learned how to work by consultation and consensus.

In an information-rich polity, the very definition of *control* changes. Very large numbers of people empowered by knowledge— coming together in parties, unions, factions, lobbies, interest groups, neighborhoods, families, and hundreds of other structures—assert the right or feel the obligation to "make policy."

Decision making proceeds not by "recommendations up, orders

down," but by development of a shared sense of direction among those who must form the parade if there is going to be a parade. Collegial not command structures become the more natural basis for organization. Not "command and control" but "conferring and networking" become the mandatory modes for getting things done.

"Planning" cannot be done by a few leaders, or even by the brightest whiz-kids immured in a systems analysis unit or a planning staff. Real-life planning is the dynamic improvisation by the many on a general sense of direction. The sense of direction is announced by a few of the many, but only after genuine consultation with those who will have to improvise on it.

More participatory decision making implies a need for much information, widely spread, and much feedback, seriously attended, as in biological processes. Participation and public feedback become conditions precedent to decisions that stick.

Secrecy goes out of fashion, because secrets are so hard to keep. That means more openness, not as an ideological preference but as a technological imperative.

In a nobody-in-charge society, where decisions are made by consensus and committee work, policy is made by an upside-down version of the traditional pyramid of power. Russell Baker, probably the best satirist currently on active service, captured its essence in an ironic dialogue with himself several years ago:

What does this country need today?
Leadership. . . . The country yearns for new leadership for a new era.

If led, will the country follow?
If given the right kind of leadership, the country will surely follow.

But what kind of leadership is the right kind?
The leadership that leads the country in the direction it wants to take.

And what specific direction does the country want to take?
Who knows? That's for the leader to figure out. If he is the right
kind of leader, he will guess correctly.

*. . . Am I wrong in concluding that it isn't leadership the country
wants in a President but followership?*

Russell Baker was not wrong. High policy—that is, major change in
society's sense of direction—is first shaped in an inchoate consensus
reached by the people at large.

If you find this upside-down pyramid hard to visualize, you are
in distinguished company. The classic expression of wearied cynicism is still Walter Lippmann's brooding book *The Phantom Public,*
in which he announced his conclusion that "we must abandon the
notion that the people govern. Instead," he continued, "we must
adopt the theory that, by their occasional mobilization as a majority,
people support or oppose individuals who actually govern. We must
say that the popular will does not direct continuously but that it
intervenes occasionally." The task, Lippmann thought, was "to find
ways for people to act intelligently but in ignorance."

Walter Lippmann was the most brilliant pundit of his time, but
he never ran for office or even ran an organization. No political
leader or organization executive could operate on his premise and
survive.

Tick off in your mind some major shifts in U.S. policy these past
twenty years:

The federal government was the last to learn that the war in
Vietnam was over.

Richard Nixon and his immediate staff were the last to tumble
to the fact that the president had fumbled his way out of office.

The tidal waves of social change in our time—environmental
sensitivity, civil rights for all races, the enhanced status of women,
recognition of the rights of consumers and small investors—were not
generated by the established leaders in government, business, labor,
religion, or higher education, but boiled up from people (and new
leaders) who had not previously been heard from.

The nuclear-power industry was derailed by the very large numbers of people who concluded that the experts had not done their homework on nuclear safety, on nuclear proliferation, or on the disposal of radioactive waste—yet were nevertheless pushing this new source of energy down the people's throats.

American women had stopped having so many babies long before school boards and government planners adjusted to no-growth or slow-growth assumptions.

The people at large were opting for smaller cars well before Detroit caught on.

People-in-general moved rapidly toward an ethic of qualitative growth while government and business leaders were still measuring progress by quantitative aggregates.

People-in-general got interested in energy conservation and solar energy while the ranking alarmists on energy policy in and out of government were still pooh-poohing sun-based alternatives to imported oil, driving around in gas-guzzling limousines, and failing to practice conservation in their own organizations.

Sprinkle on your own illustrations, to taste.

What seems to happen is that if the question is important enough, people-in-general get to the answer first. Then the experts and pundits and pollsters and labor leaders and lawyers and doctors and business executives and foundation officers and judges and professors and public executives, many of them chronically afflicted with hardening of the categories, catch up in jerky arthritic moves with all deliberate speed. The press serves as a gatekeeper, moving all this information from its specialized sources to the general public, where it is then circulated through informal but powerful interpersonal networks. And only then, when the policy decision is long since made and the experts have finally done the programming, written the editorials, raised the money, painted the directional signposts, and staged the appropriate media event, the publicity heroes and heroines come forth, the people that *People* magazine thinks are our leaders, to climb aboard the train as it gathers momentum and announce for all to hear the new direction of march—speaking by television from the safety of the caboose.

It's more and more obvious: those with visible responsibility for leadership are nearly always too visible to take the responsibility for change, until it becomes more dangerous to stand there than to move on. It is not a new idea: "I am a leader," Voltaire wrote, "therefore I must follow."

There are exceptions, but they are rare. Anwar Sadat was a leader who presumed to break through the barrier of conventionally expert advice, which counseled him not to practice dramatic public diplomacy in so touchy a matter as Egyptian-Israeli relations. But Sadat's crowning initiative—the simple announcement: "I will go to Jerusalem"—was one of only very few acts of personal leadership by a publicity hero, getting well out ahead of any perceived consensus, that I have witnessed in forty years of observing and practicing international politics. Sadat's sudden move was in a class with Gandhi's nonviolent protests, or Churchill's rallying cry, or Roosevelt's Lend-Lease proposal, or General Marshall's speech at Harvard, or Tito's break with the Kremlin, or John F. Kennedy's nuclear-test-ban proposal. (Nixon's opening contact with China doesn't make this list; his tactics were dramatic enough, but by the time he moved the American people had long since made the underlying policy decision to recognize the People's Republic as the government of China.)

John Stuart Mill's comment is even more up-to-date than when it was written: "That so few dare to be eccentric marks the chief danger of the times."

Most of the history we learn in school is so narrowly focused on visible leaders that it may give us the wrong impression about leadership processes even in earlier times. We learn that Genghis Khan or Louis XIV or George Washington or Ibn Saud or the Emperor of Japan said this and did that, as though he thought it up by himself, consulted with nobody, and wrote without the help of a ghostwriter. But even in ancient, "traditional" societies I suspect that effective leadership consisted in being closely in touch with where the relevant publics were ready to be told to go.

Consensus is a prominent feature of many cultures now dismissed as "primitive." The Polynesians in the Pacific islands with their circular village councils and the American Indians around their campfires made (and in some degree still make) decisions by fluid procedures that may induce more genuine participation than a "modern" meeting run by parliamentary procedure. In the agora of Athens and the "Senate and people of Rome" (the SPQR), there seems to have been lively participation by those (well-born male citizens) qualified to take part.

The difference in the current scene is the sheer *scale* of the relevant publics. In "democratic" Athens slaves, women, tradesmen, and other noncitizens didn't presume to play in the decision games. The notion that "all men," let alone whole peoples, had inalienable rights came in only with the Enlightenment, a scant three centuries ago, and has been made effective, still in a minority of the world's nations, only in the twentieth century.

Even Moses, with all the apparent authority in his hands—because he was God's instrument for governing the Israelites—had to learn the hard way about executive leadership. In the biblical story, when he descended from Mount Sinai with the two stone tablets of the law and saw the children of Israel making merry around the golden calf, he flew into a rage and broke the tablets. Later, after a good deal of retributive violence, Moses went back up the mountain and carved the Ten Commandments into two more stone tablets "like unto the first."

In the first action, says historian Sidney Hyman, Moses was conceding that law that lacks a consensus of support is unenforceable. "In that sense, law and life must be in accord, and no leader can get too far in advance of his people if he expects to be followed. But the fact that Moses proceeded to hew out a duplicate table of the law seems to say that he understood (upon reflection) that law itself is a great teacher—that its enforcement can in time create a consensus in its own support."

In the 1980s A.D., anyway, it is clear enough that the policy announcements by publicity heroes we hear on radio and television or read in the newspapers should not be confused with "policy-making." That noble function is more complicated and more interesting, the product of a continuous multilogue between the real leaders (the million or more Americans and their counterparts in other nations) and the general public.

The same is true of less visible decisions in, for example, corporations, universities, and hospitals. When Procter & Gamble launches a new product, General Motors unveils a new model, or college tuition and the cost of a day in the hospital go up again, you can be sure that the real policy-making was the product of staff work, internal arguments, and external consultation, not only with experts but with consumers or other constituents whose acquiescence is essential to making the decision stick. (A decision that doesn't stick isn't a decision no matter how loudly it is announced.) Indeed, in complex matters and especially if it is bad news like a price increase, new policy may even be announced by the "executive committee"— with the visibly responsible "leader" out of town or otherwise unavailable for direct quotation. This luxury of anonymous visibility is not available, of course, to public officials; for the political executive, there's no hiding place down here.

The upside-down model of policy-making is well described, curiously enough, in *The Thoughts of Mao Tse-tung,* the little red book that is available in several languages as visitors to the People's Republic arrive at their airport of entry into the enigma of Chinese communism. The booklet contains a good deal of warmed-over Lenin and some editor's effort to rewrite nuggets of ancient Chinese to make them sound like Marxism. But the *Thoughts* also contain a few passages of practical advice from a crafty and experienced executive leader who, like it or not, put together the largest (and still potentially the most successful) revolution in world history.

In one of these, Mao is addressing the cadres (read "experts and executives") and he says, translated into American, something like this: Look, you cadres, don't get the idea that you're making the policy. The masses (read "people") are making the policy. Your job is to get out and sniff around and figure out where the masses are going. Then you've got something to do that they don't know how to do. You've got to codify the policy, program and budget it, and organize to carry it out. But then you had better go back and check again with the masses, to make sure you keep up with their changing sense of direction. Then you recodify, reprogram, rebudget, and reorganize. This continuous cyclical dialectic between the leaders and the masses, says Mao, is the correct "theory of knowledge."

Mao and his political heirs have never been able to bring themselves to give the Chinese masses that much rope. (When and if they do, Chinese governance will again be, as it has been before in history, one of the world's prime political and cultural magnets.) But Mao's comments about process are not a bad description of how big decisions do, in fact, get made in the United States of America in the latter part of the twentieth century.

If you prefer to take your political philosophy of executive leadership from American classics, I can offer the comment of Chester Barnard, a corporate CEO who became a public official and provided in *The Functions of the Executive* one of the earliest analyses of modern executive leadership. "When I have been asked: 'What do you *do*?' I have been unable to reply intelligibly." A leader, he argued, often takes ideas about what to do and how to lead from the very people he leads: " . . . this sometimes gives the impression that he is a rather stupid fellow, an arbitrary functionary, a mere channel of communication, and a filcher of ideas. In a measure this is correct. He has to be stupid enough to listen a great deal, he certainly must arbitrate to maintain order, and he has to be at times a mere center of communication. If he used only his own ideas he would be somewhat like a one-man orchestra, rather than a good conductor, who is a very high type of leader."

John Gardner puts it this way: "Very few—almost no—major policy innovations are enacted at the federal level that are not preceded by years (say, three to ten years) of national discussion and debate. The national dialogue is an untidy but impressive process. Ideas that will eventually become the basis for some major innovation in federal policy are first put into circulation by individuals and small groups." These individuals and small groups are often sensing a public mood before the public has yet been told by the communications media what their mood is supposed to be.

47

This bubble-up (rather than top-down) process, equally untidy and impressive, is to be found not only at the federal level but wherever complex and innovative decisions have to be made and carried into action. When a pollster asks the right question, a journalist senses a trend, a marketing strategist tests a new product sent over by the R & D people, a professor tests a new idea derived from working with graduate students, a legislator proposes something fresh after talking with constituents, he or she helps convert the inchoate policy into programmatic form.

A political leader may sense a change of mood and ride into office on it. Jimmy Carter did this in 1976. He correctly guessed, for example, that after Vietnam and Watergate people yearned for honesty and plain speaking; that religious virtues were still good politics; that people had already grown out of their post-Vietnam despondency and were waiting for a leader to articulate a post-post-Vietnam policy that combined a strong defense with a strong effort to reduce the cost of defense through arms control.

Ronald Reagan also skillfully caught a wave in 1980. He guessed that resentment of big government and high taxes were at near flood tide; that people were worried about the steady buildup of Soviet military power and impatient with abuses and waste in social programs; and above all that Americans were tired of having to think of themselves as impotent in international affairs, unable even to protect half a hundred Americans on the premises of our own embassy in Tehran. Again and again in the 1980 campaign, he stressed his upbeat philosophy: We're Americans. We can do whatever we set out to do. He used a similar theme in his 1984 reelection campaign; the Democratic challengers never absorbed the idea that people are moved more by hope than by fear.

But in the 1980s a new wave is forming: the special concern of women has propelled the "peace issue" toward the center of electoral politics, and the polls report that close to 80 percent of the people favor a mutual, verifiable freeze in the manufacture and deployment of nuclear weapons.

Participatory fever is contagious. Public policy used to mean "what the government does." Now it includes corporate policies, collective bargaining agreements, the cost of health care, the recruitment of university presidents, lobbying practices, equal employment opportunity, environmental protection, tax shelters, waste disposal, private contributions to political candidates, the sex habits of employees, and just about any other "insider" activities that outsiders think are important enough to engage their time and attention.

The biggest issues so far have to do with the quality of public responsibility that shows forth in the actions of corporations, universities, hospitals, and the thousands of other structures in which executives make the decisions that serve people, cost them, anger them, or please them.

The rising tide of participation is reflected in dramatic organizational changes. Big corporations now usually have a vice-president for keeping the corporation out of trouble with nosy outsiders, or even with their own stockholders and employees, who raise questions about what the company ought to produce, who it ought to employ, and how it ought to invest its money.

Should "my" company, or any American company, make and market nerve gas, even if the government does want to buy it? Should "my" company, or any American company, promote nuclear proliferation by selling to developing countries nuclear power plants that make plutonium, the fuel for nuclear weapons, as a by-product of generating electricity? Shouldn't "my" company have more women, and blacks, and American Indians in its employ, and especially on its board and in top management? Should a company whose stock I own invest my money in South Africa? Should "my" company, or any American company, pass the social costs of its profit seeking— overcrowding, the paving of green space, radioactive risk, dirt, noise, toxic waste, acid rain, or whatever—on to the general public? Should our community hospital perform abortions, splice genes, change people's sex, invest in expensive equipment that can help only a few affluent patients? Should our state university do secret work for the

Defense Department? Should the CIA recruit our students for who-knows-what clandestine wars in other people's countries?

Such questions cannot be brushed aside without raising their decibel level. There are ways to deal with all of them: shifts of policy or diversionary moves or consultative processes or public explanations—in descending order of probable effectiveness. But the visibly responsible leaders had better build into their organizations staff members competent to help develop strategy on such issues as these, not as a public relations frill but as an essential ingredient in bottom-line budgeting. And the visible executive had better be personally competent to defend the organization's public posture in public debate. These "public responsibility" issues can make or break companies, products, and executive reputations. If you don't believe that, take a Nestlé executive to lunch and ask him about marketing baby formula in the Third World.

As every surfer knows, it is not easy to catch a wave even when you know from what direction it will be coming, and it's impossible if you do not watch it very carefully. The task of leadership, then, is most often to help the followers go where they want to go—and if a publicity hero gets too far behind, as President Nixon helped us all understand, he gets wiped out.

4

Secrecy:
Costs and Benefits
of Openness

The push for participation by all kinds of people and the inherent leakiness of the information resource combine to produce the modern executive's most puzzling dilemma. The dilemma must have been familiar to the first cavepeople who tried to bring other cavepeople together to get something done. But for us moderns, the scale of the perplexity is without precedent. The dilemma can be summarized in one question: *How do you get everybody in on the act and still get some action?*

The contemporary clamor to be in on the act is certainly impressive. In business, customers are feistier, more likely to complain; stockholders are more numerous and less passive; policyholders are more inclined to follow through on their insurance claims; union members and other citizens give advice on what's wrong with the steel and automobile industries; employees assert the right to judge whether their employers should make fragmentation bombs; maritime unions decide whether shipments should go to the Soviet Union; advocacy agencies excluded from the United Way organize their own competing drives for community funds deducted from payrolls. Ethnic groups keep a watchful eye on investments in South Africa and business with partisans of Israel and the Arabs. More and more parents have a world population policy; teachers organize to tell school systems what ought to be taught; students want tailor-made courses of study. Environmental groups are articulate and effective beyond the wildest dreams of Gifford Pinchot and Teddy Roosevelt. New kinds and colors of people are breaking through the oligopoly of influence long controlled by businessmen and male lawyers from early-arriving ethnic groups. Even those deadly predictable circuses, our national political conventions, become increasingly interesting as minorities and women fill more delegate slots, and live television coverage enhances the risk that a delegate will be seen making a deal, picking his nose, adjusting her shoulder strap, or falling asleep in millions of living rooms at once.

Openness, then, is the buzzword of modernization. In its firmament the deities are the public hearing, the news conference, the investigative reporter, "60 Minutes" and "20-20," Ted Koppel, Phil Donahue, and the *National Enquirer.* Its devils are also well known: smoke-filled rooms, secret invasions, hidden or edited tapes, and expense-account luncheons at which the establishment decides what to do next.

In consequence, compared with a generation ago, most public officials—and a rapidly growing number of private executives conscious of their ultimate public responsiblity—are much more inclined to ask themselves, before acting, how their actions would look on the front page of *The Washington Post* or *The Wall Street Journal,* or on the evening telecast. Even former Vice-President Agnew has conceded that taking cash from contractors in his government office might be wrong if judged by what he called post-Watergate moral standards. No one doubts that raising the risk of public exposure will improve the private behavior of executive leaders as they ask themselves, "How would I feel about this action if everyone were able to see me take it?" The moral of Watergate is plain: If the validity of your action *depends* on its secrecy, better decide to do something else.

But the yen for wider knowledge and broader participation has gone well beyond this nationwide sensitivity training for visible leaders, and raised new questions about the "cost-benefit calculation" of more openness. A generation of experience suggests that it is high time we faced the *next* question: How much openness is enough?

Because this isn't a mystery story, I shall reveal at the outset the conclusion of the analysis that follows. Experience teaches that the procedures of openness are well designed to stop bad things from happening and ill designed to get good things moving, unless the consensus for action has been built in private ahead of time.

This is a difficult subject to discuss without being misunderstood. I have complained for years, in writing and at length, about the malignant effect of secrecy on public policy. In a paper for the Senate Watergate Committee, historian Stuart Gerry Brown and I argued that secrecy and confined circles of consultation may have been the main reasons for some of the classic boo-boos of our time: the Bay of Pigs fiasco, the escalation of the war in Vietnam, the Nixon shock in Japan, and of course the *opéra bouffe* of Watergate. (That article was written before President Carter's hostage trouble in Tehran and President Reagan's "peacekeeping" trouble in Beirut; both would have lengthened our list of America's self-inflicted wounds.)

In most areas of social, economic, and political concern, we are nowhere near the limits of useful openness. But the evidence is piling up that the very great benefits of openness and wide participation are being offset by the risks of making it difficult or impossible to get done the complicated things that have to be done if we are going to protect our communities, our surroundings, our bodies, and ourselves.

The practical dilemmas of openness were awaiting me when I arrived in Hawaii, to become president of its state university system, in the fall of 1969. The Vietnam War was still in full swing. Hawaii sometimes follows fashions a year or two late, so we were having in 1969 the kind of turbulence that hit the Berkeley campus of the University of California in 1967. We even had a few restless alumni of the Berkeley demonstrations who had come to Hawaii to help generate a second round in the gentler land of Aloha.

It did not take long to notice that some of the campus demonstrations started when someone anonymously called the three commercial television stations to say, "There's going to be a demonstration at noon at the corner of Dole Street and University Avenue." A sizable part of the more than twenty thousand students on the university's central campus would be going somewhere near that busy intersection anyway at noon. The television cameras would obediently turn up at the appointed time, several hundred persons would wander by, see the cameras and a small knot of activists, and come over to see what was going on. The resulting crowd would look impressive by Hawaii standards; their pictures would be duly taken and reported on the evening news as a large campus kerfuffle.

We decided that the situation might be amenable to reason and we took our complaint about the cameras attracting the demonstrators to the Honolulu Community-Media Council, a mediating body that had just been started at the university's initiative. After a good deal of negotiation we prevailed on the three stations to adopt in common a new policy: They agreed to send reporters only to nose around, but not to send cameras or other conspicuous technology unless there was something to photograph other than what was induced by the presence of the television equipment. The incidence of one-day dramas dropped off sharply. (Plenty of real drama remained; that was the season of the Cambodia invasion and ugly incidents at Kent State and Jackson State universities, and every large campus was oscillating between turmoil and unease.)

It was also in Hawaii that I became fascinated with the dilemmas and contradictions that arise when leaders genuinely try to get everybody in on the act. The swelling demands for participation and openness culminated in controversy about legislation requiring public boards to do their business and keep their records "in the sunshine." In the 50th state, so recently a colony, the idea of opening up all sorts of decision-making processes had a wide appeal. The benefits were all too obvious in a society where most of the land belonged to a few big companies (because so much land had been given by the Hawaiian monarchy to members of the old missionary families, of whom it was said that they "came to do good and did well"), and most of the political power belonged to a well-established Democratic organization based on block voting by the ethnic Japanese and run by John A. Burns, an astute and talented Irishman in his fourth term as governor.

To my surprise I found myself, at first, almost alone in publicly questioning the form of sunshine proposed for the 50th state. Under an early draft of the law, two legislators passing each other in the corridors of the state capitol would be forbidden to talk about anything "likely to come to their attention in their official capacities" unless seven days' notice had been given, the press and public invited, and the subject to be discussed advertised. I wondered aloud what the Founding Fathers, who believed in representative government, would think of such a doctrine. In one debate I observed that those two legislators would have to stick to pleasantries about the weather and, given the scientific potentials of changing the weather at human command, even talking about the weather might soon be ruled out. (The law that eventually passed was much modified from the version thus ridiculed.)

This brand of sunshine, which I described at the time as moonshine, struck me as the product of linear thinking carried to the limits of absurdity: if more openness improves the quality, relevance, fairness, and acceptability of public policy, then total openness is bound to produce the best policy of all. The logic is appealing, and a great deal of steam has been generated in its support. There is almost no political constituency in this country where a visible leader can oppose more openness and survive.

Let us take, as one slice of the openness trend, the experience so far with these state open-meeting, or sunshine, laws, and look honestly at some illuminating examples of where our experiments with openness might lead.

Open meetings are not the only form of legislative sunshine. Open records (the federal Freedom of Information Act and its counterparts in the states), "open appointment" procedures, radio and television coverage of courts and Congress, and the growing demands to open up "private" companies and agencies (because they are all ultimately affected with the public interest) are also part of the picture. But we will start with the open meetings issue and work out from there.

The idea that openness should be legislated by government does not come down to us from the common law or even from the U.S. Constitution, which made it possible to restrict voting to white men and leaned heavily on the notion that the people's representatives, not the people themselves, would be the real policymakers. Thomas Jefferson once suggested applying a kind of "sunshine" to the proceedings of the constitutional convention; it didn't happen. (It is an interesting speculation: if no private caucuses among delegates had been permitted, would the resulting Constitution have proved to be so durable?)

Openness as a principle of governance does not appear until 1898, in a Utah statute; Florida, which has appropriately been a bellwether "sunshine state," followed suit in 1905. A remake of the Florida sunshine law in 1954 generated a small tidal wave of similar laws. A second burst of sunshine developed in the wake of the Watergate scandals in the early 1970s. Their purpose clauses are full of resentment and fury against deception, corruption, and cover-up in high places. By 1974, forty-six states had sunshine laws, and by 1977 meetings of public bodies were required to be open in all fifty states. Federal legislation followed the lead taken by the states—an interesting reversal of the way civil rights and women's suffrage became law (first by federal action) during the same period.

Rooted in the thinking of Jefferson and other Founders was of course the idea that a democratic republic would not survive unless its people were thoroughly informed. The people Jefferson and his friends thought worth informing were still a smallish minority of "the people," but the rhetoric was meant to be universal ("all Men") and survives in some of this modern legislation. The California sunshine law derives its justification from the same robust populism that underpins the First Amendment, in wording borrowed by many other states:

> The people, in delegating authority, do not give their public servants the right to decide what is good for the people to know and what is not good for them to know. The people insist on remaining informed so that they may retain control over the instruments they create.

The principle is persuasive, but conflicting notions, equally basic, are also at issue. Three principles, each represented by powerful gladiators, contend in the policy arena. One is **the public's right to know,** rightly and righteously defended by the media, as self-appointed surrogates for the public, brandishing the First Amendment to the U.S. Constitution as a devastatingly potent weapon. But there is also, say the public executives and members of governing boards, **the right of the public to be served by agencies that can operate effectively** in getting their jobs done in the public interest. And of equal importance there is **the individual's right to privacy** to be considered as well.

Too seldom do the gladiators pause to consider that "the public interest" includes all of these, and that the outcome in any particular case will have to be a creative blend of three principles, which means that no one of them can be overriding.

The state laws and the court cases they have generated so far do not provide a clear signal of how far openness is supposed to go. Every state buys the broad principle that meetings of public bodies should be open. But there is plenty of room for differences on important details. Which bodies are considered public? What constitutes a meeting (should conference phone calls or computer teleconferencing be covered)? How many people makes it a meeting ("two or more members," a quorum, a majority)? What kinds of discussion should be exempted and can still be confidential? How about recruitment of top officials, and evaluation of their performance? Do individuals have a right to privacy when their own cases are discussed in a public body? What about collective bargaining on labor contracts? Or a board's consultation with its attorney about litigation? Or a discussion of buying or selling land or other investments where the public discussion itself could affect the market in ways injurious to the "public interest"?

The states' answers to these and dozens of other knotty questions are far from uniform. Everybody is for openness, but the spectrum of definitions is very wide, ranging from Tennessee's no-nonsense law that opens up all meetings of public bodies, to the cautious approach of Pennsylvania, which is currently judged to be the least "open" state.

The issue extends far beyond governmental processes. The public's right to know is being pressed in domains that used to be considered private; corporations, nonprofit agencies, and foundations also have to decide how much openness is enough. Board members and executives in thousands of parapublic and pseudoprivate enterprises will face the same basic question from their own employees, constituencies, stockholders, policyholders, customers, clients, and critics: Shouldn't we somehow have a bigger part in the decisions you make that affect us?

The case for openness has been so effectively made, and is so much a part of the contemporary American consensus, that it needs no elaboration from me and I am far from wanting to quarrel with it. Apart from the moral justification for open systems—that they give access to people who have been excluded from access—a substantial degree of openness is, as we have seen, a technological imperative of the information society.

In this sense a very large benefit of openness is simply that complex social systems work badly if they are too centralized. (In managing their agriculture, the Soviets have put this proposition on public exhibit for two-thirds of a century.) The opposite of centralization is of course *not* "decentralization," which is simply an effort to preserve hierarchical workways when your organization gets too large for grandpa to know everything. The opposite of centralization is what Charles Lindblom calls *mutual adjustment*: in a generally understood environment of moral rules, norms, conventions, and mores, very large numbers of people adjust their behavior by watching each other and modify their behavior just enough to accommodate the differing purposes of others, but not so much that the mutual adjusters lose sight of where they themselves want to go.

Imagine (the image was suggested by Lindblom) a large clump of people on either side of a busy downtown intersection, waiting for the traffic light to change before crossing the street. There is *macro* discipline here. The convention of the red light means the same thing —danger—to all the participants in this complexity, though there is no physical barrier to violating the norm at their own risk. Then the light changes. It would be theoretically possible, with the help of a computer, to chart in a central *micro* plan the passageway for each pedestrian to enable him or her to get to the other sidewalk without bumping into any other pedestrian. But not even the most totalitarian system tries to plan in such detail. What works is mutual adjustment: Somehow those two knots of people march toward each other and there are no collisions; each adjusts to the others, yet all reach their objective—a positive-sum game if there ever was one.

It is not only at the micro level that mutual adjustment works. It works also in global markets. Even in markets dominated by cartels or monopolies, most of the decisions are not made by giving orders; the price mechanism is an information feedback system that instructs people all over the world how to adjust their behavior to live with the system.

What makes mutual adjustment work is the wide availability of relevant information, so each mutual adjuster can figure out what the others might do under varied conditions, and give forth useful signals about his or her own behavior. The market principle doesn't guarantee smoothly working systems, of course; perfect competition among buyers and sellers with full information is to be found only in textbooks for sophomores. Speculation by big operators can defraud the smaller ones; the herd instinct so prevalent on the floor of the New York Stock Exchange can produce wide swings in basic signals such as prices, out of all proportion to the underlying economic conditions. Yet very large systems, many of them global in scale, based on massive information outputs and feedback systems, have been developed in this century. In recent years systems unimaginable before the marriage of computers and telecommunication (currency and commodity markets, worldwide airline and hotel reservation systems, global public health controls, and weather forecasting systems come readily to mind) are accepted now as routine. These "markets" still mostly require the services of middlepersons: stockbrokers, bankers, travel agents, airline reservation clerks.

The next step, already beyond the experimental stage, is for the producer and consumer to get together without so much intermediation. Tellerless banks and clerkless reservation systems are already spottily in place. The ambitious French test, furnishing an entire community with two-way computer terminals from which a family can book train and airline reservations, buy theater tickets, do comparison shopping, and get the latest news, is only spreading to a whole French city what could be done now in a Minneapolis suburb from my home computer, if I could plug into large computerized data bases and interactive communication systems already in place. I can see already that the limiting factor in the use of the new power that knowledge brings into my home is going to be not the availability of information but our family's capacity to absorb what's out there and the time we will be willing to sit in front of a screen.

But more openness is not always better than less. Aristotle was wise to warn against carrying any principle to its extreme. My research associate, Sandra Braman, and I recently conducted an inquiry (for the Association of Governing Boards of U.S. colleges and universities) into the costs of openness as they affect the governance of higher education in this country, and I have to report that the costs are already high and evidently rising.

We did not have the resources to probe all the ways executives have invented to bypass (and therefore live with) the sunshine laws —the lunches, the (they hope) unrecorded phone conversations, the contrived accidental meetings at the homes of mutual friends. (That would have been an interesting project, like studying speakeasies at the time of Prohibition.) Our analysis nevertheless raises insistent questions with which executive leaders in every field will be grappling in the coming years. So, on the basis of experience and observation, and at the risk of sounding "anti-open," which I'm not, here is an inventory of the costs of openness.

First. The costs of open meetings as such can be summed up this way. An open meeting is likely to be large. The larger it is, the higher the ratio of emotion to reason, nonsense to common sense. An open meeting favors simple formulations over complicated ones, certainty over ambiguity, the loudmouth over the reflective private person. An open meeting is more apt to generate confrontation than compromise, it will probably result in inaction rather than action, and it will likely be prone to caution and delay rather than innovation and impetus.

From interviewing a range of people in half a dozen states with different attitudes toward sunshine laws, we found general agreement on the costs. Open meetings tend to induce:

- A loss of candor.

- A "loss of freedom of speech among decision makers."

- The distortion of complex issues by oversimplification.

- A net reduction in governance. (A university trustee in Iowa put it this way: "We can't go into executive session to discuss an issue of great sensitivity, such as organizational problems. So we just don't govern as much.")

- An inhibition on foresight, prediction, brainstorming, and "blue sky" speculation. ("A public audience can turn a description of possible events into a crisis, a range of alternatives into *faits accomplis,* and constructive criticism into major program weaknesses.")

- A tendency for boards and administrators to delegate major decisions down to levels in the organization that are not covered by the sunshine laws.

•A tendency to do everything with a primary eye to "how it looks." ("The outcome itself is oftentimes different from what it might have been were members of the body solely concerned about finding the best solution to the problem, and not so much about how they appeared while they were doing it.")

•Major changes in the recruitment of university executives, and sometimes the abandonment of any real effort by boards to evaluate executives once they are in office. (More on this below.)

Second. It is obviously easier, and more fun, to advocate openness than to use it. The student movement of the late 1960s and early 1970s achieved greatly expanded opportunities for student participation in college and university decision making in the United States. But an honest reckoning in 1985 would have to feature the massive student absenteeism from the committees where the hard work of budget making and curriculum building is done. "It turned out," a University of Hawaii administrator said to me several years after I had left the Islands, "that the students didn't really want to participate in managing the university. They wanted to watch it being managed, through an open door." (That's a form of openness, too, and may sometimes be the most practical way to get everybody who is really interested in on the act and still get some action.)

Third. Public-interest lawyers and a climate of litigious paranoia have brought the courts into public administration and corporate governance in a big way.

Some of the short-run results are gratifying, but do we want what they lead to? The longer-run effect is to cause every public agency, sizable corporation, or foundation to write down all its procedures. This puts greater power in the hands of lawyers and management specialists, which is nice for them. (Indeed, for some in the legal profession it came along at about the right time. Just when the negligence business was being ruined by the no-fault principle and ambulance chasing was no longer lucrative, along comes a new requirement for legal talent in the form of class-action suits to enforce newly legislated rights; a lawyer of my acquaintance calls this "social ambulance chasing.") But making the administrative process more legalistic also produces those spastic movements and muscle-bound rigidities you see in almost all large organizations these days.

The progress of this degenerative disease can now be traced clinically. Rights are adjudged to be better protected when they are written. If they are written down, they have to be scrupulously fair to equal and unequal alike. Exceptions are then increasingly frowned on, bucked to higher authority, or taken to court. The professional planners and executives lose the flexibility and discretion that attracted them to their professions in the first place. They drift away, to be replaced by instruction-reading machines in human form. The moral climate degenerates with the widespread feeling that whatever really needs to be done is obviously impossible given the existing procedures, and that if there is something wrong, it must be somebody else's turn to fix it.

Fourth. The passion for public hearings, too much of the time, serves only the purpose of having a public hearing so that it cannot be later said that a public hearing was not held. When, exceptionally, the public hearing actually attracts an audience, the news reports feature the most extreme and partisan statements heard and ignore as unnewsworthy the voices of reason and counsels of compromise. The provoking and advertising of controversy is not, actually, the same as openness, but it is a hallowed tradition of journalism that if there is no controversy, if there is merely cooperation and consensus, there must not be anything worth reporting.

Fifth. Voting is in vogue and *Robert's Rules of Order* reign. Some days I think General Robert's little book is the most subversive volume in the university library, so useful is it to those who would wrap a do-nothing purpose in the tinfoil of procedure.

The trouble with writing everything down in whereas clauses and then voting on some clear two-sided proposition is that it eliminates from the process of getting things done the very ambiguities that leave room for discretion, improvisation, imagination, and plain common sense.

Sigmund Freud was probably right when he defined maturity as the ability to live with ambiguity. But if he had not mixed this perception with all that talk about sex, his books would never have sold. I have been trying for years to sell the notion that Freud's definition of maturity is the essence of the executive function, and it is a hard sale. "How can ambiguity *ever* be constructive?" a community college student once asked me in a public forum on the island of Maui. I asked him in return: "Who *really* makes the decisions in your family?" There was a long silence, then a beatific smile of comprehension lit up his face. "I see," he said slowly. "It *depends.*" "Hang on to that thought," I told him. "It will come in mighty handy when you get to be secretary of state."

In those international organizations where the Western nations imposed a parliamentary model for administrative decision making, there is much voting but little action; the United Nations General Assembly is of course the prime example. But in those international bodies that tend to act by consensus and expect their executives to take a policy lead (the World Bank is one kind of example, the North Atlantic Council another), much action is taken and very large budgets are spent by processes that involve little or no voting.

For some purposes, voting may still be the best and fairest way to make decisions. It is hard to improve on voting as a way of selecting those who will act as the people's representatives in a legislature where public policies must be negotiated and agreed. But for those so chosen, and especially for the executives and experts who propose the policies and then have to carry them into action, procedures of consensus better fit the complex issues and variant interests involved in the macroproblems of modernization than our Western tradition of choosing up sides in an adversary process and taking a snapshot of the resulting disagreement.

Sixth. In the age of participation, the open meeting is more likely than the private conversation to substitute procedural moves for substantive action.

You may have noticed in your own experience what so often happens in mine: People who disagree with what you are doing will seldom say so in public. The complaint usually appears in camouflage: You failed to follow the correct (that is, the written) procedures; you did not consult his or her group, or at least not early enough or long enough, or with the right members of the group; you neglected to prepare, in the proper form, a budget justification, an estimate of cash flow, an environmental assessment, an organization chart; you omitted to quantify the costs and benefits, request the attorney general's opinion, call a public hearing, give proper notice for this meeting, or provide enough copies of your proposal.

Such procedural objections, even trivial ones, can devastate a plan of action. Especially in a large meeting, most of those present are sufficiently distracted, apathetic, confused, or hungry to favor postponement of the matter by means that do not require hard thinking about the substantive course of action proposed.

As we analyze the power of openness to inhibit action, however, let's keep remembering the other side of the paradox. Many proposed actions ought to be aborted at conception, or at least smothered at birth. It is nice that we have invented such effective ways of blocking them. If the Roman Catholic Church had been operating by *Robert's Rules,* Joan of Arc could probably have engineered such a procedural tangle at her trial for heresy that her martyrdom would have been averted.

Seventh. The age of fairness is, paradoxically, producing lifetime tenure for everyone who is already there. This tends, of course, to discriminate against those who haven't made it yet. (One ironic result is that some of the unemployed seem to have tenure, too.) Procedural rigidities, established in the name of fairness, often prevent executives from discriminating between those who function well and those who function poorly, and even make it easier to reward, rather than release, the weaker members of the team.

A 1984 study commissioned by the National Institute of Education found only eighty-six cases of tenured teachers being fired in the forty-three years between 1939 and 1982—that's two per year in the United States as a whole. "Although incompetent teachers are a major problem in public education, they are seldom fired because schools are wary of court fights that can cost upwards of $100,000."

During my several stints as an academic administrator, I have been struck with the willingness of students and colleagues to sign petitions in defense of teachers who are by common (private) knowledge less than fully competent, just when their contracts are being quietly and compassionately terminated to protect the rights of future students to the best available teaching. The academic executive has two options: to take on the protesters, publicly explain the teacher's weaknesses, and spend several years in court as defendant in a defamation suit; or else inflict the inferior teacher on the next thirty years of students. In too many cases the second option looks more inviting; short-run benefits traded for long-run trouble often do. But each such choice brings the executive's institution, and our society, closer to participatory mediocrity.

Eighth. The clearest and most dramatic consequence of openness, in university governance at least, is the difficulty it creates in recruiting first-rate chief executives and evaluating them after they are in office.

Most of the people best qualified to run large universities (which are among the world's most complex organizations to manage because they are the least vertical in structure and process) are seldom looking for work. Typically, they are happily employed and at home in their communities. The last thing they need is the fact that they are being interviewed by a search committee somewhere else to become known. Even less do they need the loss of face if they are considered for juicy positions elsewhere and are then found wanting.

The impact of "sunshine" on the search for university presidents varies, of course, from state to state. In Florida the whole process, including interviews with the final "short list" of candidates, is conducted in the open, sometimes with television cameras present for the interviews. In Pennsylvania, by contrast, the exception to sunshine for personnel matters covers the whole search process until the final selection is announced. But even there, candidates (or "non-candidates" who are "allowing their names to be considered") have to assume that, in this as in all human endeavors, interesting information is quite likely to leak out.

Several recent studies have shown the following to be the net result of too much sunshine.

- The best "candidates" decide that they don't want a job they have to "run for" in public. The ultimate horror story has become all too well known: One candidate in a process that was supposed to be confidential, but leaked, found that the news of his candidacy at one institution created enormous problems for him in his current position as president of another. Ultimately, distrust and suspicion caused loss of the job he had been holding; he was not the first choice in the search process he had been undergoing; and with a new reputation as a second-choice administrator found it next to impossible to find any job at all. Finally, he took a position with much less responsibility rather than remain unemployed.

- Letters of reference are hardly worth reading, because they have to be written on the assumption that they will be read by the candidate and printed in the newspapers. (David Riesman, who has researched this subject in depth, says that "it is widely appreciated in academic life that letters of recommendation lose all credibility if confidentiality for them cannot be guaranteed.")

- Openness can be, and frequently is, manipulated for political ends. ("The press can be used as a tool to create an atmosphere of favor or disfavor for a particular candidate, or to prevent a rival campus from obtaining a president whose light would outshine one's own.")

My own experience of secrecy in a presidential search was more comic opera than tragedy.

In the spring of 1969 I was brought late into the search process at the University of Hawaii, after the Regents had at length decided not to appoint either of two qualified internal candidates and had interviewed some outsiders who had not been clearly preferred over a promotion from within. My wife, Lois, and I were invited to

Honolulu for a week in March, first-class air travel, all expenses paid —almost unfair, as we came directly from Brussels and had not seen the sun for several months. The purpose of my visit was supposed to be a secret; the "cover story" was a lecture at the East West Center, a credible yarn frayed by a week of visiting all the state's most visible movers and shakers, including the governor and the leadership of the Hawaii state legislature. The newspapers and television stations had somehow been sworn to secrecy. Lois wanted to see the house that went with the job, and was driven past it on the condition that she wear dark glasses and crouch down in the car so that no one would notice an unknown woman eyeballing the conspicuous real estate.

When the time came, at the end of the week, for my lecture on U.S. foreign policy (I was still ambassador to NATO at the time), the East West Center's lecture hall was crammed—but not, I suspected, because the largely student audience of predominantly Oriental parentage was engrossed in the subject of mutual deterrence in Europe. When the floor was opened for foreign-policy questions, the first student came right to the point. "The rumor is you've been offered the presidency of the University of Hawaii," he said. "Are you going to accept?" I did a quick calculation and figured that to deny all would damage my credibility later on. "The rumor isn't quite right," I replied, "nobody has offered me the job. But if someone does," I asked the questioner in return, "do you think I ought to take it?" This was taken as good-humored confirmation of why I was in town; the newspapers and television stations burst forth with their bottled-up biographies. As things turned out, I was by that time the only viable candidate (perhaps because I was the person the Regents knew least well), and as a Democratic holdover in a presidential appointment in the Nixon administration, I was obviously going to need a job. So neither the Regents nor Lois and I were embarrassed by disclosure.

Once a university executive is in office, the canons of participatory governance require some kind of evaluation process, typically at five-year intervals. This is often combined with an effort by the members of the governing body to assess how they themselves are performing their duties as regents or trustees. It is not clear to me that this trend toward formalized evaluation of board members and chief executives is an advance in the history of civilization. But whether it is or not, openness is rendering it impossible.

If an independent evaluator is called in, he or she has to talk to people in and close to the university. If they know their comments will be made public, or might even get back to the president or trustees being evaluated, they are going to be reticent to a fault. Evaluations are still being done in states where there is a clear exemption from the sunshine laws for this kind of activity; but in the other states the tendency now is to drop the idea of a formal evaluation altogether.

In Minnesota, one of the more open states, the president of the University of Minnesota was recently evaluated after ten years in office by an external evaluator from the University of Wisconsin. The strengths and weaknesses of the president could not be presented to the Board of Regents; such a report, and the discussion thereon, would have been a public circus of intense interest to every newspaper and radio and television outlet in the state. Therefore no written report was ever made. The evaluator's oral comments were presented to each regent personally, one on one, and were never discussed collectively by the board.

This procedure was adopted to place the process beyond the reach of the sunshine law, on the assumption that such an evaluation, to be worth anything, must be confidential. It was challeged in court by the *Minneapolis Star and Tribune,* however, on "open records" grounds; the Minnesota Data Privacy Act covers oral information that would have to be made public if it were to be written down. The newspaper secured a court order forcing the regents to record what they remembered of the oral evaluation, beyond any material that was strictly personal in nature. Each regent who had talked to the evaluator then solemnly swore out an affidavit that there was nothing in the conversation with the evaluator that didn't fit that exception. The whole affair kept several lawyers and a judge gainfully employed, but made it difficult if not impossible for the regents of the university to do the main thing they are supposed to do, which is to govern the institution through executives they hire, evaluate, and if necessary fire.

A similar impasse develops when governing boards try to evaluate themselves. At the University of Minnesota the regents have been trying every five years, by self-analysis, to improve their capacity to govern. A succession of court decisions about the sunshine laws expanded the definition of a *meeting* to apply to a majority of a quorum of any body, whether meeting formally or informally. This amounted to an open invitation to the media to join the Board of Regents in its retreats, in background discussions—and in its self-evaluation process. Small wonder that the board has curtailed the occasions for candid self-evaluation.

A 1984 case in the Montana Supreme Court may be a straw in a new windshift. It ruled directly on the collision between each person's right of individual privacy (explicitly protected in that state's constitution) and the public's right to know. Privacy won. University presidents, the court said in effect, do not lose their right of privacy by virtue of their public office; it permitted the Board of Regents to close the sessions in which the performance of campus presidents are appraised. The court also added this reinforcement to the arguments of those who want to limit openness: "[T]he public's interest in maintaining a smoothly running university system, of which frank employee evaluations are an essential part, serves as an additional justification for closing the meeting."

All of these problems point to the difficulty of keeping in front of the public eye all *three* elements of the public interest: the public's right to know, the individual's right to privacy, and the right of the public to be served by efficiently functioning public institutions. Overweighting one or the other of these elements of the public interest leads to tension, conflicts, and sometimes nonsense.

The great benefits of openness and wide participation are flawed, then, by oversimplification and confrontation, by apathy and nonparticipation, by muscle-binding legalism, by too many public hearings, by an excess of voting and parliamentary process, by the naysaying power of procedural objection, by the protection of mediocrity, by the inhibition of excellence in recruitment and the absence of candor in evaluation, and by one thing more. Mythology has it the other way around, but it seems clear now that wide consultation *early* in a policy process tends to discourage innovation and favor standpattism.

More openness in decision making is a radical litany, yet the multiplication of those consulted tends to water down radical reform. During the Vietnam War, I used to conduct seminars on this subject (among others) during the long hours spent with student leaders on the barricades. Why, I asked them, do you advocate openness with such passion when the reforms you want would be voted down if you put them to a big public meeting? They were regularly nonplussed by the question; evangelists, in David Riesman's phrase, often "mistake the righteousness of their cause for its marketability."

An action proposal, especially if it is new and unfamiliar, will seem threatening or at least postponable to most of the experts who haven't already been involved. It is no accident that so many memorable U.S. public policy initiatives (much of the New Deal and the Lend-Lease idea in the 1930s, the Marshall Plan and Harry Truman's Point Four in the 1940s, the Open Skies proposal in the 1950s, the Peace Corps and Food for Peace and the War on Poverty in the 1960s, the Nixon Doctrine and the Carter human rights initiative in the 1970s) began as the products of leadership hunch and thinking-out-loud rhetoric, with most of the professional staff work and the needed consultations at home and abroad following after. In each case the executive leaders were sensing a trend the American people would buy if a credible salesman came forward to peddle it. But if all the relevant experts had been asked for their opinions before launching them, some or all of these important ideas might well have shriveled in the womb. Too many people, in Washington and abroad, would have said, "Let's study it some more."

Bold initiatives for change can thus be killed by premature exposure to the rough winds of public debate. Yet let us again remember that this cuts both ways: Timely openness is also well designed to stop foolish change. Earlier and wider consultation would almost certainly have killed the ill-fated Bay of Pigs operation, drastically modified the Vietnam escalation, and illuminated the grotesquerie at Watergate for the fatuous scheme everyone, including President Nixon, later judged it to have been.

In sum, early openness is bad for bad ideas and bad for good ideas, too. Openness later in the process of consent building for a new idea is good for good ideas, but may be good for bad ideas too. Participation is paradox. So what else is new?

How do you get everybody in on the act and still get some action? A true dilemma can never be resolved by choosing one of its horns and ignoring the other. In a Portuguese bullfight, where the matador shows his mastery not by killing the bull but by jumping over it, the man who tried to swing himself over the oncoming animal by grasping only one of its horns would have to have superhuman strength to bring it off. But if he can catch hold of both horns at once, a reasonably athletic bullfighter can vault over the bull with grace, applause ringing in his ears.

The bestiary contains no example of a bull with three horns, and the dictionary provides no word for a three-sided dilemma. Yet the matadors advocating the public interest on the issue of openness have the exceedingly difficult task of grasping three horns of a *tri*lemma. Those who defend the public's right to know will also have to get used to defending the individual's right to some degree of privacy and the right of organizations that are supposed to serve the public interest to be effective. The advocates of privacy will likewise have to take account of the public's right to know and the public agency's duty to serve. And the leaders (governing boards and executives) of organizations claiming to act in the public interest will have to widen their lenses to encompass individual privacy and the public's right to know in their definition of the wider public interest. Once again, the ramparts of the whole need to be held against the assault of the parts.

5

Ownership:
Knowledge as
a Shared Resource

The openness which the informatization of society brings in its train is raising fundamental questions about the idea that knowledge "belongs" to a person or an organization. Like waves eating away the foundations of a seashore hotel, the propensity of this "sharing resource" to leak is eroding the doctrine that knowledge can be owned, exchanged, and monopolized the way "real" resources can. Those who persist in treating their knowledge as property are apt, like King Canute, to get wet.

That you or I can *own* a fact or an idea, that a message of any kind *belongs* to a person or a corporation or a government, is a rather peculiar notion to begin with. The person from whom you got the fact or idea or message didn't lose it; any right you acquire to the message is at best shared with the sender, the carrier, and whomever else is privy to it. Even if you paid to get the message (if, for example,

---

it was a piece of research you hired someone to do), or if someone paid to send it to you (a friend who sent you a telegram, a company that sent you a commercial), it was the assembly or delivery service, not the information contained in the message, that was paid for. The researcher could not *own* the facts and ideas he or she strung together for your use, and neither can you, even if you use them as your *own*.

Colin Cherry, the British communication theorist, wrote it this way: "the word *communication* comes from the Latin: *communicare* = to share. It does not mean 'sending messages,' for messages cannot possibly be 'sent' in the sense that we speak of sending goods or commodities. Communication is always a social activity, an act of sharing."

Even as it applies to information in traditional delivery vehicles, such as this book, the idea of property rights in knowledge is tattered and torn. This was brought home to me when a young Chinese scholar, the nephew of an old friend, wrote to me from Hong Kong to say that he had translated an earlier book of mine (*The Future Executive*) and had arranged to market it in the People's Republic of China through a university press. I thought at first that my correspondent wanted to buy the Chinese rights to this copyrighted work, or at least was seeking my permission to use *my* words in *his* book. Not at all; my friend's nephew never raised those questions. Instead he asked me to write a new introduction for the Chinese edition of my book. Intrigued by the prospect of sharing my thoughts on management with a billion Chinese, I sat down the very next weekend and wrote an introduction to this politely pirated edition of a copyrighted work.

The new tide of information technologies makes the ownership of intellectual property more detached from reality with every new invention.

Four kinds of waves are rolling in. Dynamic high technology keeps developing better and faster *techniques of piracy*—xerography, videotape, the backyard dish for picking up signals from satellites. The knowledge explosion also produces new *kinds of works* (computer software), new *means of delivery* (microfiche, videocassettes, computerized videotext over a telephone line), and new *ways to assemble* great complexities of facts and ideas in more readily accessible form (computerized data bases, inventory controls, energy use data, on-line reservation systems for airlines and car rentals).

In this environment, laws written to protect books and phonograph records and broadcasts, the products of the past, are getting harder and harder to apply. Laws that address technologies not yet invented are hard to write.

Yet the Canutes persevere.

The Association of American Publishers sued New York University and nine professors for infringing copyright when they helped students learn by photocopying useful literature. They had to settle for vague promises to be good, and for only four years. The publishers didn't even get their court costs back.

The Columbia Broadcasting System thought it could establish a proprietary right to what it reported on CBS News. It sued Vanderbilt University to prevent its library from distributing videotapes of CBS News for study by students of journalism. "They think they can 'own' history," said one outraged scholar. That case was settled not in court but in Congress: a powerful senator from Tennessee, Howard Baker, got a law passed making clear that the CBS executives didn't have the rights they thought they had.

Home Box Office is still trying to prevent people from building dishes on their roofs to pluck HBO signals from the public's airwaves. Even in jurisdictions where the law is clear, its enforcement is a nightmare.

Universal City Studios tried for several years in the early 1980s to get Sony to ban the sale of its videocassette recorders for use by people in their own living rooms, usually for recording broadcast programs they would otherwise miss, to play them back at more convenient times. Not only that, but a panel of federal judges in the Ninth Circuit agreed with Universal, in an opinion which for sheer effrontery to common sense won the King Canute prize for 1982: "Off-the-air copying of copyrighted materials by owners of videotape recorders in their own homes, for private non-commercial use, constitutes an infringement of copyrighted audiovisual materials."

Sometimes the law resembles Kipling's Elephant's Child, its nose pulled out of shape by the crocodile of reality. I have struggled through the turgid prose of *Universal City* v. *Sony* and diagnosed the appeal judges' problem: a dynamic technological environment makes them acutely uncomfortable. In the tradition of the law, which looks back at precedent and past legislative intentions, they hitched their wagon to what Congress in its ignorance meant to say about technologies it couldn't yet imagine.

Courts are inhibited (though not precluded) by training, tradition, mandate, and structure from recognizing the nontraditional. The great dissenters such as Oliver Wendell Holmes and Louis Brandeis were willing to peer into the future, but their dissents didn't become "the law" until, much later, the future arrived. Where there is no past to cling to, some judges become disoriented, and the resulting obscurity of their language doesn't really hide the fact that they are at sea.

The Supreme Court agreed to review the Sony case, thus giving itself a chance to show that horse sense is not necessarily incompatible with the law. By a 5 to 4 margin, the court told the 2 million owners of VCRs to rest easy on their living-room sofas.

For judges thus afflicted with the uncertainties of information technology, Lao Tzu has some advice that may help:

> To know that you do not know is the best.
> To pretend to know when you do not is a disease.

The nervous breakdown of copyright protection may be retarded in some degree by technological fixes. Satellite broadcasters can scramble their signals to prevent pirating. Elaborate codes have been devised by the creators of some computer programs, though teenage computer hackers have been showing how inherently porous they are. Recording your unique insights on videodisk may keep them a secret, at least from people who cannot afford videodisk technology.

When I first acquired a home computer, I found the ethical dilemma right up front: in the instruction manual. On its cover sheet I was threatened with jurisprudential mayhem if I copied any of the software. On the very first page of the manual I was told that before I did anything else I should make at least two backup copies of the floppy diskette provided with the manual.

Since then, the technological fix is increasingly in vogue. A couple of recently purchased software packages contain diskettes that self-destruct after the first backup copies are made. Other vendors have tried sending an "official" backup copy along with the original, to dissuade the customers from replicating the diskette ad infinitum and furnishing it to their friends. A computer-user group is like a medieval guild, a society of peers in which mutual help is a higher ethic than protecting some outsider's property rights. A few software producers now send their creations to prospective users, asking them to pay if they prove useful—an interesting break with market behavior down through history.

The leakiness of the information resource seems destined to overwhelm the Canutish efforts to imprison it. The history of arms control and the success of computer pirates teach us that there is always a technological fix for a technological fix.

Is the doctrine that information is owned by its originator (or compiler) necessary to make sure that Americans remain intellectually creative? In most other countries creative work is overwhelmingly controlled by organizations and carried out by salaried people. In Japan, even the most inventive employee is likely to have a lifetime job and receive salary raises in lockstep with his age cohort, his morale sustained not by personal ownership of his ideas but by togetherness in an organizational family.

Most U.S. patents are held by organizations (corporations, universities, government agencies), not by the inventors. Many copyrights, perhaps most, are held by publishers and promoters, not by the authors and songwriters the Founding Fathers may have had in mind when they sewed information-as-property into the U.S. Constitution.

An author or songwriter who helps a publisher make money

should certainly participate in the proceeds. But direct agreements about profit sharing or joint venture arrangements (the movie industry is already full of relevant examples) seem a less fragile basis for such cooperation than the fraying fictions that the author owns the words in a book or that shared information is being "exchanged."

In U.S. universities and research institutes, creative work is already rewarded mostly by promotion, tenure, and tolerant traditions about teaching loads and outside consulting. We generate a respectably innovative R & D effort in public-sector fields such as military technology, space exploration, weather forecasting, environmental protection, and the control of infectious diseases without the scientists and inventors having to own the ideas they contribute to the process.

In the private sector, the leaders of industries on the high-tech frontier are already saying out loud that their protection from overseas copyists doesn't lie in trade secrets but in healthy R & D budgets. John Rollwagen, chief executive of Cray Research, which produces the world's most powerful computer, put it this way: "By the time the Japanese have figured out how to build a Cray 1, we have to be well along in designing a Cray 2—or we're out of business."

The notion of information-as-property is built deep into our laws, our economy, and our political psyche—and into the expectations and tax returns and balance sheets of writers and artists and the companies, agencies, and academies that pay them to be creative. But we had better continue to develop our own ways, compatible with our own traditions, of rewarding intellectual labor without depending on laws and prohibitions that are disintegrating fast, as the Volstead Act did in our earlier effort to enforce an unenforceable Prohibition.

The idea of ownership is in trouble not only because laws about intellectual property are fraying around the edges and splitting at the seams. It is also in trouble because it is the basis for the distinction between what is private and what is public in our mixed economy, and that distinction is already irretrievably blurred.

In our capitalist system, we draw a sharp line between what the government (the public sector) does and what private individuals, clubs, associations, foundations, and corporations (the private sector) do. The line between public and private is drawn according to whether a government or a nongovernment owns the capacity to do what is done.

Socialists draw the same line, believing (contrary to much evidence in the century just past) that government ownership of the means of production is the way to assure a fairer society.(Central economic planning, even though it was popularized around the world by industrial democracies that do not practice it themselves, is everywhere in disarray.)

The line between public and private is still clear enough—in our heads. It is looking more and more like a mirage in the real world, because more and more of what we all (governments and nongovernments) do is information work.

Governments at all levels have long been essentially information industries. The same is true of schools, colleges and universities, health services, financial services, publishers, law firms, and consultants of all kinds. Even the production functions each year contain larger ratios of information work, as compared to the traditional factors of production: land, labor, and capital.

Both capitalist and socialist thinkers, caught in their common nineteenth-century doctrine that ownership would be the key to industrial success, are obstacles now to the *re*thinking that might explain the huge success of systems that are neither private enterprise nor public enterprise but a combination of both.

Most of the genuinely private enterprise in the United States is what isn't counted in the Gross National Product: the "informal economy" of household work, bartered services, organized crime, and other activity not officially counted as working. Many of those counted in the official statistics as unemployed youth, superannuated retirees, and illegal immigrants are very busy indeed making a living the Internal Revenue Service never hears about.

The rugged automaticity of the market seems to be shoved aside whenever the project is so large that the government has to be ushered in as a risk-taking partner, and also when important private enterprises prove to be insufficiently enterprising. The efforts to rescue Lockheed, Chrysler, Big Steel, and the New England fishing industry come to mind; sometimes transfusions from the rescue squad revive the accident victim, and sometimes the trauma gets worse. (Some political leaders have trouble understanding that there may be more economic nourishment in helping the industries that are the potential worldwide winners in their fields.)

Traffic is two-way across the blurring frontier between private and public. Private interests are encamped inside legislatures and public bureaucracies; but governments are also doing their best to get public functions performed by the private sector.

From Franklin Roosevelt to Lyndon Johnson, we thought that if there was a problem of national scope, the solution was obvious: create another government agency, appropriate more money, hire more government employees, build more public buildings, and put the problem in the buildings along with the government employees. Let's not knock the system; it worked pretty well for nearly half a century.

In the 1980s and 1990s, we the people have not lost our taste for more governance, but we want it with less government. The only way to deal with that paradox is to induce more private institutions to perform what used to be thought of as public functions. Already we find that more and more managers, still organized as corporations, styling themselves *firms,* or calling themselves *consultants,* are really in the public management business.

We poke fun at "Japan, Inc.," and nervously note that cooperation between business and government seems to pay dividends on the other side of the Pacific Ocean. Our rhetoric, which takes the line between private and public as a given, obscures from us the similar trend in the United States.

In practice if not in theory, the U.S. government farms out to private organizations some of its most sovereign functions: inventing and manufacturing weapons systems, delivering health and welfare services mandated by law, building transportation systems, collecting taxes through the withholding device. (Just think what an enormous agency the IRS would have to be if it didn't delegate most of the tax collecting to the private sector, and instead collected taxes the way the Census Bureau collects information, by going from door to door.)

Private nonprofit agencies exist as artifacts of the tax-exemption code. And private corporations cheerfully go public when necessary, through the bankruptcy courts or through ingenious (and often socially useful) "public-private partnerships." For several years before its big bail-out loan was repaid, Chrysler was for practical purposes a public corporation and Lee Iacocca in effect a political executive, temporarily underpaid for his valiant efforts at a dollar a year. His effective board of directors, after all, was the Federal Loan Board, which consisted of three very public officials: the secretary of the treasury, the chairman of the Federal Reserve Board, and the comptroller general of the United States.

Most U.S. urban development these days engages a combination of private investment and public subsidies, coordinated by a "developer" who may be a private entrepreneur but is sometimes a public planner. In Minneapolis, for example, the Loring Park development, several hotels, and the Metrodome that now houses the Viking football team and the Twins baseball team and, in St. Paul, the Lowertown development and the World Trade Center are all imaginative combinations of private and public enterprise. These and a thousand other urban projects around the country would not have been possible if partners from either side of the blurred line had been missing.

The many varied ways we have invented to mix private enterprise and public enterprise are not properly described by the word *privatization*, because some form of public action (usually a decision about fairness, or the use of tax money or tax exemption to sweeten an otherwise unprofitable pot) is a priceless ingredient. China's well-advertised "decentralization" of agriculture isn't privatization either; government quotas for each commune have to be met before farmers can accumulate wealth from the private sale of residual harvest; and food prices are still controlled.

Out in the U.S. countryside, of course, the agricultural sector has long been energized by public price supports, parity payments, and rewards for not farming too much land. The miracle of agricultural productivity on private U.S. farms is partly the consequence, of course, of a wise public policy that funded farm research and extension services to make sure that government-supported science reached the individual farmer.

In the United States at least, even the formulation of public policy is done increasingly by nongovernments, profit and nonprofit. The reasons are obvious. Precisely because nongovernments are *not* responsible, they are faster on their feet and can be more flexible and futuristic in their thinking than governments are. They can work, ahead of time, on problems that are likely to be important but are not yet urgent enough to command political attention; they can test assumptions that are not yet "official"; they can write and speak more freely about "alternative futures"; they can bring people and ideas into the discussion without implying approval by the government of the day; and they can organize dialogue across disciplinary boundaries and international frontiers, escaping some of the rigidities of responsibility.

There is even a rough and ready test of their relevance: Is the nongovernmental organization working on issues that are still too vague, too big, too interdisciplinary, or too futuristic for governments that are too busy, too crisis-ridden, and too politically careful to think about?

Creative mixtures of private enterprise and public authority made the United States of America a great nation and can keep it that way. We would do well to glory in the blurring of public and private and not keep trying to draw a disappearing line in the water.

In international politics the notion that knowledge is owned by sovereign states is in maximum disarray. Every newly miniaturized recording or micrographic device and every new satellite launched for communication or photography or remote sensing make it more difficult to sustain the doctrine that national governments can own, or even control, their information resources.

In 1979 the U.S. government sent two delegations to two world meetings about the control of information. At a UNESCO conference in Paris, the delegates righteously advocated the "free flow" of information, meaning information furnished by U.S. news agencies, U.S. television producers, and U.S. movie studios. A few weeks later at the UN Conference on Science and Technology for Development in Vienna, an equally righteous group of Americans came out against the free flow of information, meaning "information" as a technology we were eager to hoard.

Both principles are authentically American: the right to choose, the right to own. In the international discourse, we will hardly be able to have it both ways. Yet there is no evidence that the two groups of delegates, and the government that instructed them both, perceived the irony or the contradiction.

The U.S. State Department, which instructed both delegations, earned the King Canute Prize for 1983 with its ruling that Western European owners of IBM computers could not move them from, say, Birmingham to Manchester without first seeking U.S. permission. This assertion of extraterritoriality over equipment produced by a multinational company with headquarters in the United States was designed to prevent "strategic" equipment from flowing indirectly to communist countries. Regardless of the merits of the case, the edict is simply unenforceable. In the global information society, the long arms of ownership and control are shrinking fast.

If information is inherently hard to bottle up, policies based on a long-term information monopoly are likely to have a short half-life. For the 1980s and beyond, the principle of action is clear: If the validity of your action depends on its continuing secrecy, don't depend on it.

In our generation-long arms race with the Soviet Union, successive U.S. administrations have managed to persuade themselves that each new U.S. weapons system (its made-in-America technology a continuing mystery to our adversaries) would enable us to stay ahead. In the most Canutish of these actions, in the early 1970s, the United States decided to stuff multiple independently targetable reentry vehicles (MIRVs) into single missiles. Despite elaborate secrecy on our part, the Soviets soon figured out how to do likewise.

But since they (for other reasons) had built much bigger missiles boosted by more powerful rockets, they were able to stuff more MIRVs into their canisters than we could. Thus did we outsmart ourselves by taking an action that depended for its validity on technological secrecy and created the famous "window of vulnerability" instead.

A prime example of Canutish behavior in my personal experience was U.S. reluctance to tell our NATO allies what we knew from satellite reconnaissance about Soviet deployment of missiles aimed at European targets, when the Europeans were bound to learn about them sooner or later. A wave of common sense undermined that policy in 1966 when Robert McNamara, as U.S. secretary of defense, handed to allied defense ministers, in the top-secret precincts of the Joint Chiefs' War Room, the satellite photos we had been withholding until then. That was almost two decades ago, but I can still vividly recall the shocked expressions on the faces of the security men lining the walls as McNamara dove into his briefcase and tossed onto the table for international inspection the prize examples of our space-based photography. After that it became routine to share with our NATO allies what our declared adversaries already knew.

In the management of mutual deterrence, the overclassification of information about what we could do, if we had to, may actually increase the danger of war by miscalculation. The core of the nuclear deterrent, that remarkably stable if unattractive substitute for peace, is the Soviet leaders' uncertainty about what the U.S. president would do in the event of Soviet moves against our allies or ourselves; combined with the Soviet leaders' certainty that we have the means to retaliate no matter what. Keeping our intentions credibly uncertain is easy: We cannot know what we would do "if," until we know what the "if" is. But keeping from our adversaries full knowledge of our capabilities merely adds another element of madness to the mad momentum of the nuclear arms race.

Our own government has for three decades engaged in half-hearted and demonstrably ineffective efforts to own strategic U.S. science and to keep foreign nationals out of sensitive university research. In our mostly open society, it never worked very well. Americans have no corner on the market for brains; scientists talk quite freely across frontiers to each other; our European and Japanese allies never had much enthusiasm for controlling transborder information flows (because sales of equipment mean jobs for European and Japanese workers); and Soviet technological espionage, like ours, has long been a thriving industry.

Keeping our R & D to ourselves is a policy that depends for its validity on secrecy. As informatization intensifies in the postindustrial world, strategic secrecy can be expected to work less and less well.

Similar government behavior used to work better for dictators and totalitarian bureaucracies in societies where keeping information from spreading is honored by doctrine and practiced ad absurdum. Xerox machines still have to be licensed by the government in the Soviet Union; in Bulgaria, even typewriters are closely controlled. Ideas are harder to license. Russian youngsters readily learn about jeans and hard rock, and scientists on both sides of the porous Curtain seem to know how far along their peers are in unraveling (for example) the puzzlements of rocketry and space travel.

Television executives in West Germany are still chortling over a prize example of information power. Most East Germans are able to watch West German television without interference, but residents of the important city of Dresden used to have trouble (for topographic, not political, reasons) getting an acceptable West German picture on their television tubes. In consequence, the East German authorities found that people were reluctant to take jobs in Dresden; and that whenever there was an important event, such as a World Cup soccer match, people would stream out of Dresden on energy-wasting missions to find decent television reception. The East German government found no repressive measures that would help, so they built a tower with a transponder to capture the West German television signals and beam them into Dresden—so the Dresdeners wouldn't be disadvantaged by their *lack* of contact with the West!

The good news is that information is leaky, that sharing is the natural mode of scientific discovery and human communication. The changing information environment seems bound to undermine the knowledge monopolies that totalitarian governments convert into monopolies of power. In the horoscope of the USSR and the Soviet blcc, a future looms where nobody is in charge.

6

Privilege:
The Fairness
Revolution

The informatization of society may destabilize more than the Soviet bloc. It may help undermine the systems that keep 2 billion people in relative poverty, and more than a third of those in absolute poverty. In many ways the most exciting and puzzling question about the new knowledge environment is whether it will be good news or bad news for the global fairness revolution—and for that revolution's U.S. precinct, the upward mobility of women, minorities, and the poor.

The most arresting trait of the information resource is that it is inherently more accessible than other resources and that, once accessed, it unlocks the other resources. What does that imply for access to the power and affluence that knowledge brings in its wake? Theoretically at least, compared to the things-as-resource, information-as-resource should encourage:

- •the spreading of benefits rather than the concentration of wealth (information can be more equitably shared than petroleum or gold or land or even water); and

- •the maximization of choice rather than the suppression of diversity (the informed are harder to regiment than the uninformed).

In the industrial era, poverty was explained and justified by shortages of things; there just weren't enough minerals, food, fibers, and manufactures to go around. Looked at this way, the shortages were merely aggravated by the propensity of the poor to have babies.

In the information society, the physical resources are joined at center stage by information, the resource that is harder for the rich and powerful to hoard. Each of the babies, poor or not, is born with a brain. The collective capacity of all the brains in each society to convert information into knowledge and wisdom is the measure of that society's potential.

But whether the informatization of the globe will actually mean a fairer shake for those who have been the victims of discrimination depends mostly on what they do. Most of the fairness achieved in world history has not been the consequence of charity, good-heartedness, and *noblesse oblige* on the part of those in power. Always in history, it seems, fairness has been granted, legislated, or seized when there was no alternative. And usually the reason there was no alternative was that the "downs" were determined (or at least perceived by the "ups" to be determined) to cast off their shackles and take the law into their own hands.

In the United States, women have latterly been determined. We are consequently moving, very rapidly by historical standards, from a man's world to equality of the sexes.

The subordination of women has been built deep into nearly all the world's cultures throughout recorded history and doubtless before that. Formal matriarchies were few and far between, and instances of real equality even rarer. There were of course always influential women "in their place": making a home for the male hunters and gatherers to come home to, doing most of the farm work in agricultural civilizations, and meanwhile bearing and rearing the next generation. Occasionally a Cleopatra or a Madame Pompadour or a Mrs. Woodrow Wilson would make history with intelligence or charm or opportunity or all of these. But they were one in a million or more.

An American in the mid-1980s may have to pause for a moment to realize how very recent the status-of-women revolution is. I am writing in the year when Geraldine Ferraro was nominated for vice-president of the United States. But I can without effort remember the put-down about the powerful men in FDR's entourage "and the women they married when they were very young." Or listening to the radio as Mrs. Wendell Willkie, wife of the Republican candidate for president, was asked at a press conference what *she* did and replied, "Oh, I'm just a bit of fluff." Or even in the JFK administration, less than a quarter-century ago, when the earlier put-down was reformulated by a female society columnist: "the women hanging on the arms of their husbands, wearing them like name tags."

Now the status of women is dramatically different, if not yet equal. In public agencies women get many of the top jobs, but you can still meet with the top fifty executives in a multinational corporation, as I have done, and see only men in the room. Sex stereotyping still hangs heavily in the marketplace for "work"; there are male nurses and female welders, but they are still eyebrow-lifting rarities. Nevertheless, "equal access" is being very rapidly achieved.

The trouble, of course, is that equal access to similar jobs is not nearly enough to bring about equality of opportunity. Education is, as we shall see, the key to equal opportunity, in the information society more than ever. If few women are trained for engineering careers, the most painstaking equal-opportunity search will turn up only women who have a choice of a dozen jobs because of their high scarcity value. The proportion of women in law schools, medical schools, and schools of public affairs and administration (sometimes as many as half the entering class) is not yet matched in the graduate programs of the business schools; the results out in the marketplace for professional work are preordained.

Neither does equal access guarantee equal pay for equal work. Overall, in the mid-1980s, women are paid about 60 percent of what men earn for doing the same or similar jobs. The "equal opportunity" movement has only recently gotten to work on the knotty issue of "comparable worth"—how to compare, within the same organization or community, a female teacher or nurse with a male autoworker or junior executive.

The tidal wave is now irresistible and is not overtly being resisted, though many rearguard actions are fought every day inside U.S. organizations. Moreover, what's happening in the United States is contagious. Women from developing countries may disorient American feminists by arguing that *their* liberation has little to do with gaining access to corporate leadership and everything to do with an escape from poverty for the whole family. But the reality of feminism sells even when the rhetoric misses the mark. World population growth, which seemed on a runaway to disaster a generation ago, has been drastically cut back; effective chemicals combined with women's choices have certainly been the main factors in the turnaround.

From experience in the United States and Western Europe, we can trace a pattern that, with cultural differences, may play itself out in many other more-or-less democratic societies.

Stage 1 features militants shouting to get the attention of "the (male) establishment" and seeking access to the places and positions that are presumed to be "making policy." Under cover of the verbal artillery comes the organizing: mobilizing women as a potent political bloc to produce a "gender gap" with which established authorities have to reckon.

Stage 2 is a pervasive change in attitudes, which is the real policy-making. It turns out not to be enough to establish that women are the same as men—a proposition hard to sustain even, as Elizabeth Janeway puts it, by wearing pinstripe suits so as not to look out of place in the executive suite. The goal is to produce a differentiation of equally valid functions, so that both sexes come to regard woman and man as equally valuable to the society they build together.

Stage 3 is to reorganize social institutions to match the changing attitudes—for example, to make marriage as much a partnership in law and social policy as the best marriages are partnerships in love; to build child care into every aspect of the world of work; to automate the house (already quite far advanced) and to staff the home (by personal contracts and by electronics) so that the functions left for the family to perform are compatible with a need, economic or psychological, for the adults to work outside the home. At the same time, home computers hitched to telecommunications will be creating more opportunities for home-based work. But making the home a workplace isn't the answer to making the home a home. The idea to be preserved, or recaptured, is expressed in the old saying: Home is where you can go and they have to take you in.

The social flow the feminists have helped create has left one large and disturbing eddy: a rhetorical downgrading of full-time home-based work. Like other specialists, some feminists may have been mesmerized by the way statistics are collected. In the Gross National Product, "work" is what is paid for outside the home. Indeed, a woman who leaves home to work in an office often contributes twice to the GNP, once by the salary she earns and a second time by what the family pays other women to do: the housekeeping and taking care of the children and the old folks. Meanwhile, women working equally hard as "support systems" to their husbands and children, and perhaps an elderly parent as well, are not counted in the GNP at all. (I have long been puzzled why this never became a hot "women's issue": the statistical put-down still affects half of half the population in even the most "developed" countries.)

Stage 4. It is not accident or coincidence that women are breaking into the executive market just when the key to success in executive work is working-with-other-people skills. Psychologists tell us that in our culture most boys have typically been socialized for the "action skills" (the rougher sports, running precariously along the top of a wall, challenging schoolyard rivals, and ordering people around), whereas most girls have been socialized for the consensual skills that enable them to get their way without seeming to take the lead. In growing to maturity young men have to learn how to "get everybody in on the act" without giving orders, and young women have to learn how to "get some action": that is, learn that there is a limit to the utility of making people happy by consulting them.

By the time they arrive together as executive leaders, both women and men will have to be good at both consulting and acting. But in the age of participation, the female of the species may for now have a cultural edge. Think about this generalization as you read on.

The United States has always been a multiracial society, but until recently we have not been acting like one. Members of races other than white, and some of the later-arriving Caucasians, too, have been stacked mostly near the bottom of the hierarchical heap. It wasn't a sorting by color or culture alone; it was more like the definition of *disadvantaged* I once proposed, with serious intent, be applied to the state of Hawaii by the Department of Health, Education and Welfare: "if your folks got here too early or too late."

In our first two hundred years we have managed, against a backdrop of civil war and community violence, to abolish slavery, to accept millions of nonwhite immigrants, and to integrate buses, lunch counters, rest rooms, professional sports, a good many schools, most colleges, and some residential areas. All this was, it seems, the easy part. The hard part is achieving fairness in employment and education.

There is no doubt that in the job market the recurring recessions of the 1970s and early 1980s, and the rapid shift from a production to an information economy, have been setbacks for racial fairness. Laborsaving automation and robotics, the loss of a competitive edge in world markets for steel and automobiles, and the growth of high-tech and knowledge industries have hit hardest the kinds of well-paying jobs, skilled and semiskilled as well as unskilled, in which millions of blacks and other minority Americans had found niches of protected fairness in the workplace. Moreover, the shrinkage of opportunity in the public sector (some 60 percent of all black college graduates have been employed by government agencies) has slowed the formerly rapid development of a black middle class.

At the same time, according to civil rights leader Bayard Rustin, "the collapse of black-family structures—a result as well as a cause of the black plight—and the alarming increase in the number of unwed black mothers, most of whom live in poverty," has contributed to "the continued growth of a black underclass of poor and indigent which in 1978 stood at 30 percent but [in 1984] stands at approximately 36 percent."

U.S. policy for American Indians focused for more than a hundred years on "protecting" them by treaty on "reservations"; in practice, this sealed many Indians off from economic growth and the kinds of education an industrial society and a science-based agriculture required. A hundred years on the reservation resulted, for example, in a life expectancy of thirty-nine years for native Americans at a time when the U.S. population as a whole reached the biblical vision of three score and ten. The federal presence in the life of native Americans became pervasive and intrusive; at one meeting with federal officials, an Indian leader with a sense of history and a sense of humor asked whether the bureaucrats could please stop referring to his people as "the target population." More than half of those identifying themselves as American Indian are now urban residents, with special problems and opportunities for which there is little room in government programs oriented to welfare and other forms of "aid." The net result is that the people "whose folks got here too early" are still stacked mostly near the bottom of the heap.

Fairness for Hispanics is complicated by the dual-language issue (does English have to be the passport to full citizenship in a multicultural society?) and by the enormous overhang of U.S. residents politely styled "undocumented." Fairness for Asian Americans is complicated by the cross-cultural abyss between the majority's European-oriented heritage and the old civilizations and (for Americans) extremely difficult languages of East Asia. Of all the minority groups, the Asians seem to develop and sustain the greatest urge to get educated; during my time as salesman for the University of

Hawaii, I used to claim that our undergraduate student body, much more than half of Oriental parentage, probably had the highest average level of student motivation on any college campus in the nation.

In an information-drenched society, fairness is above all a product of education—but education is also a product of fairness. Education is prerequisite both to knowing your entitlements and to making sure you get them. The scandal of educational disadvantage in the United States is the result of many factors, past and present: segregation and discrimination, absence of books, records, and grammatical speech in the home, communities uncommitted to educational excellence, constituencies unable (or sometimes unwilling) to pay for it. Whatever the reasons, the statistical record is stark.

The black minority, some 12 percent of the U.S. population, produces only 6.5 percent of U.S. college graduates, 5.8 percent of master's degrees, and 4 percent of doctoral and first-professional degrees. Taken together, black, Hispanic, and native Americans make up 19 percent of the U.S. population but earn only 8 percent of doctoral degrees. A 1983 survey by the National Research Council found racial minorities most severely underrepresented in engineering, biological science, physical science, and mathematics. In 1981–82, 606 blacks got their doctorates in education, 29 in the physical sciences, 20 in engineering, 6 in mathematics, and 1 in computer science. That's not a misprint: *one* in computer science, in the year computers and telecommunications got married.

There are many outstanding cases of highly educated minority Americans finding successful vocations in key sectors of our society —in all levels of government, in corporations (still the most resistant to this kind of change), and in the nonprofit sector (Franklin Thomas, president of the largest nonprofit, the Ford Foundation, is black). But, according to another black educator, Clifton Wharton (president of the seventy-three-campus State University of New York and chairman of the board of the Rockefeller Foundation), the overall picture is "a dispiriting conclusion . . . the facade of progress that has been erected in recent years actually masks the reality of sluggish change."

The next phase in building a multicultural America may surprise some members of the white majority who grew up, as I did, in the tradition that taught that each person has to "make it" on his or her own. I was brought up with this liberal mind-set, and for many years I thought the road to "integration" was for me (and sooner or later everyone else) to deny the racial distinctions that skin color makes obvious. But I have come to think that tolerating, even emphasizing, the differences is what will make possible a truly multicultural society called the United States of America.

I had to think especially hard about this when I moved to Hawaii. In Hawaii, everybody is a minority. Everyone who lives in the 50th state has to be impressed with the variety of its people and their comparatively tolerant attitude toward each other. (It's only "comparatively"; just under that society's surface the mutual suspicion among racial groups is still strong enough to be a major factor in politics and employment.) On closer inspection, paradise seems based on paradox. The tolerance is not in spite of the variety, but because of it. It is not through a disappearance of distinctions in a melting pot that the people of Hawaii have achieved a level of cultural equality and racial peace (expressed in the Polynesian word *Aloha*) that for all its inadequacies and unfairnesses has few parallels around our discriminatory globe. Quite the contrary. The glory is that Hawaii's main ethnic groups retained or developed enough pride, enough self-confidence, and enough sense of their cultural history—in a word, enough distinctiveness—to establish their right to be separate. This group separateness seems, paradoxically, to be the first phase in establishing the rights of individuals in each group to equality with individuals of different racial aspect, different ethnic background, and different cultural heritage.

Perhaps, after all, Hawaii's experience is not so different from the transatlantic migration of the various more or less white Caucasians. On arrival in New York, they didn't melt into the open arms of the white Anglo-Saxon Protestants who were already there. Again, the contrary is true. Each new group of arrivals cleaved to their own kind, shared a religion and language and humor and discriminatory treatment with their soul brothers and sisters, and gravitated into occupations that didn't too seriously threaten the jobs of the ethnic groups that had arrived before them.

In Hawaii as along the east coast, waves of new Americans and older Americans have been thrown together in the tide-rip of democracy and have learned in time to tolerate each other, first as groups, and only thereafter as individuals. As they rubbed up against one another in an urbanizing America, they gradually discovered not the easy old Christian lesson that all men are brothers, but the hard new multicultural lesson that all brothers are different.

Maybe the lesson from both the Atlantic and Pacific migrations is that each ethnic group must find its own identity before members of other ethnic groups will treat its members as individual human beings, as respected and valued citizens of a common polity, as sisters who are different and *therefore* sisters.

The lesson from Hawaii has plenty of modern relevance for the next decades of what Henry Luce, the founder of *Time* magazine, used to call the permanent American revolution. The lesson is, for example, that the black Americans who want to establish their blackness and glory in their roots are on the right track. It is important, surely, that black children know where they come from—relive the history of their ancestors, feel the shame of historical failures and the pride of historical contributions, use the flexible English language in ways that are distinctive, and bring forcibly to the attention of all Americans that the various colors called "black" can be beautiful.

A similar principle applies to other Americans called minorities, and indeed to "white ethnics" who are rediscovering their roots too. It is interesting that, a generation ago, it was only the elite who were parading their heritage and boasting of their "roots." But the Daughters of the American Revolution, who wouldn't let Marian Anderson sing in their Constitution Hall in Washington because she was black, were in eclipse by the time "Roots," a story of slavery and struggle by an underclass, became prime-time television fare.

Only where racial and cultural distinctions are fully accepted, widely regarded as interesting rather than threatening, will a reasonable tolerance be likely to follow. For equality is not only the product of similarity. It is also the cheerful acknowledgment of difference.

Worldwide, the achievement of racial equity and cultural pluralism still awaits a very long footrace between feudalism and fairness. Most countries are still governed on the (explicit or implicit) assumption that one race of people will provide the aristocracy of achievement.

This is true, for example, in Japan, China, Indonesia, the Philippines, Thailand, Malaysia, and Singapore; it is true in India, Pakistan, Iran, the Arab nations, and Israel, and in all these countries particular religious persuasions are also part of the struggle for political power. It is true in Europe with its whites-only governments and in most of the new nations of Africa, where blacks-only governments are the rule. It is less true in some Latin American countries, where skin colors are (as they say in Hawaii) "all mix up"; but in this century there is not yet a case of an ethnic American Indian rising to national leadership in the Western Hemisphere.

The rich nations—and the rich people in the poor nations—face a global fairness revolution, multiplying the demands on a world economic system that knows how to include only a minority of humankind in its benefits. We are witness in consequence to a shredding of international law by those who think markets are unjustly rigged to favor the already favored, and to a growing resentment of a money system that helps the rich get richer by making more and more unrepayable loans to the poor. Both among and within the nation-states of the twentieth century, the old French warning retains its relevance: *Entre le fort et le faible, c'est la liberté qui opprime et la loi qui affranchit* (In relations between the strong and the weak, it's freedom that oppresses and law that liberates).

The arguments (and terrorism and wars) are about what kind of law liberates. The kind we have had, the law that was written by the big brothers in the brotherhood of man—sanctity of contract, property rights, nondiscriminatory trade, freedom to use and exploit the international commons—has been seriously eroded by nonobservance. If law is too rigid and universal, as Aristotle had already figured out two and a half millennia ago, equity is required to correct the law. "Always," Aristotle wrote in his *Politics,* "it is the desire of equality which rises in rebellions."

Reiteration of the legal principles is about as operational as the mandatory health warning in cigarette advertising seems to be. What is happening is an ironic extension of another legal doctrine *rebus sic stantibus,* the notion that a change of conditions justifies a fresh shuffle and a new deal. The prime threats to world security, inside nations and among nations, arise when newcomers to the political bargaining table reach for the cards before the earlier arrivals are ready to make room for more chairs.

Societies flexible enough to adapt to the pressure from the "downs" (as the United States has been doing, not without conflict and coercion, on school integration, voter rights, sex discrimination, and equal employment opportunity) manage to keep change comparatively peaceful.

Societies that try to maintain rigid hierarchies (and especially those that, like the shah's Iran, at the same time encourage education for most of their people) get blown out of the water. In Iran it was the marriage of convenience between those who harbored two powerful resentments, about tradition (the mullahs, who had been bypassed and downgraded by "modernization") and about fairness (the Iranian students at home and abroad), that brought the shah down.

The Ayatollah Khomeini, even while railing against the corruption of Western industrial society, saw the potential in its information technologies. From his base in Paris he sent streams of powerful rhetoric, recorded on audiocassettes, to his supporters in Iran. These were played by the mullahs to their Shi'ite Muslim congregations in their mosques, which were off-limits to the shah's security forces; incensed, the faithful poured out onto the streets to join the student-led partisans of fairness in making Iran ungovernable. When they succeeded together, the tradition defenders and the fairness advocates went after each other, and the fairness people lost.

Similar examples of the "triple collision" (modernization versus equity versus tradition) can be found in a hundred different countries, in tactically very different forms. Part of the stew of resentments is always the complaint we learn to make from infancy: "It isn't *fair.*"

I spent a week in Iran in 1975, as one of a group of Aspen Institute consultants asked to critique Iran's development plans. During a seminar on the government's impressive efforts to get a whole generation educated as engineers and economists and managers of a very rapidly modernizing society, I couldn't resist the temptation. "Do your plans," I inquired, "include the probability that, if you get thousands of your young people educated in a former royal colony now called the United States of America, quite a number of them are going to start asking out loud, 'What do we need a king for?'" It was the wrong time and place, of course, but I still think it was the right question.

The key that unlocks "growth with fairness" in this changing context, in the United States and elsewhere, is indeed widespread access to relevant education. More than any other one factor, it was that forward-looking nineteenth-century decision to offer free public education to every citizen that enabled the American people to pull themselves out of underdevelopment. It was another wise educational policy, the Morrill Act of 1862, to use federal land grants to set up university-based agricultural research stations and build a county-by-county extension service to deliver the resulting science directly to the farm. That made possible the U.S. food production, and the resulting U.S. agribusiness, that is now the centerpiece of the world food and feed market.

At the other end of the global scale, the absence of educational opportunity is all too evident. Of the world's 4 ⅔ billion people, nearly 2 billion are under the age of fifteen. Educational opportunity for them is summed up in heavyhearted numbers published by the International Pediatric Association: 300 million six- to eleven-year-olds in developing countries do not go to school. Fifty percent of all children who actually enter elementary school don't stay until the end of the second year. Only 25 percent will finish elementary school. Only 10 percent of the children in developing countries are immunized against the six basic childhood diseases.

Development is, more than anything else, education. Today,

around the horizon of the developing world, in Asia, Africa, Latin America, the close connection between education and "growth with fairness" is now crystal-clear. The poor can get rich by brainwork. The Japanese have amply illustrated this theorem of wealth creation in the information era, and the hustling, educated people of South Korea, Taiwan, Singapore, and Israel have in their different fashions provided a more recent but similar demonstration. Their economies have not only grown faster than those in other developing countries, but the benefits of that growth have been spread more fairly among their own people than in developing countries that are "favored" (as they are not) by oil or hard minerals or good soil or moderate climate.

The growing importance of information in creating wealth has to be good news for countries less endowed with geological riches and arable land than the early arrivers of the industrial age. Around the developing world, in fact, the striking paradox is that the most successful countries are precisely those *not* blessed with natural resources.

A country such as Japan, with virtually no fuels or minerals, with a short growing season and much farmland we would call marginal, is forced by physical poverty to bet on the only sure resource it has: the minds of its own people. Getting them all, not just an elite few, educated, turns out to be the most profitable investment of all. The educated minds seem able to pull in from the global information flow the data, knowledge, and insights needed to create a development strategy of their own. Nor does it mean that they have to swallow Western culture whole along with the agricultural and industrial technology. The Japanese are still strikingly Japanese, the Koreans still strikingly Korean.

The richer countries are not very good at helping the poorer ones; we act in Canutish ways, trying to limit access to our markets, hoard our technologies, and starve our educational exchange programs. But the developing countries that bet on universal education for their own people, and thus learn how to seek facts and ideas about technology, management, markets, and governance, can readily secure these hardest-to-hoard of resources; then they start treading on our tails.

By contrast, in the countries whose people have been kept in ignorance (by colonial policies, or their own leaders' mismanagement, or first one and then the other), it doesn't seem to matter what riches lie in the ground they occupy. Most of their citizens become the peasants of the global information society (along with the dropouts of the postindustrial regions). The physical riches get siphoned off to the educated folk huddling in the affluent sections of their central cities, and to the information-wise foreigners who "come to do good and do well."

If the rich and powerful believe that it's only at their expense that resources can be shared with the less fortunate, they will cast themselves as the Canutes of world politics: that is, they will dig in and resist spreading information around through education. But if information, the increasingly dominant resource, is really expandable, diffusive, and shareable, more informatization may make for more fairness.

There will be less excuse in the future than in the past for depriving whole populations of the benefits of development. There will also be less excuse for the disadvantaged to blame their condition on the barons and bosses when the accessible knowledge to even the score is already floating out there in the noösphere.

The noösphere of knowledge that is power, this *accessible* resource, has many of the characteristics of a "commons." In considering the implications for fairness of information-as-a-resource, it is an intriguingly fresh thought, worth a moment of speculation.

In earlier times sharing arrangements for a common resource were customary, for example in tribal ownership and nomadic practices. Vestiges of the idea survive in such concepts as the Boston Commons and the national park system, and in the way many major waterways, in Europe and North America, are managed.

For people in old England the commons, as Ivan Illich defines it, was "that part of the environment which lay beyond their own thresholds and outside of their possessions, to which, however, they had recognized claims of usage [not to produce commodities but to provide for the subsistence of their households]." The commons "was necessary for the community's survival, necessary for different groups in different ways, but . . . in a strictly economic sense, was not perceived as scarce."

The older commons, such as those for sheep and cattle, have disappeared through "enclosure." But the idea of commons has now been revived in a big way, as the basis for worldwide cooperation in the environments that by common consent belong to no one or everyone (which seems to be about the same thing): the deep ocean and its seabed, Antarctica, outer space and celestial bodies, and the weather.

The Mediterranean Sea, the arena of bloody ancient feuds and lethal modern rivalries, has recently been formally recognized by all the coastal states (including the Arab states and Israel) as so precious a shared commons that reversing its degradation must be a matter for cooperation even among sworn enemies. The resulting international agreement, intermediated by the United Nations Environment Programme, is self-enforcing: violating its terms would be in a literal sense self-defeating.

For the management of an information commons, a sharing environment, these exotic precedents suddenly seem not so exotic.

Illich, in a Tokyo speech called "Silence Is a Commons," argued that electronic devices (from the microphone to the computer) are a form of "enclosure," reserving to the few the privilege of breaking the silence otherwise available to the many.

I don't know about silence; I haven't had much experience with it. But on the computer as a form of enclosure, I demur. In its general impact the forced march of information technology, personal computers combined with global telecommunications, seems to me to be taking us away from the idea of enclosure. My hunch is that the fusion of computers and communications will further empower the many to participate in "making policy" in domains to which the few, with their moth-eaten monopolies of knowledge, will have to yield more and more access.

Neighborhood organizations are furnishing themselves with personal computers to deal more effectively with the banks and developers and government agencies that will otherwise make the neighborhoods' decisions for them. American Indian tribes might set up a computer teleconference to concert their political clout on fast-moving legislation. A single individual with a personal computer can even now get access to so much useful and timely information that she or he can, with a week's homework and without leaving home, intervene as an unusually knowledgeable citizen in the debate on almost any public policy issue on the national agenda.

To chart these potentials is not to fulfill them. The trends in information technology would make it possible to organize as a commons (with free, though not necessarily costless, access thereto) much of the world's most useful knowledge. That is not to say it will happen. It just helps remake the point that those who think "it isn't fair" will have plenty of opportunity to get access to almost any information that is being withheld from them to their disadvantage. But they will have to want to work at it; they will have to prepare their brains for the task. In the information society, as in its predecessors, there is still no free lunch.

7

Geopolitics:
The Passing
of Remoteness

We have considered what the informatization of society is doing to hierarchies founded on control, secrecy, ownership, and limited access to resources. The fifth of these eroding forms of power, summed up in the word *geopolitics,* is based on location.

For almost a century, from Andrew Jackson to Woodrow Wilson, the strength of the United States lay in its isolation. We could get on with our development without outside interference, except, of course, for large railroad loans and massive immigration that Americans didn't think of as "world affairs." We tried, for nearly two decades after World War I, to reenter the cocoon of remoteness, but we got involved again—this time, it seems, forever.

The idea that location is a form of power, that the political importance of communities is due to their geography, dies hard.

Cities usually developed because they were seaports or on critical inland waterways, or (earlier) on important overland caravan routes or (later) on important railway lines. It made a difference whether you were in the city or in the country; if you lived in a rural area, you were remote. There was no choice about it, you were just remote.

The importance of countries was often based on the natural resources they had discovered, and developed, on "their" territory. The spices of the Orient, the rubber and tin of Southeast Asia, the coal and iron of Central Europe, the diamonds (and later uranium) of South Africa, the fruits of Central America, the petroleum reserves of Indonesia and Mexico and Venezuela and North Africa and the Persian (or Arabian) Gulf and the North Sea, the soils that produced those "amber waves of grain" in North America—these crucial resources left an indelible mark on the national sovereignties that happened to find them in their backyards.

Then there was the sense of place in military strategy. This was the idea that a nation's power depended largely on its geography: how defendable its frontiers, how rich its mineral deposits, how fertile its soil, how plentiful its water, how extensive its coastal waters.

The political relevance of geography was one of the cardinal principles of the founding fathers (only one founding mother: Eleanor Roosevelt) of the postwar world in the 1940s and early 1950s. For issues that could not be handled by global institutions (the United Nations and its specialized agencies, the World Bank, and the International Monetary Fund), their assumption was that regional organizations, continent by continent, would take charge.

It soon developed that for the most part (a partial exception has to be made for the European Community and ASEAN, the Association of Southeast Asian Nations), regional organizations did not amount to very much; they tended to be overstaffed and underemployed. On the other hand, *functional* international organizations such as OPEC (the Organization of Petroleum Exporting Countries, which set the price of oil as long as it was in short supply) and OECD (the Organization for Economic Cooperation and Development, the club of rich countries banded together for mutual cooperation and for dealing with the poor) turned out to be fully employed.

In military strategy, geopolitics was overtaken by rocket technology. As soon as intercontinental missiles could reach anywhere from anywhere else (from unfindable submarines as well as from undefendable land silos), the location of the missile and its target became of secondary importance; from many silos in the Soviet Union, Chicago or Omaha are closer than New York City. The size and shape of a nation's landmass, and its position on a map of the globe, turned out to be not nearly as important as its relations with the states that could threaten it, no matter where on the globe their real estate happened to be.

But the major change in geography-based thinking has been the coming of the information society, and especially the fusion of computers and telecommunications.

The countries with the biggest flows of information we call "developed." But anybody can extract knowledge from the bath of information that nearly drowns us all. You don't have to find it in your own frontiers, you don't have to grow it in your own soil, you don't have to fabricate it in factories or put it together in assembly plants. You just have to "get it all together" in your own brain, and then combine your brain with others in organizations ("networks," committees, alliances) designed to make something happen.

Communications satellites and fast computers are gradually erasing distance, eroding the idea that some places are world centers because they are near other places, while other areas are bound to be peripheral because they are remote from the "center of things."

The poet Octavio Paz caught on to what was happening well before most of the systems analysts and political pundits did. "We Mexicans," he wrote in the early 1970s, "have always lived on the periphery of history. Now the center or nucleus of world society has disintegrated and everyone—including the European and the North American—is a peripheral being. We are living on the margin . . . because there is no longer any center. . . . World history has become everyone's task and our own labyrinth is the labyrinth of all mankind."

The passing of remoteness is one of the great unheralded macro-trends of our extraordinary time. You can now plug in through television to UN voting or a bombing in Beirut or a Wimbledon final. You can sit in Sydney or Singapore or Bahrein and intervene directly in the markets that determine the prices of goods or of money. Distant farmsteads can, if they will, be connected to the central cortex of their commodity exchanges, their political authorities, their global markets. Once you can participate in rule, power, and authority according to the relevance of your opinion rather than the mileage to the decision-making venue, then the power centers are wherever the brightest people are using the latest information in the most creative ways.

There are, of course, alternatives to geography as principles of organization. A revised proposition is suggested by futurist Magda McHale: In the changing information environment, civilization will be built more around communities of *people,* whether or not they happen also to form communities of *place.*

That this trend is well advanced can be seen in a quick review of the changing context of three familiar kinds of organization: state, nation, and organized religion.

The *state* is not withering away, as with their different motives Karl Marx and the advocates of world government would have desired. But power is leaking out of "national sovereignty" in three directions at once.

The state is leaking at the top, as more international functions require the pooling of sovereignty in alliances, in a World Weather Watch, in geophysical research, in eradicating contagious diseases, in satellite communication, in facing up to global environmental risks.

The state is leaking sideways, as multinational corporations—private, pseudoprivate, and "socialized"—conduct more and more of the world's commerce and operate across political frontiers so much better than committees of sovereign states seem able to do.

The state is also leaking from the bottom, as ethnic minorities, single-issue constituencies, functional communities, and special-purpose neighborhoods take control of their own destinies—legislating their own growth policies, their own population policies, their own environmental policies.

And what does *nation* mean nowadays? Increasingly it means not location but ethnicity: the Frenchness of Quebec, the tribal loyalties of the Ibo in Biafra, the separatism of the Scots, the rhetorical nationhood of the Arabs, the world's many diasporas ranging from the overseas Chinese to the Zionist, and non-Zionist, Jews outside Israel.

In the information game of global ethnicity, for example, Israel is certainly one of the advanced countries: the Jewish people have been at it for so long. The potential of real-time networking is now a powerful new means of communication with the electronic diaspora, whenever Israel has ideas to sell to, or wants to solicit ideas from, the information-rich global community that is world Jewry.

And *organized religion*? In a world of people-communities, the "parish" cannot be mostly geography-based. All of the great religious traditions have had to settle, so far in world history, for predominance in one or another part of the world. But now, even established religions are trying to break free from their national and regional parishes. The Roman Catholic pope's extensive travels and the terrorist outreach of Ayatollah Khomeini's Shi'ites form a grotesque correlation: both are breaking loose from historic geographic boundaries to appeal to a wider religious, and therefore political, constituency.

The prospect of people rather than place as a basis for community holds interesting implications for universities and school systems trying to serve a local clientele, for corporations that have bet heavily on regional organization, and for political systems that have bet heavily on geography-based constituencies. It implies that those institutions that exploit the electronic answers to remoteness will be "catching a wave" in the new knowledge environment.

The fusion of rapid microprocessing and global telecommunications thus presents all peoples with a choice between relevance and remoteness. There will be costs and benefits to either choice, but the necessity to choose is new, and inescapable.

The world's least remote people are Americans.

As of 1985 the United States of America is more pervasively engaged with other societies, more intimately involved in the destinies of more peoples around the world, than any other country. Indeed, in most senses of the phrase the United States is the *only* global power—not because of its geography (rather, in spite of it), but because Americans are able to compute and communicate on more subjects in more places, around the clock and around the globe, than any other people. This is partly because of what the U.S. government can do. But it is mostly because the American people are directly engaged, whether they know it, and like it, or not, in the making and carrying out of U.S. foreign policy.

What about the Soviet Union, you say? The Soviet Union is a superpower in space exploration and military might (which may turn out to be the same thing), but in very little else. That is why, whatever the problem, the Kremlin looks for a military solution. Quite a lot of people in the world are using Soviet weapons. But hardly anyone outside the USSR is singing Soviet songs, listening to Soviet rock, drinking Soviet colas, flying in Soviet airliners, hoarding Soviet rubles, buying Soviet computers and electronics, aping Soviet agriculture, or copying the Soviet political system. The United States, by contrast, has a global reach in all such fields, and many more.

To the surprise of many Americans disheartened by the doleful diet on television's evening "bad news," the United States is also the world's most attractive society. The evidence? There are now some 16 million refugees worldwide—a million more than all the displaced persons just after World War II—and, given a free choice, more of these refugees would like to come to the United States than anywhere else, by hook if possible, by crook if necessary.

Those of us who seek or are sought for generalist roles need, therefore, to think hard about the kind of world in which Americans are going to have to live and work as an interdependent part of the whole. We also need to think hard about the kind of world we *want;* no one runs the world, but the United States always seems to get on the executive committee.

"A civilization," Raymond Aron wrote, "is usually composed of combative states or of a universal empire." But what we have achieved is much more complicated: "quarreling states, more subjected to asymmetric interdependence than they would like . . . too different to agree, too interconnected to separate."

The world we are not remote from is leaderless, dangerous, uneconomic, unjust, and (so far) ungovernable. The problem for the "executive committee" is to exercise leadership in moderating its dangers, enhancing its efficiencies, rectifying its injustices, and arranging the governance of its necessarily international functions. I have already suggested how dangerously unfair most of its people believe it to be. Let's look at the rest of the picture.

- It is a world with nobody in general charge. That is, of course, the way we Americans wanted it. We didn't want the Kaiser or Adolf Hitler or Josef Stalin to be *über alles,* but neither did we want to be global policemen or overseers ourselves. Through alliances and aid programs, we have done what no leading power in history has done: shared some of our power with others and tried to build up other nations (including recent ex-enemies) and international agencies. Let's not be carried away with our own generosity, because it was really enlightened interest: We didn't want all those foreigners on our backs. We wanted our brothers to keep themselves.

- It is a world where what peace we have is an international balance of terror, based on the built-in uncertainty of nuclear weapons. We may have invented not just the ultimate weapon but the ultimately unusable weapon, the explosion that is too powerful to be a military instrument and cannot even be profitably brandished. (The last good brandish was Nikita Khrushchev's promise in the 1960s to "incinerate the orange groves of Italy and reduce the Acropolis in Athens to radioactive ash." That empty threat only served to galvanize Italy and Greece as loyal members of the NATO alliance—which, considering their internal politics, wasn't easy.) Strategic nuclear weapons have been usable, since 1945, only to deter their use by another.

• It is a world in transition from concepts of national security as military defense based on complex weapons systems, to concepts of security as including oil, environmental risk, nuclear proliferation, population growth, unsafe streets, Islamic revolutions, and a global epidemic called inflation. The most frightening security nightmare of the 1980s and 1990s may not be the familiar image of the mushroom cloud but the unfamiliar and unsettling collision of the modernization process in the developing world, with resentments about fairness and about the rape of cultural identity. The collision at this dangerous crossroads is what's producing the Irans, the Lebanons, the Cambodias, the Northern Irelands, the El Salvadors, and who knows how many future examples of the incapacity of governments to cope.

• It is a world full of dangerous weapons. Two-thirds of a trillion dollars of annual defense spending worldwide. Five nuclear weapons states, two more presumed to have nuclear weapons, two dozen more with a "nuclear mobilization capacity." One nation per year gone nuclear for energy production, all of them together producing as a by-product the starting kit for several thousand Hiroshimas a year if they wish. A massive trade in conventional arms, amounting to more than $13 billion per year in 1982, with American ingenuity and marketing skills accounting for 37.7 percent of that trade worldwide. The prospect of terrorists brandishing much bigger bangs than any terrorist has yet found it useful to set off. And an escalating capacity by smaller nations—or guerrilla groups, criminal conspiracies, or individual desperadoes—to make a less-than-global mess of the complexity we call civilization.

• It is a world full of wars. In 1980–82, six new wars were started and only two were turned off. In 1983 there were forty major and minor conflicts in the world, involving 45 of the world's

164 nations: ten conflicts in the Middle East and the Persian Gulf, ten in Asia, ten in Africa, seven in Latin America, and three in Europe. As many as 4½ million soldiers (of the 25 million in standing armies worldwide) were engaged in combat that year. The total casualties in these wars are uncounted, but estimates of deaths run from more than 1 million up to 5 million. The number of wounded may well have been three times the number of dead. The financial cost of these wars runs into many hundreds of billions of dollars. (The 45 nations involved in the forty wars spend more than $500 billion a year on their armed forces.)

•It is a world whose industrial democracies face a chronic crisis of governance—their leaders baffled by the dirt, danger, and disaffection that urban systems seem to generate; their young people educated for nonexistent jobs; their middle classes periodically squeezed by inflation, disemployed by recession, and harassed by regulation; their industries and farms hosting an enormous migratory proletariat; their governments revolving in endless and ineffective coalitions. The world's leading "centrally planned economy" is, by contrast, so stable as to be static—its leaders unable to generate the morale or productivity to compete in the trading world, incapable sixty-eight years after the Bolshevik Revolution of feeding their own people, incompetent to enforce their system dependably on their key neighbors, let alone to create a durable market for it around the world.

•It is a world with 4,677 million people in residence, already programmed to double in four decades. Annual population growth decreased from 2 to 1.7 percent in the decade just past, but the same period still saw global population rise by 800 million. The world food situation (not yet organized enough to call a "system") is too dependent on the North American granary, where public policy is still afflicted with a hundred-year bias in favor of scarcity. At its tenth anniversary session, the World Food Council affirmed "that hunger can no longer be blamed solely on humankind's inability to produce enough food for all. Hunger today is largely a natural and man-made phenomenon: human error or neglect creates it, human complacency perpetuates it and human resolve can eradicate it."

•It is a world where national energy policies still discourage plentiful solar sources and draw down too fast on the complex petroleum molecules that are really too valuable and versatile to be burned. The way things are going, we might have to settle in desperation for coal (which risks overheating the earth through the "greenhouse effect" of spewing carbon dioxide and other gases into the global atmosphere) or nuclear power (which facilitates the proliferation of nuclear weapons and produces radioactive wastes for which no reliable garbage dump has yet been found).

•It is a world under chronic threat of a nervous breakdown in the fatefully interconnected world economy. Whatever triggers it (at this writing, a cascade of defaulting debtors seems a likely trigger), the scenario is all too readily imaginable: bank failures, wild speculation and financial panic, the ungluing of alliances induced by epidemic inflation and depression at the same time, a hardening North-South confrontation leading to government-sponsored terrorism and the interruption of ocean choke points, violent revolutions in a dozen Irans or Lebanons at once, and paralysis of will in the world's islands of affluence as the "power of poverty" pits guilt and resentment against each other in the politics of the industrial countries.

•It is a world where science, which has always been transnational, keeps inventing inherently global technologies—for weather observation, military reconnaissance, telecommunications, data processing, resource sensing, and orbital industry. As a result, for the nonland environments at least, we find ourselves moving beyond concepts of national ownership, sovereignty, and citizenship to ideas such as the global commons, the international monitoring of global risks, and "the common heritage of mankind."

- It is a world in which a growing number of functions that simply must be performed cannot be contained in national decision systems at all: the management of transborder data flows; the allocation of radio frequencies; the regulation of satellite communications, global pollution, ocean fishing, and mining; weather forecasting and modification; the nuclear fuel cycle; the potentials of earth-sensing space vehicles; and a complexity of transnational corporations that provide much of the enterprise in world trade and investment yet remain the most popular villains in world politics.

- It is, in sum, a world whose international institutions and practices are not yet able to cope with the international functions modern science and technology have made possible, or to resolve the conflicts generated by the modernization process itself.

In the most creative celebration of the Bicentennial of our Declaration of Independence, a group of citizens in Philadelphia commissioned historian Henry Steele Commager to draft a "Declaration of Interdependence"; 128 members of Congress signed it, and the new declaration became the basis for a year of Philadelphia-based discussions of world affairs.

The Philadelphians were on the right track. Durable though the nation-state has proved to be, interdependence has caught up with most of the issues, practices, and policies that used to be regarded in the United States as essentially "domestic": energy, pollution, civil rights, race relations, feminism, poverty, education, research, science, technology, business, labor, food, transportation, population, culture, communication, terrorism, revolution, law enforcement, arms, narcotics, religion, ideology. No nation controls even that central symbol of national independence, the value of its money: Inflation and recession are both transnational.

The communications media operate all over the world. One-fifth of the world's gross product is created by multinational enterprises, more of them based in the United States than anywhere else; something like one-quarter of what I learned in school to call "international trade" is the *internal* transactions of international companies.

Nonprofit organizations, foundations, exchange programs such as Youth for Understanding and The Experiment in International Living, and church-based missionary movements have all in some degree had to internationalize their operations, some even bringing non-Americans onto their governing boards and spinning off their overseas functions to indigenous organizations. In many U.S. school systems the basics are being taught in global perspective.

In the U.S. government, nowadays, every agency has its own international relations. Actions of the Department of Agriculture are among the most important decisions made about the world food balance. The Federal Aviation Administration maintains a web of transnational relationships to make global air travel safer. Federal programs to conserve fuel and develop alternatives to oil determine the U.S. negotiating position with the international oil cartel. The Environmental Protection Agency finds that many forms of pollution require international cooperation to monitor and control. Each new technological breakthrough—fast computers, weather modification, remote sensing of crops and geological formations from orbiting satellites, new ways to fish and drill and mine and build in marine environments—brings with it a new tangle of international claims and conflicts.

In the so-called old-line domestic departments, the interdependence functions are also of growing importance: Justice's immigration controls (such as they are), Treasury's Coast Guard and debt-management operations and drug enforcement functions, Commerce's National Weather Service (one of two world headquarters for the World Weather Watch), and Interior's responsibility for minerals policy are only a few of a hundred examples. Even the quasi-judicial bodies have foreign policies of their own: The Federal Reserve Board has the dominant voice in determining the growth rate of the world's largest stock of international money, the U.S.

dollar. And the independent Nuclear Regulatory Commission has the power, which it has never figured out how to use, to veto a White House decision to export nuclear materials or equipment.

The content of international affairs is now mostly the internal affairs of still sovereign nations. At the White House level, every major issue for policy decision is partly domestic and partly international.

What we mostly want from other countries—and what they mostly want from us—are changes in domestic preconceptions, priorities, policies, and practices. By the same token, most major domestic policy actions we take—decisions about the levels of farm subsidies, the direction of research and development, the degree of emphasis on energy conservation, the supply of American dollars, the amount of unemployment we will stand for, the size and shape of our budget deficit, and many, many others—are enormously important to nearly every other nation on earth.

Despite these well-known facts, the U.S. government is still unambiguously divided between people who are supposed to work on domestic matters and people who are supposed to work on foreign affairs. To paraphrase Gilbert and Sullivan, each matter of public policy is born a little "domestic policy" or a little "foreign policy," and is so treated as it grows up through the processes of decision, both in the executive branch and on Capitol Hill.

One of the most elementary doctrines about the management of large-scale systems is that a supervisory office should not be organized in the same way as its subordinate offices are—that, indeed, it should deliberately be organized to *cut across* the vertical divisions below, in order to throw new light on their interrelationships and inconsistencies before issues come to the top executive for decision (which can mean resolution of differences or, more commonly, confirmation of a consensus already reached among subordinates). Each of the cabinet departments was established essentially to deal either with national security and foreign policy matters, or with domestic policy. Yet the White House has been organized the same way for three decades, coordinating state and defense and the intelligence community through a National Security Council and channeling the rest of the government through a domestic policy staff, the lineal successor of a function performed by White House assistants under a variety of names ever since the Truman administration.

Because the system does not fit the function, dissonance between foreign and domestic policies is normal. Review the history of the price of oil, the embargo on soybeans, the law of the sea, the use of food surpluses, the sale of arms, and the export of nuclear equipment, and you will find plenty of examples of international ramifications unpredicted, ignored, or suppressed.

Despite the melding of domestic and international issues out there in the real world, it is still almost literally true that only one person in the executive branch is overtly hired to work on both domestic and foreign policy. We call him President of the United States. The policy officials with domestic or foreign affairs job descriptions have to cheat, of course; nearly everybody with public policy responsibilities works on both.

It has sometimes been suggested that the secretary of state should be given a clear track to coordinate the foreign policy aspects of all government decisions. But those decisions reach so deeply into American politics (the oil crisis is displayed at the filling station, Soviet purchases of wheat affect the price of bread at the local supermarket, decisions about the global supply of dollars push mortgage interest rates up or down) that the secretary of state cannot become fully responsible for them without being elected president. The last secretary of state who found the job a stepping-stone to the presidency was James Buchanan, in 1856.

The only option, in the mid-1980s, is to view foreign policy, as Adam Yarmolinsky has suggested, as "not a subject matter for government decision making; it is rather an aspect of every important government decision." The implications are far-reaching, and not only for the federal government. Taking our interdependence seriously will require changes of purposes and priorities in education, in research and development, in business practices, in the orientation of labor unions, in the communications media with their global impact, and in the voluntary sector with its grass-roots base.

The necessity to make so many public policy decisions in international ways, in consultation or agreement with other nations and international enterprises, *and* the fact that the interdependence issues reach deeply into the "domestic" politics of our own and other nations, require a much wider and more intensive dialogue between "followers" and "leaders," and a broader education of people-in-general about the nature of interdependence, because if they don't understand it their leaders won't.

In the easier days of the Marshall Plan, the decisive actions needed to meet an international crisis were essentially taken by a few legislative and executive leaders; the rest of us participated in passive ways by reading the newspapers, paying our taxes, and reelecting Harry Truman. But the chronic crisis of interdependence, of which the troubles called energy and food and arms and inflation and jobs and money are only the most obvious examples, requires actions by dozens of government agencies, hundreds of state and local governments, thousands of business executives, hundreds of thousands of teachers, and millions of householders, automobile owners, investors, and organized and unorganized workers.

The style of national governance appropriate to these circumstances is akin to wartime leadership, engaging the cooperation of whole populations to take domestic actions without which the requisite international cooperation could not be arranged by even the most skillful diplomats. Such leadership goes far beyond the capacity to guide legislation through the labyrinth of enactment to the capacity to educate whole populations. For modern interdependence and national security require changes in attitudes and assumptions, lifestyles and workways—the capacity to elicit millions of willing actions, more or less voluntary, backed up by self-interest, market economics, social pressure, and only at the margin by government intervention.

In a polity where ultimately the people make the policy, even individual citizens have to try to get their minds around the whole of this complexity. A fortiori, the leaders who interact with citizens in the formulation of policy have to wrap their minds around the world, develop for their own personal use a strategic global agenda that can serve both to help educate the American constituency and to guide the day-to-day tactical actions and reactions that constitute American foreign policy.

To me as an American, the most prominent feature of this volatile and turbulent world is that it is constantly *in motion*. Everywhere, the status quo is on its way out. Half a hundred governments are likely to change next year and the year after that, sometimes by constitutional process but more often by coercion or violence.

Official diplomacy is mostly the art of getting along with the sitting government. But in so dynamic an environment, the American people have at least an equal interest in being in effective communication with the *next* government, and the one after that. What our government says and does, how and when we compromise our stated principles, should be decided with an eye to the effect on those future relationships. If, to select an example not quite at random, we encourage a sitting government to drag its feet on land reform, we can hardly expect much cooperation on strategic issues from enthusiasts for land reform who may take over next.

We have not been skillful at masterminding or even forecasting political transition in other societies. But the U.S. government can at least position itself so as not to make the unseating of each sitting government a defeat for the American people.

All peoples, however governed, are presently or potentially our friends. But no government can expect to be our overriding friend; it is as true as when Lord Salisbury said it that nations do not have permanent friends, they just have permanent interests.

So our judgment in each particular case (about trade, about human rights, about economic cooperation, about arms control, about educational exchange, about a military alliance) should be heavily weighted in favor of the long-run relationship between the American people and the peoples of the other country or countries involved. That purpose is seldom served by the effusive nonsense which so often characterizes the personalized diplomacy of summit meetings. This is not a partisan comment: it applies as well to President Carter's short-lived prediction of the shah's longevity as to Vice-President Bush's euphoric toast to President Ferdinand Marcos of the Philippines: "We love your adherence to democratic principles and to the democratic process."

In reaching out to "next governments" around the world, the United States has the enormous advantage of its credible pluralism. With marginal exceptions U.S. businesspeople, trade union leaders, farmers, scientists, engineers, professors, journalists, and especially students and other young people can travel the world without being regarded as instructed agents of their government, whatever its temporary political complexion. By the same token, we welcome here each year many thousands of key people—leaders and leaders-to-be—from nearly every country on earth. Many of them spend some time being briefed on U.S. policies, but all of them spend most of their time getting to know Americans from every walk of life, every sector of society, every shade of opinion.

In the new knowledge environment, this "getting to know you" experience should be thought of as a major part of U.S. foreign policy. It does not guarantee political support by our visitors, or those we visit, of whatever the current U.S. government may temporarily emit as "policy." But a healthy flow of Americans overseas, and a comparable flow to the United States of leaders and potential leaders from other countries, guarantee that next governments around the world will include people who understand that American governance may be messy but is not really messianic, and that democratic pluralism and nonviolent transitions of power are practical propositions even in a continental society.

It may be that the votes our senators and representatives cast each year on educational exchange programs are the most important policy they are privileged to make about the future of peaceful change in a world that is always changing but seldom peaceful.

"To make the world safe for diversity": That was President John F. Kennedy's "mission statement" for the United States in world affairs. A pluralistic world with room for many cultures, protected in going their self-selected ways and induced to leave their neighbors alone—that won't be a comfortable world, for Americans or anyone else. But for Americans, it should be a recognizable (because

Madisonian) world, even a congenial world, because diversity is where we come from.

I have had frequent occasions to try to explain the United States to people from Europe, Africa, Asia, and Latin America. It's not easy. After much trial and error, here is the essence of what I try to get across to my friends from abroad.

You have to understand, I tell them, that our purposes in the world are different from the purposes of most other societies, even of some of our closest friends and allies, because our experience at home has been different. ("When will people learn," Thomas Babington Macaulay asked, "that it is the spirit we are of, not the machinery we employ, that binds us to others?")

In this world there are a good many nations, and countless parties and organizations, whose leaders passionately believe some single national state, some unifying political doctrine, some monochromatic race of people, can and should dominate the world. But we Americans know that nations are too interdependent, doctrines too dangerous, ethnic and cultural groups too proud, and individual men and women just too ornery to give these claims and pretensions much of a chance in the long run. We know these things not because we have figured them out rationally, but because that is the kind of people our experience has taught us to be.

Visitors to the United States often find us more than a little confusing—especially visitors who can describe their goals and define their "system" with practiced words from ancient manuscripts or modern manifestos.

We do not have a "system"; we have a protected plurality of systems. The Englishman Edmund Burke, in his famous speech about how to get along with those wild men across the Atlantic, said in despair that our religion was "the dissidence of dissent." Americans, Burke thought, were a "people who are still, as it were, but in the gristle, and not yet hardened into the bone of manhood."

In the two centuries since those words were spoken we have kept relearning, from hardening, bone-building experience in peace and war, that the best and most durable way to manage our public business is the undogmatic, unsystematic, loose-reined, checked-and-balanced, part-public–part-private governance we call democracy. We have learned to distrust the idea that any one person's (or any one group's) view of society is the correct, approved, authorized version. We hold comfortably in our heads this paradoxical idea: The one essential thing about democracy is that no one individual or group ever gains the exclusive right to say, with authority, what democracy is.

For Americans, a preference for diversity should come naturally. That is just as well. With the passing of remoteness, a tolerance for diversity seems to be the first principle of world order.

8

The
Social Fallout
of Knowledge

If you chart the direction of all the conceptual changes mentioned so far in this book, you will find a common characteristic: Our basic ideas all seem to be *lengthening* to take in more of the future and *widening* to include what used to be regarded as *externalities.* That's an academic word for factors that don't fit into a traditional discipline or profession or analytical system, yet seem to be disturbingly relevant all the same—so you put them on the shelf to think about later.

We are coming to realize that we often make avoidable trouble for ourselves, that Walt Kelly was quite right to finger the enemy as us. We—you and I, not merely the other guys—have often found it seductively comforting to tunnel our vision, to focus too sharply on one issue at a time, to neglect to ask the questions that illuminate the ways in which, as the study of ecology has now taught us, every action has consequences that should be considered as part of the decision to act. The French have a wonderfully succinct way of saying this: *Il faut vouloir les conséquences de ce qu'on veut.* Freely translated: You should not only want what you want, but want what it leads to.

We plunged into the use of nuclear power for electricity without asking the hard questions about the back end of the nuclear fuel cycle —about safety, about waste, about proliferation. We pursued growth without asking, "Growth for what?" or "Growth for whom?" We were persuaded by narrow-gauge, straight-line extrapolations that we were running out of resources when we were mostly running out of imagination. We applauded a goal of national energy independence when the problem was the management of international energy interdependence. We produced new gadgets and only then inquired about their consequences. We built interstate highways and discovered with astonishment their effect on urban living. We built on land without asking how the nearby weather would be thereby modified. Some executives thought social responsibility was someone else's problem, induced consumer outrage expressed in government regulation, and then wondered how that army of government regulators happened to have become so intrusive and so burdensome.

We—and especially those of us who like to think of ourselves as generalists, executives, leaders, or all of these—would need wider lenses and a longer focal length even if the world stood still. But scientists keep probing, inventors keep inventing, and the keepers of technology keep letting it out of the cage. And with computers and telecommunications working together now, there is truly no visible limit to how complicated things can get. E. B. White must be appalled, and James Thurber guffawing with delight, wherever he is.

It is still shocking, forty years later, to realize that the Manhattan Project, the huge secret organization that produced the atom bomb during World War II, did not employ on its staff a single person whose full-time assignment was to think hard about the policy implications of the project if it should succeed. Thus no one was working on nuclear arms control. We have been playing catch-up, not too successfully, ever since.

The Manhattan Project was not an exception; it was the rule. For three hundred years until the 1970s, science and technology were quite generally regarded as having a life of their own, an "inner logic," an autonomous sense of direction. Their self-justifying ethic was change and "growth." But in the 1970s, the worm began to turn: Society started to take charge, not of scientific discovery but of its technological fallout.

The implications of this trend—for the meeting of human needs, for the security of peoples, for the very nature of "growth" and "development," for scientific discovery and technological innovation themselves, and above all for economic and political management— are enormous. Nonscientists and nonengineers will have to learn enough about science and technology to substitute a social wisdom for a guidance system based on scientific rationalism. The experts in each specialized field will have to develop the capacity to relate their own expertise to the politics of value and the values of politics. People, and nations, that fail to learn the rudiments of "technology assessment" will be handicapped, unable to participate effectively in the decisions that affect their own destiny.

Until the modern era, technological change was so gradual that it was readily absorbed and molded by, became organically part of, the cultures that accepted it. Those cultures in their turn were modified by the new technologies, at an even slower rate. The use of fire, animal husbandry, agriculture, the wheel, and celestial navigation; the progression from stone to bronze to iron to steel—each new breakthrough was limited by tradition in the pace, the scope, and the spread of its social consequences.

The norm was the law of tradition, learning by rote, living by repetition, employment by custom, and leadership by small aristocracies of status.

In less than three centuries the scientific and industrial revolutions (which were not being called *revolutions* when they started) so quickened the pace, widened the scope, and especially broadened the diffusion of knowledge that discovery and innovation eroded antique techniques (at a pace we now consider revolutionary) and called into being new kinds of organizations, such as bureaucracies, corporations, and big research laboratories.

Especially in the world's North and West, educated people came to believe that if they could only learn enough they could actually control nature. The energy that could be placed at the service of each man and woman seemed limited only by human inventiveness. A seemingly inevitable technology-based progress became the basis for new structures of value (for some, almost a new religion) and new theories of society.

The prestige of science was such that it became the leading edge of social and political philosophy. Indeed, social and political change have during these three hundred years followed in a remarkably straight line from new scientific perceptions. Isaac Newton's cosmology, with its planets orbiting around without bumping into each other, gave James Madison the courage to describe (in *The Federalist*) a politics of pluralism in which "factions" would move freely yet avoid damaging collisions. Darwin's powerful doctrine of struggle and survival led directly to Social Darwinism: If you were poor, it must be because you were unfit to survive; that made it all right to be rich and made fairness a matter of charity, not the inalienable right some European thinkers and American Declaration-writers seemed to think it was. Physical technologies led directly to copycat notions in the social sciences, reflected in phrases such as *management science* and *social engineering*. Once we learned from the life sciences and popular ecology that everything was related to everything else, *interdependence* became the new cosmology.

First in Europe, then in North America, then in Japan and Russia the new contagious norm was the law of change, learning by experiment, living with uncertainty, employment by acquired skill, and leadership by an aristocracy of achievement.

Until our own time, the direction of modernization seemed clear: more. The definition of dynamism was more energy use per capita, more material goods per person, higher wages and more protection for each worker, weapons with greater kill-ratios, speedier vehicles, taller buildings, bigger cities, growing populations, lower infant mortality, rising life expectancy—all as soon as possible. The mood was well captured in the slogan popularized by the United States Navy's construction battalions (Seabees) during World War II: "The impossible we do in a day. The miracles take a little longer."

When the UN was preparing for a world conference on Science and Technology for Development, in 1979, I was asked to team up with one of the Third World's outstanding thinkers, Dr. Ibrahim H. Abdel Rahman of Egypt, to see if we could explain what makes a society dynamic, and what the less developed countries should be doing to become more dynamic.

In recent centuries dynamism has clearly been lacking in the societies now labeled "developing." My Egyptian colleague and I did not claim to know why, and we do not think anybody else knows why. When I first worked in the early foreign-aid programs, we all thought it obvious that Western industrial dynamism had somehow to be associated with Western values, private enterprise, and parliamentary governance. But this theory has not survived the twentieth-century evidence that very modern industrial technology could coexist with non-Western value structures (Japan) and non-Western political institutions (the Soviet Union). Besides, many of *this* century's "less developed" peoples have had their own highly developed periods of scientific creativity or technological dynamism. China, Egypt, Persia, Greece, and India, the Phoenicians, the Arabs, and the Incas come readily to mind.

If we couldn't explain the differences in "dynamism" we could at least describe them—and a summary of that description may be useful as we think now about harnessing technology to human needs and purposes. We did *not* find that dynamism meant "more." We found a *process* that was common to all the dynamic societies, but that process can be used to generate quality as well as quantity, "better" as well as "more."

We found dynamism to be an effectively managed mix of four kinds of *information*: science (which we called "know what"), technology ("know-how"), values ("know why"), and social authority and organization ("know who"). Each has a role, but it's know-how that provides the dynamic thrust; technology is the instrument for continual change.

Technology, or know-how, may be derived from any or all of three sources: from the application of science (Albert Einstein's speculations leading to the use of nuclear energy); from "tinkering" (Thomas Edison, who had only three months' formal schooling at the age of seven, inventing the phonograph, the electric light, and the motion-picture machine); or from a direct response to a social-economic demand (the need for urban mass transit, hardier varieties of seed, an antitoxin, a new weapons system, a better mousetrap).

But technology is simply more information—at best, abstractly interesting if not applied. And in the societies where the most technology is applied, the dynamism seems to be the consequence of two mutually reinforcing spirals of change.

A *micro*loop, crudely illustrated in figure 1, spins together the know-how of specialized technology with an entrepreneur (private or public), capital (private or public or often both), labor, skill training, a productive facility, advertising, a market ("free" or "planned") with consumers who pay for what is produced, and the reinvestment of the resulting wealth in more capital, more benefits to workers, and especially more research for even more innovative technology. The linkage of these functions through organizations that bring people together to perform them (institutions for education and training, for financing, for farming or processing or drilling or mining or construction or fabrication, for worker protection, for marketing, for management, and for public regulation to protect the public's interest in the whole process) closes the loop and keeps it spinning.

At the *macro*level, in a working society we can see hundreds, thousands, hundreds of thousands of these loops, some running down, some cranking up, and some spinning with continuous innovation. Taken together, in figure 2, they form a composite picture of the society as having a certain level of technology (T), a definable set of values (V), and a variety of social organizations and authorities (A) in dynamic equilibrium with each other.

A change in technology (say, the widespread use of small computers), a change in values (say, an environmental movement), or a change in authority (say, a major electoral change or a coup d'état) may well unbalance this composite equilibrium, until changes in the other two elements produce a new equilibrium. (Natural disasters, and policy disasters such as the Great Depression, also upset the preexisting equilibrium and induce changes in all three of the dynamism factors—technology, values, authority.)

In the modernized societies, each new equilibrium is different from the last and at a more sophisticated level of technological complexity. What makes their "development" not circular but a spiral—that is, what makes their social change a *dynamic* equilibrium—is the continual injection of innovation through technology, plus the slower but not less important changes in values, attitudes, and social structures.

There is a rough analogy here to the harmonized functioning of

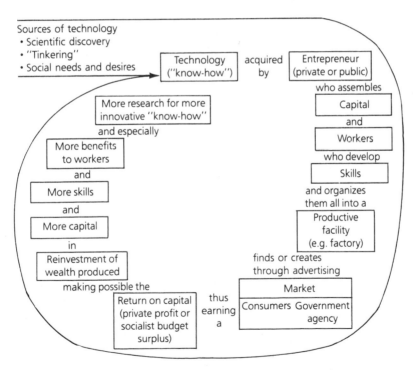

Figure 1. Technological application: the microloop

the human body, with its daily functions needed to maintain life and health, its growth functions that enable each of us to be physically a slightly different person each day, and the higher functions of intelligence, communication, learning, and appreciation.

The priceless ingredients of dynamism are different forms of information; people who can't convert information to knowledge they can use are going to be uncomfortably, even miserably, dependent on those who can. So strategy for a developing nation (or indeed for any disadvantaged neighborhood or ethnic group) begins and ends with their people getting educated and thus taking charge of decisions about technological innovations that will affect their destiny. Dr. Abdel Rahman and I concluded our report to the UN this way:

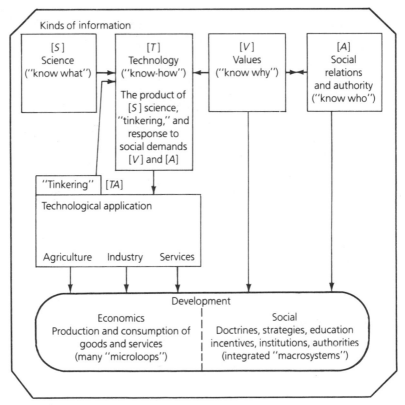

Figure 2. The active ingredients in development

[T]he key to the effective application of technology for development is still and always educated, self-reliant indigenous people—including women, that often neglected human resource. When developing-nation leaders can bargain from a base of clear national purpose and stable social authority, there is essentially no limit to the kinds and amounts of technology they can afford to import. A nation's ultimate resource is the quality of its own leadership. That is the one component of the development spiral that cannot be purchased from abroad.

Some years ago a precious drop of wisdom was added to the ocean of international discourse about science and technology for development. The speaker was Paul Hoffman, first Administrator of both the Marshall Plan and the U.N. Development Programme. "Technical assistance," he said, "cannot be exported. It can only be imported."

We the policy-making people have high expectations of those men and women who make a living by using the scientific method to theorize, experiment, discover, and innovate: the scientists and engineers and managers of research. We expect them to provide, in language we can understand, the indicators and insights and intuitions that will enable the rest of us to build the institutions, push through the laws, and mobilize the consensus to point technological innovation in socially determined directions.

They will have to give us as much early warning as they can, expose their guesswork somewhat sooner than when they are "sure." The final recommendations in nearly every report by the National Research Council include a plea for more research funds. But the authors don't get their research budgets unless they can explain *why* the scientific uncertainties make for bad public policies or business decisions.

We have learned from bitter experience about the cost of waiting until hardware is built and tested to start thinking about the institutions we will need to contain, channel, and control it. The Manhattan Project was only one of many instances in the generation just past. We know from this experience that it takes at least as long to invent, negotiate, finance, organize, staff, and make operational a complex institution as it does to get from a scientific idea to a working prototype of a complex physical system. And we have even done it right a few times already.

The United States Navy's Polaris program, which produced forty-one nuclear submarines, each with sixteen one-megaton nuclear weapons aboard, is an excellent example of a successful systems approach.

The human purpose was carefully thought through in advance: to deter strategic attack from intercontinental missiles by threat of massive counterattack with a weapons system that would itself be invulnerable to attack—the perfect *second-strike* weapon. Several science-based technologies were developed for the purpose: nuclear propulsion, satellite-assisted inertial navigation, rocketry and missile mechanics that produced extraordinary accuracy for a shot fired from a moving platform. But training of the duplicate (Blue and Gold) crews, their willingness to stay undersea for months at a time, and the concept of a one-way communication link (so the subs need never surface to transmit messages) were just as important as engineering the hardware so it would work.

Until some research physicist discovers a way to see through water, the nuclear submarine deterrent is still the least vulnerable and most stable part of the balance of terror that passes for peace in United States–Soviet relations. It's successful because it was conceived, from the outset, not as a collection of technologies but as a *system*.

In my personal experience, the most successful effort to build an institution to use a set of emerging technologies has been the World Weather Watch.

Until the 1960s weather forecasters looked at the bottom of the clouds as they circled the globe, probed the upper atmosphere with undependable balloons and radiosondes, and pieced together maps of the world's weather that looked very much like jigsaw puzzles. The World Meteorological Organization (WMO), a specialized agency of the United Nations, did little more than arrange schedules, codes, and ways of observing the weather so that meteorologists from different language and geographic areas would know how to exchange information with each other.

My job in President John F. Kennedy's administration was as an assistant secretary of state, responsible for the bureau that handled U.S. relationships with international organizations (we belonged to fifty-three of them at the time) and for instructing U.S. delegations to the 700-odd intergovernmental conferences that were held each year. One of the fifty-three organizations was WMO, and our chief delegate to its annual meeting was naturally Robert White, the chief of the Weather Bureau (what's now called the National Weather Service) in the Department of Commerce. Scarcely anyone else was interested in the agenda for meteorological meetings, so it fell to the State and Commerce departments to decide what I would instruct him to say on behalf of the United States at the WMO.

That was why I had lunch, one day in the summer of 1963, with Bob White and Herb Holloman, the Assistant Secretary of Commerce for Science and Technology. With no idea what it might lead to, I started to tease them early in the meal. "You scientists and technologists, you never tell us institution builders what man-made miracles are going to be possible far enough ahead of time to allow us to wrap them in political and financial and administrative clothing, before they start running around naked!" I suggested as an experiment that they undertake to tell me, before our luncheon ended, in words I could understand, what revolutions in weather forecasting were in store.

They did. By the time we parted, I understood that in the decade of the 1960s four new technologies would be combined to revolutionize weather forecasting. One would be picture-taking satellites, keeping track of the cloud systems from above, giving a synoptic view covering the whole world, supplemented by but not depending on surface and air observations. Another would be measurements, from remote-sensing satellites, of temperatures and air currents at places around the earth that could not be matched by observations from balloons or other probes launched from the ground. A third would be communication satellites, which would be able to get digitized data from anywhere to anywhere else in a big hurry. And the fourth part of the coming miracle would be much faster computers, which would process the complex information coming in from all over the world and get it onto the forecasters' desks in time—that is, before the weather changed.

Over a second cup of coffee we looked in awe at this prospect; the obvious policy conclusion occurred to us as a kind of simultaneous equation. If these new technologies could be pulled together in a workable *system,* the human race would be able for the first time in history to treat the weather as a single envelope around the globe, the way God had presumably been thinking of it right along. But because the weather impertinently ignores the land frontiers and ocean jurisdictions we humans think are so important, it would require the cooperation of nearly every nation to make a global forecasting system work.

My recollection is that we decided, then and there, to launch a U.S. initiative at the next global assembly of the WMO, a few months away. I no longer remember who first suggested calling it the World Weather Watch; as some wise person has said, success has many parents. A plan was developed by hardworking staffs in both departments; I was ready to authorize Bob White to launch it, and he was champing at the bit to sell it to the national weather services around the world.

Then we got lucky. Another part of my job was to backstop the United States Mission to the United Nations in New York, headed by an authentically great man: Adlai Stevenson had been governor of Illinois and twice (1952 and 1956) the Democratic candidate for president. Ambassador Stevenson, with help from my bureau and support from Secretary of State Dean Rusk, was trying to persuade President Kennedy to come to New York that autumn to make an international policy speech to the UN General Assembly, in his capacity as chief of state of the host nation. The president was interested; the General Assembly was then a world forum without parallel, an impressive environment for a major policy speech. But he was petulant about the content of such an address. I don't want to go up there, he said in effect, and mouth all those clichés that are usually heard in UN speeches. Is there something fresh for me to say?

The opening was too inviting to pass up. "Well, Mr. President, we just happen to have developed a proposal for a World Weather Watch using satellites our space program is about to launch. We were going to float it at the WMO, but why not float it at the General Assembly instead?"

The president was more than receptive; he was so enthusiastic that I was puzzled at first. Then the political barometers on the White House staff explained the tie-in with "domestic" politics. The president had received a heavy dose of editorial flak for announcing that the United States would put a man on the moon before the end of the 1960s. We can't even clean up our urban slums, the editorial writers were writing, and this guy wants to go to the moon. What a waste of the taxpayers' money! If President Kennedy could, at the UN, hang up a new vision of a space-based system that would move us from chancy three-day forecasts to more dependable predictions five days ahead—and eventually, if the most ambitious scientists had their way, out to the theoretical limit of two weeks—he could dramatize the prospect that the exciting but expensive U.S. space program would benefit every farmer, every business, every picnicker, every citizen who needs to guess, with the help of the atmospheric sciences, what the weather is going to do next.

Thus it was that the World Weather Watch was included among the Kennedy initiatives in the General Assembly in the autumn of 1963. It was unanimously endorsed there and referred for action to the WMO. And there, Bob White and several other U.S. scientist-statesmen managed to arrange the endorsement and participation of nearly every country in the world. The two big data-collection centers, it was agreed, would be near Moscow and in Bethesda, Maryland, a suburb of Washington, D.C. And, because the politics of the World Weather Watch had been drained out through its approval in the UN General Assembly, no one at WMO felt the need to hold up the gathering global consensus by introducing political issues. (Then as now, such issues as the rights of the Palestinians were always available as an alternative to discussing action items on the agenda of a UN technical agency.)

By the late 1960s, the World Weather Watch was up and running—the satellites and ground stations communicating with each other, most of the world's nations contributing to the expenses and adding their local observations to the global data pool, the resulting information being converted into forecasts by thousands of meteorologists (and, on television, a good many pseudometeorologists) around the world. Even the People's Republic of China, which stayed aloof at first, in time sent a junior officer to deposit weather data at the Bethesda headquarters, sidling into the World Weather Watch without having to say they were mistaken to stay out in the first place.

In short, when it comes to handling the social fallout of science and technology, a much better model than the Manhattan Project is the World Weather Watch. We started to invent a new kind of global data-exchange system and to figure out how it could be governed and financed, *while* the hardware (the picture-taking and remote-sensing satellites, the communication satellites, the faster computers) was still being procured and deployed.

One unanticipated result is a powerful assist to global education. Our children are instructed by watching the weather on television each day. The education doesn't come so much from the chummy charisma of the television weatherpeople; it comes from following those satellite photos of the clouds as they sweep from west to east across the map—the best textbook yet for a global perspective and for an appreciation of science.

We the people, and not only our children, are better informed about the weather than ever before. If you go out on the street and ask the first three people you meet what the weather is going to be, you will notice that they no longer feel their joints or even look up at the sky, but instead will tell you in semiprofessional language about the cold front moving in over Canada and due to arrive in their hometown early tomorrow afternoon.

Even the mass-entertainment industry sometimes contributes to our meteorological education. During the excitement about the possible damage to the ozone layer from aerosols, an inspired scriptwriter managed to combine the world population problem and the depletion of ozone in one five-minute segment of "All in the Family." Michael didn't want Gloria to have a baby—the world was already too full of people and besides, how could they bring a child into so depressing a world, where not even the ozone layer was safe from Gloria's hair spray? But Gloria won the day with a classic global bargain: "All right, Michael," she said. "You let me have my baby and I'll let you have my hair spray!"

The next atmospheric policy questions may focus less on what the weather does for humanity and more on what humanity is doing to the weather. The students of climate change (*climate* means weather beyond a couple of weeks from now) are talking and writing about a new actor in the atmosphere, and the actor is us. As Roger Revelle puts it, humankind is conducting a global geophysical experiment, and we cannot now guess its outcome.

Awesome climate changes may be produced over the coming decades by doubling the amount of carbon dioxide (mostly from burning fossil fuels) as well as other gases in the global atmosphere. It is only recently that we've begun to understand the aggregate effect on our climate of the "other gases," some growing by several percent per year. (Among the most prolific producers of carbon dioxide and methane are the plentiful termites; there are about 1,500 pounds of them for every human being in the world.) Scientists are now estimating that the combined warming effect of all these other gases together with that of carbon dioxide will be at least 4° C, and perhaps as high as 12° C at the poles. The resulting "greenhouse effect" (these gases hold in the sun's radiation as it bounces off the earth, the way the glass roof of a greenhouse does) would probably be enough to move the corn belt several hundred miles north, make a dust bowl out of Kansas, melt the Arctic icecap and raise the level of the ocean surface, threatening most of the world's coastal cities with extinction.

This degree of change would be unprecedented within human experience, and exactly what it would be like we're not yet sure. No scientist is yet willing to say just how fast the greenhouse effect will change the face of the earth and the depth of the oceans; a dwindling few are still unsure whether we should be worried about warming or cooling. But people won't wait until all the facts are in. By the time the statistics are ruled "significant," the choices that might have been made (for example, about energy policy) may no longer be available even to consider.

We are thus faced with a new—because more long-range—type of environmental issue, different in kind from smog or acid rain or radiation poisoning, where obviously bad trends need to be reversed. In this case, by contrast:

- •Nothing bad has happened yet. How does a consensus for policies involving millions of people get built around an issue that is still in the minds and calculations of the experts? It's not like acid rain, where any amateur sleuth can see the fish turn belly-up in the lakes, measure the pockmarks on Grandpa's gravestone, and watch the defoliation of a nearby forest.

- •The warming effect may not be bad for everybody, especially in its early stages. One of the possible gainers could be Canada, where a warming trend might extend its growing season. Another might be the USSR, which could gain not only a longer growing season but also warm-water ports up north.

- •There is as yet no international consensus to match that which is growing among U.S. experts. Concerted global decision making is still well out of reach.

- •Some elements of the problem are not readily manipulated. The increase of methane in the atmosphere, for example, comes from the cultivation of rice paddies (where the swampy soil emits the gas), from cattle flatulence (which grows as herds multiply), and from the activities of termites (which are on the rise as forests are cleared).

- •The implications for the policy game scramble the usual players. On energy policy, for example, environmentalists find themselves embarrassingly in bed with their old adversaries, the pronuclear lobby; both are questioning undue dependence on coal.

You may find these speculations on future climate change so long-range as not to require your immediate attention. You may even be saying, with the Lord Keynes, that "in the long run we are all dead." Personally, I'm impressed with what might happen within the lifetime of today's young people, and engaged by the puzzle of how to build a policy consensus around a contingency that hasn't arisen yet. The near-certainty that I won't be alive when "all the facts are in" seems no reason not to raise the questions and think hard about the policy options.

But let us take a more obviously urgent case to chew on—a range of new technologies already on this side of the horizon, already provoking ethical and professional and political questions that touch us all. The subject is genetic engineering, and it hits each of us quite literally in the gut.

Many years ago I asked Victor Weisskopf, one of the physicists centrally involved in making the first atom bombs, whether he would be a physicist if he were to start over again. "No, I'd want to be a biologist," he said. "What a wonderful field—they don't know anything yet, they don't know what life is, they don't know what goes on inside a cell. . . . " If I were a teenager today (with a life expectancy of at least seventy-five) deciding on what specialized ladder to climb to generalist leadership, I would start with biotechnology.

The life sciences still don't claim to know what life is, let alone why. But they are beginning to find out what goes on inside a cell. They are learning to move genes in and out of species. They have married genetics and chemistry to produce recombinant DNA. Nature and nurture—genetic makeup and environmental influence—were previously studied and taught in separate compartments, their insights used in separate professions. But molecular biology has pulled them together as part of a broader, more interconnected understanding of how a human being works.

A bewildering variety of impossibilities has quite suddenly become probable. Great increases in the productivity of plants and animals. Ways to make protein cheap and abundant, and to produce more nitrogen where it's needed. The production of human insulin from bacteria. Early detection and correction of birth defects. New and more targetable antibiotics. A fresh attack on mental illness by curing inborn errors of metabolism. Vaccines against previously intractable viruses. Who knows—maybe even a handle on the common cold?

The mass media have picked up some of the excitement. Test-tube babies are still good for a headline. Amniocentesis enters the vocabulary of any couple wanting to know if it's a girl or a boy—or wanting to be sure, before the time limit for an abortion runs out, that the fetus they created together will be "normal."

Huge research mysteries remain. How does each cell know what its function is? (You don't find a liver cell thinking it's a brain cell, says my Minnesota colleague Donald Geesaman; whence the modesty of its ambitions?) How could the manipulation of genes be used to modify behavior? What environmental influences cause only some of the people who are genetically disease-prone to get the disease? The more the scientists probe into "life," the more they run into questions that the rest of us must also participate in answering.

The social fallout of the life sciences was a lively topic at an Aspen Institute for Humanistic Studies workshop on Critical Questions in Genetic Medicine in 1982. The workshoppers agreed that open discussion was needed of the "fundamental questions of ethics, morality, and the organization of society."

The Aspen experts were able to think up and openly discuss an impressive range of misuses for genetic science, ranging from biological warfare to such curiosities as the decision to do sperm counts on the Apollo astronauts before they took off for the moon. (Nobody explained why.) They agreed that some "genetic anomalies" could now be remedied. But, they asked themselves, once we start down the path of eliminating genetic anomalies from humans, is there any logical stopping place? And who gets to say what is anomalous?

If we as a society acknowledge that parents specifically and society in general have the right to genetic "editing" of the

newborn, where do we draw the line between genetic characteristics which are undesirable for health reasons and those which
may be regarded as undesirable for other reasons? For example,
can one visualize circumstances under which society would
authorize selecting those who are to be born in accordance with
desired characteristics of sex? Size? Intelligence? Appearance?
[Or, the rapporteur was too polite to add, the shape of the nose
or the color of the skin?]

One participant, sociologist Amitai Etzioni, opposed any intervention in human breeding. "An easy, free method of control over the
sex of a fetus would result in a 7 percent surplus of boys," he said.
"Would the value of girls then increase and make choice processes
move toward a preference for girls? It would take fifteen years to
discern what had happened and take corrective action."

Harvard's Paul Doty worried about the self-inflicted gene. How
could all the many biological molecules that would become widely
and cheaply available from DNA be controlled? "Will everybody
give himself a jab of human growth hormones?"

The popular nightmare about genetic abuse—"something es-
caped from its bottle"—was dismissed by some experts as fanciful.
But the rapporteur, Martin Klein, was not so sanguine. His trees had
been defoliated the previous summer by caterpillars descended from
gypsy moths that fled from their escape-proof bottle in a scientist's
laboratory some years before.

This is but a sketchy sampler of the long laundry list of ethical
and moral choices, and issues of secrecy and control, that inhere in
the new biology. The questions are just as naggingly tough as those
the leaders of the Manhattan Project were not asking themselves on
company time (but which he and Robert Oppenheimer were ear-
nestly asking themselves over lunch, says physicist I. I. Rabi, the
Columbia University Nobel laureate) about the control of nuclear
energy after the war was won. The difference, forty years later, is that
many scientists have been actively trying to get the rest of us interested in the social problems they are creating with their laboratory
experiments.

Biologists as a group should not be expected to come together and speak with a single voice on issues touching the ethics and politics of a free people. (It would be more than a little frightening if they did.) In a nobody-in-charge society each of us—scientists, as citizens, included—carries part of that moral burden.

Each parent and family adviser will have decisions without precedent to make or neglect. Physicians will be, as they have always been, mediators between their patients and science, only now the sciences on which medicine rests will be increasingly hard to keep up with, and patients will be disconcertingly well informed about the ethical tangles in modern medicine. Each corporation, university, hospital, and insurance company has to rethink its plans and policies in the light of the new potentials of biotechnology. Academic executives are already wrestling with their souls over university ownership of genetic engineering companies—and genetic companies' ownership of university professors.

That the hard questions have begun to be asked is good news. Every field of scientific inquiry should be so lucky. Organizing to *answer* questions about the social fallout of science, and to harness the resulting technologies, is harder yet—so that task is left to the knowledge executives.

9

A Harness
for
Technology

While many of the world's nations have been trying to catch up with America in dynamism and development, Americans have been moving to a new stage of development, featuring the social assessment of new technologies before they are deployed and not waiting for the next Newton or Darwin to point the way. It would be foolish to date the beginning of the turnaround. But its latter-day signals are clear enough.

"The 'control of nature' is a phrase conceived in arrogance, born of the Neanderthal age of biology and philosophy, when it was supposed that nature exists for the convenience of man." Rachel Carson wrote that in her influential book *Silent Spring,* published in 1962. In the quarter-century since then, peoples and their governments have begun much more seriously to question the automaticity of modernization, to insist on tests of relevance, safety, and appropriateness, to cast doubt on the direction and pace of "progress" and to experiment with *technology assessment.*

The gathering mood was expressed on a lapel button handed me at an educational convention in the early 1970s: "Technology is the answer, but what was the question?"

The lead horse was a broad-based environmental movement, capitalizing on public resentment of urban smog and stream pollution and a public perception that some corporate managers were gashing the land with strip-mining technology, "relieving themselves" (as Ralph Nader expressed it) in the nearest lake or stream, slashing the forests for lumber production, and maybe endangering us all by promoting nuclear power, the way station to nuclear weapons.

The National Environmental Policy Act, passed in the 1969 Congress, took effect on January 1, 1970. It provided the opponents of technological change with a lethal procedural weapon: the Environmental Impact Statement (EIS). Most environmental clearances on federally assisted projects could be handled by routine review in a subordinate office. But those who wanted to hold up the project could readily escalate the perceived magnitude of either the undertaking or the environmental impact by calling for an Impact Statement, which often led to a long debate about procedure. For large projects, an EIS had to be prepared. In practice, the EIS turned out to be a great way to say no, and an expensive one—the proponents of a new development or industrial plant had to do what lawyers always say is impossible: prove a negative, prove that their proposed changes would *not* be harmful to the state of nature.

Saying no can have an important purpose. The EIS process made the study of second-order consequences respectable. It provided a forum for more information to be exposed, motivations to be revealed, arguments to be made and listened to. Because the EIS process loomed on the horizon some projects just never happened, because it was clear from the outset to their proponents that the case for going ahead with them would not survive such public scrutiny. (If the Manhattan Project had had to produce an Environmental Impact Statement, wouldn't its leaders have had to put a staff of analysts to work on arms-control policy?)

It was during the 1970s that the United States, after a long public debate, decided by a Senate vote *not* to build a supersonic air transport, even though we knew how to do it. The old ethic was different: If we knew how to build it, surely it ought to be built, whether *it* was a weapons system, a public facility, or an industrial innovation. If the SST issue had arisen in the 1950s, it would have been built, such was the technological optimism of the time. But large projects such as the SST always require some kind of government subsidy, so the stage was set for a 1970s-style public debate.

Some of the arguments that killed the SST have since turned out to be factually wrong. For example, scientists now doubt that the jet emissions from supersonic planes erode the ozone layer that protects us from skin cancer. But in the heat of the moment, the environmental fears prevailed over the technological hopes. The SST decision became the symbol of a new ecological ethic. (The British and French governments, which bet heavily on subsidies for the supersonic Concorde, subsequently lost their budgetary shirts and wished they had made the same decision the United States was forced by public opinion to make.)

It was also in the watershed decade of the 1970s that U.S. dreams for nuclear power dissipated, the people's growing doubts fed by the experts' sloppy staff work on safety, on waste, and on the proliferation of nuclear weapons. And it was in the 1970s that the city council of Cambridge, Massachusetts, asserted political jurisdiction over the pace and direction of genetic research at Harvard University—a caricature of the new mood, perhaps, but remember that a caricature is merely the enlargement of a feature that is already all too obvious.

The politics of "growth versus environment" was never "science versus people." Some of the most effective contributors to the environmental movement were scientists who uncovered negative effects of technological innovation. A physicist friend of mine was fired from the Livermore Radiation Laboratory (nominally a part of the University of California but wholly funded by the U.S. Atomic Energy Commission) for the devastatingly accurate arguments against "the plutonium economy" developed in the course of his work. No claim was made that his work was flawed or his conduct improper; it was just extremely inconvenient for a government-funded weapons laboratory to find one of its professional employees on the wrong side of the public debate on commercial nuclear power.

Science can underlie harmful technologies, but it can also display good conscience. It frequently happens that flags of caution are waved first by the scientists most involved. This happened when the fluorocarbon effect on the ozone layer came to light: it was scientists who first blew the whistle. And of course it happened right after the first two nuclear bombs were dropped, when, in the classic case of guilt-driven responsibility, some of that generation's best-known physicists became instant political scientists and helped produce a wildly unrealistic proposal to turn all nuclear energy over to the United Nations. (The resulting "Baruch Plan" was quickly vetoed by the Soviet Union, so the United States never had to decide whether, on sober second thought, it would have been ready for sudden world government.)

Almost everybody knows now that rational discovery and energy-based progress can produce outcomes that create big new problems and do not serve human purposes. Warnings about physical "limits to growth," even though they proved to be greatly overstated, have helped induce a widespread ethic of prudence. Socially determined limits are increasingly being set to the damage people may do to their physical environment (air and water pollution controls, preservation of wilderness areas, protection of coastal zones, urban planning and zoning); to the rate at which people use up nonrenewable resources (coal, oil, uranium, and other minerals); and to practices that affect the renewability of renewable resources (soil erosion, destruction of wildlife, overcropping of farmland, overcutting of forests, overfishing of lakes and oceans).

With that unsystematic intuition by which the governed so often catch a wave before their governors do, public opinion in the industrial world may simply be guessing from recent experience that there are, after all, some natural limits to the application of technology—

not "limits to growth" but limits to material affluence and even material power.

Two generations of cheap energy skewed the priorities of industrial development toward energy-intensive goods and services and centralized systems. The decades of rising energy costs that are evidently ahead of us will make it more and more necessary to count costs in terms of energy as well as of money. Bankers as well as engineers know this, and it's already affecting thousands of business decisions every day.

In agriculture the torrid pace of government-sponsored innovation, including soil conservation and the application of energy (directly through mechanization of production, harvesting, processing, storage, and delivery, and indirectly through chemical fertilizers and pesticides), has driven productivity up and driven people out of full-time farming, so that in the United States 2½ percent of the people can produce a large surplus of food even after the other 97½ percent are fed. It is hard to believe that the ratio of rural producers to the rest of society can be cost-effectively reduced much further. (What seems to be happening now is that more and more people are becoming part-time farmers, financing their deficits by the incomes they earn in the cities and by government subsidies designed for full-time farmers.)

Part of the turnaround is a change in our assumptions about the nature of affluence. We used to think that what John Kenneth Galbraith called "the affluent society" would be more and more resource-hungry, gobbling up the biosphere's energy and minerals and biological potentials at an ever faster clip. But in industrial societies, it turns out, most of those near the top of the pyramid of affluence do not seek an exponential increase in their material wealth.

As the work of John and Magda McHale has shown, what once seemed an exponential rise in quantitative demand and resource depletion now looks more like the familiar biological S-curve. (It's known to many high school students as the "fruit-fly curve," from a classroom experiment in which fruit flies in a box multiply until there is no more room in the box, whereupon they stop multiplying so fast.) There is, it seems, a natural limit to the usefulness of more and more things.

The McHales put it succinctly: "As material goods become more freely available, their value and importance have declined." (Do you hoard dishes and place settings the way your grandparents, if they could afford it, did?) For many people in the affluent societies, human development, based on more varied knowledge, is now prized above material possessions. People who can afford "more" are spending not on quantity but on quality: not more houses but quality homes, not more food but better cuisine, not more travel but quality destinations. A McHale metaphor said it all: For the affluent family, the first automobile may be a Cadillac, but the second may be a small sports car (already less steel) and the next increment may be entirely symbolic—a magazine about auto racing.

The minority of conspicuous consumers is highly visible. But for most of the affluent what lies beyond "enough" is satiation; and beyond satiation are many choices that are neither resource-hungry nor environmentally destructive. Ultimately, fewer goods are purchased and more services are demanded. In the United States, as we have seen, we have already reached the point where only about one-seventh of what we "produce" is goods; all the rest is services, and two-thirds of that is the production and distribution of information.

The worm, then, is turning. The man-bites-dog headline of the 1980s is that human needs, human rights, and human purposes, socially determined, are beginning to drive science and technology. But the turnaround comes just when the instruments of social determination, and especially national governments, are demonstrably beyond their depth.

Science and industry first made possible a nationalism featuring the concentration of power in the hands of a few at the expense of the many. But the growing complexity of it all has produced national governments unable to cope.

"There is many an indication," says Ralf Dahrendorf, the German scholar-politician who was for ten years director of the London School of Economics,

> that the institutions created for two centuries of economic growth are no longer capable of coping with the potential for satisfying human life chances developed within them: Concern with environmental problems, the so-called "energy crisis," the headache and charm of our cities, the separation of education from its economic purpose and, last but not least, the persistence of the "new inflation" as a caricature of growth . . . are significant symptoms pointing to a change of the theme of historical development.

If people-in-general are going to decide about technology, instead of the other way around, they will need more and more help from a different kind of expert—an expert on experts, a generalist well enough grounded in scientific rationalism to be able to critique its outcomes. The need is for systematic expertise in pulling into one system of thinking all the elements that bear on decisions about new technologies. This new kind of get-it-all-together thinking has come in recent years to be called technology assessment.

Technology assessment is still in its swaddling clothes. In the United States, it is represented in the federal government mainly by smallish staffs reinforced by outside consultants, in some of the big cabinet departments, and in three agencies that help Congress make policy about technology-intensive issues—the Office of Technology Assessment, the Congressional Research Service of the Library of Congress, and the General Accounting Office (which, despite its antiquated name, was converted by Comptroller General Elmer Staats into the world's largest management consulting organization). Some large corporations also have staffs engaged in comparable work in their own fields, partly to help their own strategic planning, but partly to avoid being at a disadvantage in dealing with Congress and the executive departments. And there is a growing industry of consultants who do technology assessment for hire.

Before this infant profession comes of age, it will have to overcome two temptations to which some of its early practitioners have succumbed. Experience has shown that it's evidently much easier to say no than yes to any given technological innovation. And it's also easier to get stuck in the rut of microeconomics and cost-benefit analysis than it is to do genuine situation-as-a-whole thinking. Let us exorcise these two kinds of bewitchery.

The first danger in science-and-technology's new social accountability is that the pendulum of reaction swings too far. Short-term human purposes, narrowly defined by transient political leaders and managers on limited contracts, may come to dominate decisions about the long-term direction of discovery, invention, and innovation.

Industrialized societies have been innovative because they have bet on individual creativity as a matter of public policy. An insistence on science's social relevance places the future in the hands of a very few leaders of a very few countries, rather than entrusting it to the pluralistic creativity of very large numbers of individual scientists and inventors in many countries.

If in the coming era the perceived human needs of societies will increasingly be driving scientific research and technological development, it will be more and more important to make a clear distinction between science policy and technology policy:

- *Science* should remain free, open, and transnational in its search for demonstrable truth at the frontiers of knowledge. This freedom for the scientific enterprise should be regarded as a social goal and as part of every nation's development strategy.

- *Technology* that flows from scientific discovery should, on the contrary, be socially managed and directed with a view to serving human needs, enhancing the human environment, and maximizing choice for individuals in society.

No national government should, under the guise of technology assessment, try to inhibit the processes of scientific discovery and invention. But deciding whether scientific perceptions will be translated into working technologies, even deciding what technologies will be developed to the point of having to decide about them, cannot be automatic.

Whether or not a nation elects to encourage, and people elect to use, electronic banking or nuclear weapons or urban skyscrapers or village biogas plants or diesel automobiles or nitrogen fertilizer is a matter of their own development strategies, their own choices. And the social decisions involved will be the product of whatever procedures (democratic, authoritarian, revolutionary) are in vogue in each national society at the moment when the decision has to be made.

There is a related hazard in the emerging tendency of man to bite the technological dog. Technology assessment got its first boost from the widespread disillusion with the social fallout from technological change: congestion of cities, pollution of air and water, nuclear dangers, and the like. But if the pendulum swings too far, political and business leaders and their technology-assessment advisers may too quickly, too easily, and too often say no to innovation. The purpose of examining issues in the round is caution, not stagnation.

Despite the patina of systematic thought and statistical quantification, science is by nature intuitive in its sense of direction, happenstance in its discoveries, and unprecedented in its consequences. The purposes to be served by scientific discovery are always going to be morally ambiguous at the start. New knowledge will always make possible new closets of darkness as well as new windows of light.

Most human beings are by nature suspicious of change. A colleague on the University of Minnesota faculty tells of a neighbor with whom he often discusses gardening. "Dora once told me of finding a strange small animal in her garden: 'I didn't know what it was so I killed it.'" The new idea, the still unrecognized chain of reasoning, often suffers a similar fate.

The well-advertised excesses of modernization, the frequency with which we find ourselves going rapidly and efficiently to where we don't want to be when we get there, have made us all more skeptical of "progress." Paradoxically, those who have benefited most from industrial progress are the most skeptical. Organized in groups designed to reinforce this reluctance, people can readily be persuaded to turn away from new ideas, new doctrines, new ways of living and working, just because they are new.

It is, to be sure, a major advance in civilized behavior that modern societies are learning how to say no to unneeded weapons systems, toxic chemicals, nuclear proliferation, air-polluting fuels, and environment-guzzling land development. Procedural gadgetry that makes it mandatory to be reflective—the Environmental Impact Statement, the Arms Control Impact Statement, the effort to relate foreign aid to "basic human needs"—has served a useful purpose.

"Stop, Look, and Listen" has always been a useful signpost at grade-level railroad crossings. But its purpose is not to freeze the oncoming cars in their tracks; it is to enable their drivers to proceed, while avoiding collisions with useful yet dangerous technologies like speeding locomotives. Technology assessment cannot be merely a device for naysaying by multiplying the complexity of decisions and lengthening the time it takes to make them. The environmental movement has had to graduate from merely *preserving* the physical environment to *enhancing* the human environment (which includes not only the natural biosphere but the man-made technosphere as well). Similarly, the profession of technology assessment will have to graduate from its status as a good way to stop bad things from happening, and become a continuous search for technologies that say yes to human-centered innovation.

The very term *technology assessment* implies that the assessors start with technologies that someone else has already invented and wants to deploy, like auditors catching up with business decisions after they have been made. But technologies should increasingly be selected, on the advice of assessors, *because* they are likely to generate beneficent social effects. Only thus can we hope to design weapons systems to be more easily verifiable in arms-control agreements, invent urban transport systems that do not depend for their success on exhorting people not to use their automobiles, develop curative drugs that are effective yet nonaddictive, and produce children's pajamas *because* they don't catch fire.

The other big challenge to technology assessment is to widen our analytical framework beyond traditional economics to include the needs of human beings in the round.

In earlier times, most business judgments and much government policy-making were made easier for the executive leaders by keeping the framework of analysis narrow. What innovations are *possible* has always been determined by the roulette wheel of scientific discovery and technical tinkering, both the province of the creative individual. But *which* inventions became widespread innovations has been determined mostly by quantitative economic analysis —the old economics of profitability and efficiency that also gave us irreducible unemployment and uncontrolled inflation; the old economics of indiscriminate growth that counted useful products and useless products with the same positive signs and didn't count the harmful side-effects at all; the old economics of short-term costs and benefits measured in money, that analytical concentration camp in which professionals from capitalist, Marxist, and developing nations are bound in misery together, wondering how to get out.

The narrow framework of the old economics has been blamed for the excesses of modernization, but it has also been responsible for holding back the processes of useful innovation. That useful gadget, the zipper, was invented in 1891, but not marketed by an innovator until 1918. Vladimir Zworykin's invention of television in 1919 waited until 1941 for its innovator (the Westinghouse Corporation). The criterion of innovation has typically been "effective demand"— not what people *needed,* but what they could be induced through advertising to afford.

Technology assessment, then, introduces a new value structure about the human adventure and requires, to support it, a new, broader frame of analysis for leadership decisions.

The new analytical system we now require is not a set of *substitute* concepts. The conventional criteria of comparative costs and benefits, of profitability and efficiency, still have an essential place in it. What the framework does is to *add* criteria of judgment about the direction of technological advance that fundamentally change the purpose to be served by the analytical assessment. That purpose can no longer be defined as an ethically neutral equilibrium, but as sustainability of a dynamic flow system aimed at specified human purposes.

For each people and its government, for each enterprise and its executive leaders, the human purposes to be specified will vary. In the public policy arena, some will think that overcoming absolute poverty should have the highest priority. For others, the maximization of choice by individuals, or the cooperation of all citizens in a collective national effort, or the reduction of the nation's international interdependence, or the fairest possible sharing of whatever resources are available, or some combination of these purposes may be selected. What's different about the "new economics" is that there is room for varied purposes that can't be summarized in a government budget projection or a corporate bottom line.

The factors excluded from the earlier, narrower systems of analysis were often called *externalities,* which I defined earlier as considerations that may be relevant but don't fit into the analytical system you're using. You can think of what's happening now as "internalizing the externalities." An example is the extent to which business judgments and budget allotments now include many forms of spending for environmental protection and "corporate social responsibility" that never before were included in the bottom line by which a company's profitability is measured.

That's what the turnaround is all about: Inner logics and invisible hands and indiscriminate growth are on their way out, in favor of decision-making systems based on human needs, human rights, and human purposes.

We can derive from the primitive experience of technology assessment to date a minimum list of the new criteria that are taking their place alongside the conventional ones. I will formulate them as questions applying to the study of any new technology.

- **Energy balance.** Aside from costs and benefits expressed in money, what are the costs and benefits expressed in energy use and availability?

• **The environment.** What are the likely effects on the preservation of what needs to be preserved, and on the enhancement of what ought to be enhanced, in the human environment? And what are the implications for our genetic heritage?

• **Security considerations.** What effect will development and deployment of the new technology be likely to have on the security of the people who develop and deploy it, and on others whose counteractions also have to be taken into account?

• **Equity considerations.** How well or badly is the new technology likely to serve the purpose of fair access to resources, to jobs, and to the chance for human fulfillment of all members of a society?

• **Quality of life.** How does the new technology fit into the growing tendency, especially among people in knowledge-intensive societies, to prefer "better" to "more"?

• **Distribution of power.** What are the likely effects on the distribution of personal and political power—in the society making the decision, in other societies that may follow suit, and in the relations between and among them?

• **Implications for education.** Does the new technology require for its development new kinds of education (for example, more emphasis on integrative thinking)? Will people need to be retrained from obsolescent occupations for jobs the new technology may create?

• **Implications for decision making.** How will the new technology affect the ways in which and the time periods for which business, social, and political decisions will need to be made? Will it tend to widen or narrow the opportunities for participatory process? Does it require more long-range planning than is normal in executive suites, government bureaus, and legislative chambers? (I was reaching for a criterion such as this when, long ago, I complained to a congressional committee during a foreign-aid hearing: "We're still tackling twenty-year problems with five-year plans staffed with two-year personnel working with one-year appropriations. It's simply not good enough!")

The process of defining, asking, and answering these questions can and should be hard-headed, analytical, and objective. But there are value judgments to be made at each step. In widening their lenses and deepening their probes, technology assessors should not kid themselves (or their generalist "clients") that their work is conducted in an oasis of purity, in an environment otherwise dominated by values of self-interest and personal political ambition.

Technology assessment is not a substitute for the politics of decision making; it is a newly essential ingredient in a rational politics for making decisions in the human interest.

10

The Generalist Mind-Set

In the early days of that modern morality play called the Watergate hearings, there was a moment of striking relevance when Senator Howard Baker of Tennessee was questioning Herbert Porter, the thirty-five-year-old staff man who had passed large sums in cash to Watergate conspirator Gordon Liddy to use in the "dirty tricks" part of the presidential reelection campaign.

"Why?" the Senator asked. "Where does the system break down, when a person . . . abdicates his conscience? . . . Did you ever have qualms about what you were doing?"

"I think the thought crossed my head, Senator," the witness replied, "in all honesty, that I really could not see what effect it had on reelecting a president of the United States. On the other hand, in all fairness, I was not the one to stand up in a meeting and say that this should be stopped. I kind of drifted along."

The option is always temptingly there for each of us to drift along, *not* to take the lead, not to reach for or even accept broader responsibilities as our lives and careers move along. The choice is always there to sit on the telephone wire until it's quite clear where the rest of the birds are going. But each of us who does think he or she is "the one to stand up in a meeting" will be more than fully employed. The need for people who can bring other people together to make something different happen is growing much faster than the supply.

The context sketched in the preceding chapters is overstuffed with problems. They stem from the fragility of complex systems, the blurring of familiar distinctions, the erosion of hierarchies, the passing of remoteness, the dilemmas of openness, the challenge to settled privilege in a worldwide "fairness revolution," and the rapid spread of knowledge that is both cause and effect of all of these.

But leaders are problem solvers by talent and temperament, and by choice. For them, the new information environment—undermining old means of control, opening up old closets of secrecy, reducing the relevance of ownership, early arrival, and location—should seem less a litany of problems than an agenda for action. Reaching for a way to describe the entrepreneurial energy of his fabled editor Harold Ross, James Thurber said, "He was always leaning forward, pushing something invisible ahead of him." That's the appropriate posture for a knowledge executive.

What does it take to be a get-it-all-together person? I shall not rehearse in detail the qualities I have called in previous writings "a style for complexity." But I will outline them as a basis for suggesting how the new knowledge environment reinforces them all—but some more than others.

- The physical energy to concentrate harder and work harder than most of your associates.

- A good brain, and the willingness to use it. If you are not yourself plowing through the analysis, you are not making decisions; you are merely presiding while others decide.

- A soft voice, a low key, and a willing ear: the natural style of consultation and consensus. Effective leadership doesn't necessarily show, and it never shows off.

- The "unwarranted optimism" that sets the woman or man of action off from the well-documented prophet of doom. The ethical content of planning need not be limited to a lugubrious comparison in which the future always seems less attractive than the present.

- The capacity to enjoy the exhilaration of choice in motion.

These qualities of executive leadership still apply in the new knowledge environment—indeed, they now apply in spades.

Now, in the twilight of hierarchy, I would reinforce and supplement that earlier catechism with five attitudes and aptitudes I have found to be especially important for the generalist executive who takes the lead in the perilous, problematic, and participatory climate for policy making that information-richness is bringing in its train.

First is a genuine interest in what other people think and what makes them tick, which means you have to be at peace with yourself for a start.

Second is a highly developed intellectual curiosity, reaching out ever more widely with that "good brain."

Third is an attitude that risks are there not to be avoided but to be taken.

Fourth is an approach unafraid of newness, a passionate interest in the future, which is the new face of optimism.

Fifth is the courage to face squarely the most puzzling dilemma of leadership in an information society: how to reconcile the personal power knowledge confers on you with the personal responsibility it requires of you.

The ranks of executives used to be very full of people (men, mostly) who went through life, in E. B. White's phrase, pushing doors marked "pull." There is no room for them anymore. The knowledge executive, "leading while being led," simply has to have, or develop, a genuine interest in what other people think, what makes them drag their feet, what motivates them to "delegate upward" the authority to act.

It would take more arrogance than I could sustain to prescribe for the human relations of hundreds of thousands of others; keeping my own in tolerable repair is already an overfull-time job. But I have found that working at "getting to know you, getting to know all about you," every day of the year, builds the muscle of consultative talent. The exercise is simple and mostly painless. It consists of asking people you meet to tell you about themselves.

Ever since I managed a Carnegie study about Americans abroad in the 1950s, I have been fascinated by the series of accidents that make up what people call their careers and the skill with which most people are able to rationalize what has happened in their lives so far, as if they had sort of planned it that way.

So my opening conversational ploy with a new acquaintance is likely to be a puzzled, "How did it happen that you . . . ?" or, "How do you happen to be living here, doing this kind of work?" I am impressed and delighted each day at the ease, fluency, and unselfconsciousness with which almost anybody, given a receptive ear, can recite the highlights of personal history, and at how interesting most people's life histories can be and how often they uncover some intersection with my own.

There are, of course, boring exceptions. But in my experience they are usually the people who tell me all about themselves before I ask.

The human relations dilemma for get-it-all-together people is sharp. We are likely to be acutely aware of our own shortcomings and inadequacies: how little, after all, we really know of the subject-matter to be integrated, how little of all the available reading we have done, how important in their own spheres are the people we are supposed to be coordinating, how silly it is, really, for all those people to be looking to *us* for "leadership." Ray Bradbury, best known as an imaginative novelist, speaks of this in a charming piece addressed to business managers:

> Have you ever, as employee or employer, powerless or with power, sat at a meeting with your peers, as I have, and looked around suddenly in panic to think:
> What am I doing here!? These people are all forty-five, fifty, and fifty-five years old! They know what they're doing! And I? I am ten, twelve, thirteen at the most, and know *nothing*!
> Sound familiar?
> It happens to me all the time. Not just once a month, or once a week, but almost daily when people turn to me and ask my opinion. At museum conferences, in film studios, following plays where I am asked onstage to be part of an analytical panel, or when one of my daughters comes to look in my face to chart the future. Sometimes a large moment of panic ensues. If not that, at least a small one, and then I regain my calm and think: But we are all this age, aren't we, trapped in the older self, still feeling a lack of education, still sensing we have not yet learned to think? Yet here are all these curious folks, craning their heads like dinosaurs in a swamp, staring at me as if I were Tyrannosaurus rex, when at most I am simply the boy who holds the nervous rabbit on his lap, waiting for others to begin.

The honesty to perceive how much you have to be modest about is far from a fatal flaw; it may even be on the fringe of wisdom. Yet it is surely no crime to let others assume that, because of the position you hold in their scheme of things, you are better prepared than you know you could possibly be. The cardinal sin would be kidding yourself on this score, but there is a second sin to be avoided as well: apologizing for the excessive expectations of others, just because you can see more clearly than they how excessive they are.

Here, at least, the prescription is clear: *a healthy modesty, suitably veiled.*

You may have noticed that the get-it-all-together people of your acquaintance are the folk who seem to be interested in everything and find that this intellectual curiosity pays some very practical dividends. After studying closely a number of people he called super-leaders, Warren Bennis placed first on his list of leadership qualities "the management of attention." "All leaders," he concluded, "are *interesting*; they get your attention." They become leaders partly because they exercise their curiosity, day in and day out, year after year.

Four hundred years ago François Rabelais set out to know everything that could then be known, and managed to be a bon vivant besides. Such an ambition in the mid-1980s, in the midst of a worldwide knowledge explosion, would be put down as mental illness. Nevertheless, it is still a healthy ambition to be *interested* in everything. At least, I can testify from personal efforts that it pays to try. If you are going to practice catholicity of interest, serving as a university president provides an almost daily occasion to learn something wholly new—if you can avoid spending all your time on campus politics, budget cutting, and fund raising.

At the University of Hawaii one of my tasks was, of course, to bring the Aloha of the university community to innumerable gatherings of specialized scholars and expert practitioners, in fields ranging from ocean engineering to Oriental philosophy. In accepting invitations to cut these intellectual ribbons I routinely insisted that my Aloha would include five or ten minutes of personal comment on the subject-at-hand. Since I usually did not know anything about the subject-at-hand, that required me to interview the key faculty members involved, sometimes at considerable length.

In this manner, during one illustrative month, I could critique the turgid prose of Martin Heidegger; develop some instant prejudices about music education in the public schools; explain our floating city experiment to federal site visitors; describe the "Nixon shock" in Tokyo to a visiting convention of UPI editors; comment on the governance of Honolulu while introducing Mayor John Lindsay of New York at a National League of Cities convention; and, in preparation for a conference on Korean traditions, learn that the first ironclad warships were not the *Merrimack* and the *Monitor,* as our American history books would have us believe, but vessels designed by one Admiral Yi a couple of centuries earlier.

One dividend of this self-induced continuing education was a wide acquaintance among the university's best scholars in fields far removed from international politics, economic development, and public administration, my previous academic beats.

In the process I worked out a nearly infallible method of evaluating members of a university faculty. I found I was judging my faculty colleagues by whether, when I talked with them, I learned something from them. (They were doubtless judging me the same way.) It seemed probable that if a professor was not arousing my curiosity and stimulating my mind, he probably was not doing that for his students either. I do not suppose there is any way to patent this evaluation system, but it is certainly less laborious than baking that three-layer procedural cake of teaching, research, and committee sitting that is widely used in making academic promotion and tenure decisions.

Another dividend of this continual exercise of intellectual curiosity is that it provides welcome relief from the deadening effect on the human brain of constant preoccupation with the administrative process itself.

Anyone who helps govern a university, or any other complex system, soon learns the Gresham's Law that procedure elbows substance off the executive's desk. It takes only a little longer to realize that procedure is quite often the surrogate for substance, in the politics of education as elsewhere. (We have already considered this, among the costs of openness, in Chapter 4.) To focus for twelve hours a day on untangling procedural snarls, and neglect to participate in the substantive excitement that is unleashed by your administrative action, is to get mesmerized by the misery and miss all the fun.

The role of executive leadership has always been both a risky and a risk-taking one. The new knowledge environment has greatly multiplied the risks and consequently the need for risk-loving entrepreneurs, not only in the narrower sense of venture capitalists and inventive small businessmen and -women, but also in the broader sense of people who like to live and work beyond the frontiers of custom and convention.

Warren Bennis calls this aspect of leadership the "Wallenda factor," and quotes the famed aerialist in his prime: "The only time I feel really alive is when I'm walking the tightrope." Later, after the Great Wallenda fell from a high wire to his death, his wife said he had been getting too cautious: "He put his energies into falling, not walking the tightrope."

Each of us is presumably born with the built-in genetic capacity to jump offside, get out of line, start before the starting signal. But this inborn aptitude is mostly smothered as we learn to conform to family traditions, religious ritual, lockstep schooling, traffic patterns, social customs, and the criminal code. It needs to be revived and cultivated by those who would be executive leaders by function, not just by position. The day-to-day risks taken by what James McGregor Burns calls "transforming" leaders are the key factors in the dynamism of a single organization or a whole society. Without the Wallenda factor, the microloops stop spinning. In a hesitant, fearful society, the larger systems slow down.

I cannot prescribe an elixir of entrepreneurship, so I shall instead try to describe something of what goes through the mind of a risk taker as a choice is presented to do the unprecedented thing. Two incidents culled from the memory bank arose in very different settings: in China, where I was incautious in a young man's way, and in Washington, where I took the uncalculated risk of challenging a veteran politician on the subject of politics.

By a wonderful series of accidents too complicated to relate, I was sent to China in 1947, at the age of twenty-nine, to take over the final year's leadership of the China Office of the United Nations Relief and Rehabilitation Agency (UNRRA)—a mission of four thousand people, scattered around China in fifteen regional offices, stuffing $650 million of relief supplies into an underdeveloped country torn up by a decade of war, trying (because we were the UN and by definition impartial) to deliver relief supplies on both sides of a raging civil conflict.

Our headquarters were in Shanghai, but we had a couple of men even younger than I who traveled back and forth across the battle lines to keep in touch with Mao Tse-tung's Chinese communists (then still in the northern city of Yenan), supplementing our close regular contacts with the Nationalist government of Chiang Kai-shek, then still at his capital in Nanking, up the Yangtze River from Shanghai.

UNRRA's biggest single project in China, already well under way when I arrived in the spring of 1947, was to rebuild the dikes of the great Yellow River in the northern part of the country. The river had been diverted by the Chinese as a defense mechanism against the Japanese, and had been roaming all over the landscape for almost a decade. Our task was to put it back in its old riverbed, an enormous earth-moving operation comparable to building the Panama Canal.

But the Yellow River was also the scene of the sharpest clashes between Chiang Kai-shek's demoralized troops and the well-led communist guerrillas. The dike work was behind schedule, because workers (paid with food imported by our mission and supervised by our multinational engineering team) were understandably reluctant to work in a military no-man's-land. We appealed to both sides to arrange a cease-fire, but the mutual suspicions precluded any real communication, even through the UN. I volunteered to fly to Yenan, if that would help; that drew an objection from the Nationalists and a stony silence from the communists.

In desperation we conceived the idea of using the UN's prestige, then very high, to *declare* a cease-fire ourselves on behalf of the world community—which was, after all, spending a lot of taxpayers' money to help the Chinese people. I could imagine the weeks of diplomatic pussyfooting such a proposal would engender if I asked for permission from UNRRA headquarters in Washington, ten thousand miles away. So one day, without advance notice to either side, I announced a cease-fire in the valley until UNRRA finished getting the Yellow River back where it belonged.

The announcement, wrapped in eloquent rhetoric both global and humanitarian, caught both sides by surprise. Not knowing whether they were supposed to take us seriously, they both did—at first.

To our astonishment and delight the fighting stopped, the troops drew back a little, and we were able to redouble the huge dike-building effort. Neither the Nationalists nor the communists wanted to be the first to break the "cease-fire." Foreign offices elsewhere, which would have branded this a harebrained scheme if they had known about it ahead of time, were professionally cautious when confronted with a fait accompli that actually seemed to be working. From my immediate superior in Washington, Commander Robert G. A. Jackson, a notable risk taker himself, came confidential words of support.

I no longer remember just how long my unenforceable edict lasted. One night a skirmish between patrols escalated into a major firefight, and the spell was broken. But the interlude of international drama helped show how serious UNRRA was about the Yellow River project, and both sides in the civil war managed to act thereafter with enough circumspection to permit the great silty flow to be rediverted to its old bed—which was going to help millions of Chinese no matter who their government was.

In the kingdom of paradox, there is an oversupply of overriding principles. Long ago Wallace Sayre of Columbia University said of academic politics that the men of honor always seem to be outnumbered by the men of principle. The wider politics of citizenship and public affairs is also abundantly supplied with loud and effective defenders of high principles that do not need, they think, to be reconciled with other high principles.

But the executive leader's unique function is to squash together the overriding principles, shove them through that narrow pipeline called policy, and extrude them as actions that work, decisions that stick. That requires a steadier sense of direction, wider and timelier consultation (whether early or late depends on whether you're trying to stop something or start something), more unremitting toil and unrewarded homework, and more willingness to forgo an ego trip than merely deciding and announcing what is "right."

I once had a risky run-in, on just this issue, with a senior congressional leader old enough to be my father. He was Representative Harold Cooley of North Carolina, the crusty and crafty chairman of the House Committee on Agriculture, a master of the pragmatic arts of practical politics. I was in the State Department as manager of U.S. policy in the United Nations and other international organizations.

I had accompanied Secretary of State Dean Rusk to a Capitol Hill breakfast that morning, for a foreign policy briefing; Rusk had to leave early, so I was left to explain and defend U.S. foreign policy. The big issue that week, as it happened, was in my area: our tentative decision not to veto in the UN Security Council a "package deal" whereby Outer Mongolia, a pliant satellite of the Soviet Union, would be admitted to the world body along with Mauritania, one of the newest African states.

We were unhappy about admitting Mongolia, which could hardly be described as an independent sovereignty; but our main objective that year was to prevent the People's Republic of China (this was long before we kissed and made up during the Nixon and Carter years) from muscling its way into the China seat still held by the Republic of China on the island of Taiwan. The Africans had caucused and decided it was so important to them to get another African state into the UN that they would part company with the United States as a bloc on the Chinese representation question if the United States vetoed the Mauritania-Mongolia package. By then the Africans had more than a quarter of the seats in the General Assembly, and their defection on the Chinese question would be fatal to the position the president was trying to sustain.

This complex choreography had been lost in the morning headlines about the United States "capitulating" to the Soviet Union on Mongolia, and the stage was set for confrontation at our Capitol Hill breakfast. While the Secretary was still there we explained the politics of the matter, but after he departed the dialogue got out of hand.

I was being needled by experts and generally keeping my cool. Then Congressman Cooley entered the fray.

"This Mongolia thing," he asked, "isn't it a moral principle with you at all, Mr. Cleveland?"

I normally tried hard to follow the advice a wise Japanese diplomat once gave me: Never get angry, except on purpose. But this was too much.

"Mr. Chairman," I replied, trying to keep my gorge from interfering with my tongue, "the 'Mongolia thing' does indeed raise a question of moral principle. So does the question of letting Communist China take the China seat. In politics you often have to make choices, don't you? OK. So we have the veto in the UN, and we can make a moral principle out of Mongolia today if you want us to. But when I'm up here a few weeks from now explaining why, because the Africans left us in the lurch, we had to dump the Chinese Nationalists and admit the Peking government, I don't want to hear you asking me whether the admission of Communist China to the UN isn't morally repugnant too. I don't know what politics is like in the House Agriculture Committee, Mr. Chairman, but it's hardball up there at the UN."

An ominous silence fell on the large roomful of senators and representatives. Bureau chiefs from the executive branch don't talk to senior committee chairmen that way. I suddenly wondered what I would do when—it might be very soon—I left government service. Then to my astonishment and his eternal credit, Congressman Cooley broke the silence by laughing.

"Young man," he said with a broad smile, "you never talked about the UN so I could understand it before."

A dividend of both curiosity and risk taking is the executive's capacity to take with a grain of salt the predictions and warnings of a glum future that litter his desk, shout at him from the local media, and punctuate his conversations with his expert colleagues.

The central executive in any part of any kind of enterprise is likely to be surrounded by gloomily reluctant experts, bidding him or her to study the problem some more and then "don't just do something, stand there." The most breathless and computerized of the Cassandras seem very often to be wrong, and I have puzzled a good deal over the abnormal frequency of predictive error. Isaiah Berlin gives us the clue: "The experts cannot know enough."

Keeping up with trends in one's own field is difficult enough, and the expert is almost bound to assume that the factors he or she does not have time to study will cancel out the factors he or she has studied but does not understand. That leaves only a golden line of extrapolation from the corner of the great complexity he or she really does know something about, and each specialized projection, carried far enough into the future, leads to the apocalypse. The demographers, who underestimated the need for school buildings and tickets of admission to higher education, are only the most obvious examples of that troubling statistical temptation, which is to assume that what you know will not be stood on its head by what you do not know.

The get-it-all-together people, on the other hand, know by instinct what the souls in Dante's *Inferno* learned to their sorrow: they could see clearly what lay far in the future, but things blurred as they drew nearer. They learn to mistrust predictions, especially when they are so long range that when the eventual disaster is due the forecaster —and, if his prediction is correct, his readers too—will be dead. Or, if not dead, the forecaster might at least hope to be retired, preening himself on his long record of accuracy like the ancient retiree from the research department of the British Foreign Office who served from 1903 to 1950 and boasted thus at his retirement ceremony: "Year after year the worriers and fretters would come to me with awful predictions of the outbreak of war. I denied it each time. And I was only wrong twice."

Mark Twain was hard on extrapolators too. "In the space of one hundred and seventy-six years the lower Mississippi has shortened itself 242 miles," he wrote. "That is an average of one mile and a third per year. [So] any person can see that seven hundred and forty-two years from now the Lower Mississippi will be only a mile and three quarters long. . . . There is something fascinating about science. One gets such wholesale returns of conjecture out of such a trifling investment of fact."

Alice Rivlin, who guided the fledgling Congressional Budget Office to responsible maturity, probably knows as much about the pitfalls of forecasting as anyone. In 1983 she pulled together some practical learning in a talk to the Rand Graduate Institute titled "An Intelligent Politician's Guide to Dealing with Economists." A slice of her wisdom, before we move from forecasters to futurists:

> You might be tempted to say plaintively to your economists, How did we get into this mess? Aren't deficits supposed to go down if the economy gets better?
>
> At that point, the economist becomes self-righteous and perhaps a little patronizing. "It is your fault," he says; "you politicians raised defense spending and cut taxes at the same time, and you didn't cut other spending enough to compensate. Common sense tells you that those actions together will produce rising deficits." "But," you reply irritably, "my common sense did tell me that, but I thought some of the economists were saying that cutting taxes would stimulate the economy so much that we wouldn't have to worry about the deficits." "Well, yes," admits the economist, "but very few of us really believed that the tax effect would be so large, and anyway, stimulating the economy doesn't work when you have very tight monetary policy."
>
> So at that point, you sigh and resolve to abide by the two golden rules for dealing with economists:
>
> 1. Always ask an economist what will happen if his forecast is wrong.
>
> 2. Never believe an economist who tells you to abandon your common sense.

I can report that unwarranted optimism is breaking out in the unlikeliest places—an optimism, that is, unwarranted by the predictions of experts but warranted by a sense of determination that if our publicity heroes cannot figure out how to contain inflation, reduce unemployment, conserve energy, and maintain international peace, we will just have to do it ourselves.

I happened to be present in 1980, when the future arrived. More than five thousand people assembled in Toronto, Canada, for the First Global Conference on the Future. The most striking thing about this gathering of forecasters, professors, politicians, bureaucrats, clergypeople, journalists, healers, bankers, demographers, managers, consultants, evangelists, venture capitalists, and other professional dreamers was that most of them seemed to be looking forward to the future.

Seven or eight years earlier, such a conclave would have been a frightening experience. The Americans would have been glooming about their string of unprecedented troubles: three political assassinations, a losing war, the nuclear overhang, the possible impeachment of a president, the rising crime rate, the puzzlement of stagflation. The conferees would have been told that we were running out of food, water, and energy; that the spread and use of nuclear weapons was irreversible; that growth could not be sustained; that the curve of world population was exponential; that despite all the development aid more of the world's people each year were illiterate, malnourished, and poor; that women were still a neglected resource; and that the "me generation" didn't care.

The limited number of futurists who could have afforded to come to such a meeting would have felt they could not do much more than cry havoc, predict disaster, and sell books.

By the early 1980s, the people willing without a self-deprecating smile to call themselves futurists were numbered in the tens of thousands. And their mood was upbeat, affirmative, can-do. Maurice Strong, the creative Canadian entrepreneur who was honorary chairman of the Toronto affair, summed it up: "The bad news," he said, "is that the world is coming to an end. The good news is: not yet, and not necessarily."

It turns out that we were shorter on imagination than on resources, that "security" was *not* mostly a military problem, that sustainable growth *can* be managed, that population growth is *not* exponential, that we *can* abolish poverty if we get seriously to work on the task.

It turns out that the human environment has a constituency, that people make smog and water pollution and deserts and chlorofluorocarbons and toxic chemicals, and people can, if they will, control themselves. (Fifteen years ago you could choke on the air in Tokyo. Today you can't even see the air; it's made for breathing again.)

It turns out that women *do* make an enormous difference as they flood the work force with their energies and step gently but firmly into the backrooms where the boys have been making the decisions. (It's evidently both an exhilarating and a sobering experience, this new opportunity for female leadership. I congratulated Magda McHale, who chaired a panel in Toronto with charming decisiveness. "Thanks," she said, "but I don't think I've quite got it yet. I can't seem to achieve that female softness that the best male chairmen seem to use.")

It turns out, also, that the me generation *does* care. Gallup, the delegates in Toronto were told, finds that 87 percent of American teenagers pray or meditate, and two-thirds of them believe their prayers have been answered.

The self-conscious study of the future is useful not for forecasting, but to derive from a comparison of alternative destinies a strategy for what to do starting tomorrow morning. The community of futurists has its share of one-issue messiahs and purveyors of doom. But the best of the futurists, those who work on "alternative futures," have been immensely influential in the pervasive change of mind and mood from the mid-1970s to the early 1980s. They have helped enhance this emerging sense that we the people can govern after all and have reinforced the growing conviction that, despite the complexity of it all, each of us can make a difference if we try.

The trouble is that institutions—governments and political parties and corporations and labor unions and universities and establishments of all kinds—don't change as fast as people can change their minds. But if the "followers" are breaking free of the gloom of the 1970s, there is hope for the "leaders" too.

Now that so many processes of decision and action, once held close to comparatively few chests, are opening to so many for so much participation, the moral responsibility for what happens is also spread much more widely. When only the king and his courtiers were in the know, the peasants and tradesmen outside the castle gates at least had the luxury (they had few others) of believing that if something went wrong it was clearly "they," those people up in the castle, who had screwed up. But when decisions are widely debated in an open society and *then* turn out badly, something like a no-fault principle applies. "They" are us, and the blame rains on everybody.

Only it doesn't really work that way. "Everybody" won't accept the liability, but will search instead for scapegoats among the executive leaders and other generalists who are presumed, indeed are presuming, to worry about general outcomes, about what it all means and why. Therefore we who are the targets of this presumption need to think hard and straight about the responsibility that comes with the power that knowledge brings.

Our lives, our courts, and our media are crammed with incidents in which responsibility obviously resides in knowledge. But (paradox again) that is often much more obvious to bystanders who lacked the knowledge than to the people close enough to the scene who knew all about what was going on—and didn't do anything to change the outcome. The human animal, which is so good at acquiring and storing knowledge, is also adept at avoiding responsibility. What Hubert Humphrey once said of his own profession applies to them all: "We believe that to err is human. To blame it on someone else is politics."

If you know a person who witnessed a suicide without trying to stop it, you may think the witness shouldn't have let it happen. The choice was probably not so clear to the witness, who "didn't want to get involved."

You and I didn't feel responsible for the gang rape of that young woman on the pool table in a New Bedford bar. But we regard the bartender and others, who watched and didn't intervene, as partly responsible for the crime.

Millions of Americans were direct participants in the Vietnam War, shooting at the jungles, aiding the villagers, passing the ammunition, typing the commands, making the flamethrowers, reporting the war, feeling the inflation, waiting for news. We were drenched with information about our involvement in Vietnam, and much of it led rather logically to the conclusion Senator George Aiken of Vermont captured with his suggestion that we "declare a victory and get out."

Several hundred thousand casualties later, we did just that. Who was responsible for our hanging in there so long? The few advisers "in the know," unable to think of a way to win or a way to leave, hunkered down in those White House meetings with a succession of bewildered but stubborn presidents from both parties? Or the several million of us who knew enough about the situation to have serious reservations which we didn't think it "our job" to put forward?

Part of my job at NATO was to explain the war to our skeptical European friends. It didn't make much more sense to me than it did to them, so I reported their skepticism to Washington with some relish but no evident policy impact. Then President Johnson asked me in late February 1968 to canvass the liberal senators, with whom, he said, he was "out of touch," and I had a golden chance to get my oar in. (I reported that fifteen senators were determinedly ready for a long filibuster in the spring, timed to coincide with the ending of college terms, which would free plenty of people for street demonstrations. The nation was therefore due for an almost unprecedented constitutional crisis if it stayed on its present course.) But that was only a month before the president announced he wouldn't run again and called off the bombing of North Vietnam; and I acted only by invitation. Was I really so busy with my responsibilities in Europe that I was relieved of responsibility for the general outcome of a failing war that was souring every other part of our foreign policy and our "domestic" consensus, too?

Those who make and manage nuclear weapons, and those who have looked deeply into their effects, often feel a special obligation to avert their use. That's the main reason, I believe, why the third bomb has not been dropped in anger, four decades after the first two. But why was the *second* bomb dropped? If after the devastation of Hiroshima the question of devastating Nagasaki too had been thoroughly debated, with full information about the nuclear effects (and about the reaction of the Japanese militarists) available from the Hiroshima case, would President Truman have decided to use the second weapon so soon (five days) after the first as to preclude a Japanese decision to surrender on the basis of Hiroshima alone? Did the people who helped him decide to bomb Nagasaki need *not* to know (or, worse, think that the president needed *not* to know) what exactly had happened at Hiroshima and just what the Japanese militarists were thinking about it?

The responsibility that resides in knowledge produces a tension between two very human desires: the *need to know* and the *need not to know*. (The first of these phrases is the basis of the government's quixotic effort to keep some policies secret. I am indebted to Donald Geesaman for the second phrase; you may find it increasingly helpful, as I have, the more you think about it.) Both aspirations are especially functional in the new knowledge environment. Both are also highly corruptible.

Open systems built on persuasion and consensus require many people to know a great deal, so they can provide the feedback that articulates the responsibility glued to their knowledge.

If people know how a system works, they can make it work for them. Knowledge is the key to getting what each of us deserves— out of our parents, out of our employers, out of the government, out of social security, out of life. Knowledge is the key to productivity and to participation.

The catch is that the decision about who needs to know rests with those who already know. If letting others in on the secret may lead them to frustrate your ambition in some way, you're going to be tempted to decide that they lack a need to know.

Many is the time, and not just in the Watergate scandal, that a president of the United States has enveloped his actions in a cloak of "national security" so they couldn't be debated in Congress. It's just a lot more convenient to mine a Nicaraguan harbor if you don't have to explain in public why you are doing it. In national security matters our constitutional separation of powers, as Joseph Califano once said, amounts to the separation of the Congress from the power to make policy.

The need not to know is just as functional as the need to know, and even more corruptible.

If you tried to know everything, the way François Rabelais claimed he was doing, you would choke on the input and achieve no output. The human mind is well wired to protect us from information overload by use of a short-memory buffer; I am told that people with photographic memories are unable to concentrate, swamped in a morass of tumbling associations. All of us have to screen out of our minds and memories most of the information that comes through the mail and the media; that is, we don't even consider most of the items that reach our desks as candidates for becoming knowledge that we integrate with our own thinking. That's the only way we can survive in the daily struggle with information entropy.

It may even be necessary to our function in life or work to ignore facts readily accessible to us. The people who nurse the strategic nuclear missiles at the Strategic Air Command base near Omaha, Nebraska, or the security people who examine your luggage at the airport, badly need *not* to know how extremely improbable is the contingency against which they are guarding (improbable partly because they are on guard, of course).

When we reach for the "on" button of our television set, we resolutely put out of our minds whatever we may have inadvertently learned about the impact of television on real-life human behavior, the encouragement of violence in children (not *our* children, surely!), and the cohesion of the American family.

In a nationally publicized incident, a woman whose bone marrow might have saved a particular life was *not* told that by the hospital which had the dying man under its "care." The hospital people didn't think it was fair to burden her with the responsibility such knowledge would entail. She needed, they thought, not to know.

But avoidance of knowledge is all too easy a way to avoid responsibility, to cop out. In ancient China no one wanted to notice a dead body, let alone pick it up from the street; by social custom, the person who betrayed knowledge of the death became responsible for the funeral. We don't need to go all the way back to biblical times to find examples of people who avoided knowledge of nearby poverty or distress, "passed by on the other side," leaving the problem for some Good Samaritan willing to take the responsibility that goes with knowledge. Teachers understand this very well. CBS's Fred Friendly says his wife, a fifth-grade teacher, writes on the blackboard the first day of school every year: "A teacher's job is to make the agony of decision making so intense you can escape only by thinking."

During the Watergate hearings, I lost count of the number of government officials who had evidently said to themselves (and perhaps to their spouses), "I don't really *want* to know what that money is being spent for."

It was, indeed, the absence of a sense of personal responsibility, in more than a dozen supposedly responsible human breasts, that made the Watergate affair so deeply disturbing an addition to the fascinating file of American public scandals. Suppose, for a moment, that a systems analyst had been set to the task of casting up the costs and benefits of bugging the telephone in the Washington headquarters of the Democratic party. A short evening's work would surely have led her or him to conclude that what could be gleaned from listening to Larry O'Brien talk politics was not a benefit remotely comparable to the risk of getting caught at it.

Once the buggers were caught, our analyst would surely have calculated as very poor the chance of keeping the buck from passing into the White House, and at zero the chance of keeping secret the involvement of those who were in fact involved.

Yet men of great talent and intellectual power, several of them lawyers, seem not to have calculated the risks to themselves or their

president of pretending they were invisible. On matters less dangerous to them personally—the purchase of a weapons system, the
design of a housing program, the cancellation of federal aid to graduate students, the management of a budget deficit—these same public
executives had been routinely insisting on detailed justifications
based on systematic analyses of alternative courses of action. But
when it came to fundamental issues about morality in government
that directly touched their own responsibilities, the evidence is that,
one and all, they played it by ear. And in case after case the key
judgments they made, as the cover-up developed and disintegrated,
were decisions not to know what it would be embarrassing, or uncon-
donable, or illegal to know.

I sometimes hear our misadventures in foreign policy attributed
to some pervasive sickness in U.S. society, the product of "the great
American frustration" (Archibald MacLeish's phrase) or a sense of
impotence induced by foreign policy failures and domestic divisions.

But it isn't low morale or high frustration levels in the people-at-
large that accounts for the notable foul-ups of our time. The Bay of
Pigs, the successive Vietnam miscalculations, the failure to get a
strategic-arms agreement when one could have been gotten (in 1977),
the invitation to the shah of Iran that triggered the taking of hostages
in Tehran, the peace-disturbing "peacekeeping" mission in Lebanon,
the well-advertised "secret war" in Nicaragua—none of these was
demanded by public opinion; none was the subject of effective consultation with friends abroad; all were perceived as mistaken before
many of those "in the know" admitted it to themselves.

Each of them was the work of a very small need-to-know circle
of men (scarcely any women), consulting mostly with each other,
counting on secrecy for the validity of their actions, their knowledge-
input systems (misnamed *intelligence*) screening out what they
needed not to know and thus reinforcing their sense of direction, not
consulting widely enough (with Congress, with experts and generalists outside government, with allies and would-be friends abroad, or
with people-in-general, none of these being judged to have a "need
to know"), making decisions from day to day, letting one thing lead
to another, preoccupied with how they would look on the television

news that night rather than how history might judge their actions later on.

The antidote to both kinds of restraint on the commerce in facts and ideas—the narrowing of the need-to-know circle and the resort to contrived ignorance—is openness.

We have piled up in Chapter 4 the evidence that more openness is not always better than less. Yet in our changing information environment more openness much more often than not makes for better policy, especially when it brings into consultation people (or groups, or nations) who had better agree on a plan of action if they are expected to cooperate in carrying it out.

Hubert Humphrey, when he was vice-president of the United States, once visited the North Atlantic Council and spoke of the Golden Rule of Consultation among allies: "that each of us consult as soon, as often, and as frankly as he would wish the others to consult." It is tempting to speculate whether U.S. foreign policy decisions that went sour would have been more successful if they had been discussed with more non-Americans. Especially in complex and many-sided policy-making, it is comparatively easy for a single government's leaders to deceive themselves and each other. It always seems to be harder to deceive foreigners, who are more prone to ask what happened to the emperor's clothes.

Our knowledge-rich society reinforces that prescient platitude of Francis Bacon, but requires a codicil to his remembered phrase: If knowledge is power, knowledge is also the responsibility for the exercise of power—that is, the obligation to act because you know.

11

Education
for
Leadership

People are always saying that leadership is an art, not a science or a technology—a matter of intuition, not the product of reason. The classroom is indeed an unlikely place to learn charisma. But leadership is the art that determines the social fallout of science and points technology toward human purposes. The information to understand our tools and purposes, and especially to relate them to each other, is not carried in our genes. It has to be learned.

In thinking about education for leadership, we have to keep remembering that leadership is a continuous dialogue, not an act but an *interaction* between leaders and followers. The education of self-selected leaders is an important piece of the puzzle. But the whole puzzle is much larger: It is how citizens at large learn to make policy on issues that affect their destiny.

Education is the drive wheel of the informatized society. With information now our dominant resource in the United States, our leadership at home depends on how many of us get educated for the new knowledge environment, and how demanding and relevant and continuous and broad and wise (not merely knowledgeable) our learning is. If you analyze the kinds of collisions that enliven the management and politics of education in America, you will therefore find them at the intersections where decisions are made about

- who gets to learn—the familiar confrontation between the few and the many, played out as a dilemma unique to academia: the clients' access to the system on one criterion (equality) and their exit on another (merit);

- what should be taught and learned—the dilemmas of depth and breadth, disciplines and their interconnections, methodology and values;

- how to reflect in our educational systems the fact that a global perspective is now an essential ingredient of U.S. citizenship.

The Dr. Dolittle stories were favorites of my childhood reading, and as an academic chief executive I had frequent occasion to recall the Pushmi-Pullyu, that fabled creature with a head at each end: It was impossible to tell whether it was coming or going. In recent years the Pushmi-Pullyu has become reality—it's called higher education.

At one end of the system, *access,* universities and colleges are pushed by the society around them to admit students to postsecondary studies without discrimination as to race, creed, sex, or prior exposure to the skills of computation and communication.

The earlier answer to the question "Who should have a chance at higher education?" was clear enough. The brighter children of the rich and highly born had to be trained to manage things and to think of themselves as leaders. Those from other families could content themselves with physical labor or, if they were unusually talented, with specialized and preferably manual artisanry. Later on, as the more industrialized societies required more educated people, the doctrine gained favor that all should get an equal start, but if some fell behind because of early disadvantages or racial discrimination or inability to speak correctly the language of the governing classes, that was not regarded by those in charge as particularly serious because the need was still very great for common labor and skills not requiring general education.

But then machines took over more and more of the physical drudgery, and information became the dominant resource. Photocopiers, calculators, and computers were set to perform the clerical and analytical tasks. Rows of people typing copy, doing arithmetic, operating switchboards, conducting routine or repetitive analyses, or stamping and molding and drilling and packaging were freed for more interesting work, for jobs that required thinking and planning and ethical judgments. And in the climate of committee work, more and more people have to work on how to work cooperatively with other people, studying how whole systems function so as to fit their work with the work of others, and tell the machines what part they are supposed to play. In turn, as we have seen, the horizontal processes multiply the requirement for leadership and open up opportunities for almost anyone with imagination, aptitude, and self-starting energy to become tomorrow's agent of change.

By and large, the kinds of jobs high-school graduates used to do will increasingly be done by automatic systems, and the kinds of jobs left will require education and experience beyond the secondary level. Some of the new requirements for "college-level" training might well be met in the secondary schools. But the genteel poverty of both schools and teachers seems to be producing high schools less able to prepare their compulsory students to cope with the new world of work complexity.

And that is why, in the more industrialized societies, most young people will have to go to college, some kind of college. That is why most American parents today, if you ask which of their children are candidates for postsecondary education, will reply that all *their* children will sooner or later go to college.

Thus it was that by the early 1970s, "open admissions" had become the bold promise of a courageous egalitarian policy. In the

Education Amendments of 1972, Congress declared a national policy that every American is entitled to equal educational opportunity reaching two years beyond the compulsory twelve grades.

While I was in Hawaii, we said and meant it this way: Anybody who has a high school diploma *or* is at least eighteen years old is guaranteed a chance at postsecondary education somewhere in the statewide system called the University of Hawaii. During my last semester there, in the spring of 1974, one out of every sixteen persons in the Hawaiian islands (not counting tourists and vacationers from elsewhere) was a university student.

These new social intentions were the major engine of growth for American higher education for a generation. Parallel with the expansion of the whole postsecondary population from 2.3 million in 1950 to 8.3 million in 1972, graduate and professional schools were booming too. The demand for specialists to work in industry and the public service (including the armed services) seemed insatiable. And the popularity of higher education was such that public budgets and private giving kept pace with both the rising intake of freshmen and the rising production of Ph.D.s and professional degrees.

Then the bubble burst. Campus disruptions, swelling budgets, and the intolerance of most educators for systematic planning all contributed to the backlash. Governments and givers started asking before granting it how their money would be spent, and the dawn of accountability came up like thunder.

Quite suddenly, starting in the mid-1970s, a pervasive austerity sharpened, and still today sharpens, all the dilemmas that had been buried or bypassed in the continuous growth. If there is not enough money to pay all the professors (even, in some institutions, those with claims to academic tenure), it is no longer possible to teach all the students who want to study or offer all the required programs without increments of money that are increasingly hard to come by. Faculty members and administrators easily deduce that "raising standards" can result in fewer students and can permit the elimination of the less experienced (and incidentally untenured) teachers. In universities, this means that even more of the lower-division teaching can be done by graduate students, for the graduate programs on which the institution's general repute depends must of course be maintained.

But "downtown" the university's external critics, noting the sudden recession in the demand for graduate-degree holders and calculating the comparative voting strength of the many and the few, counter with proposals to drop the more elite (which they call *elitist*) forms of training in favor of wider opportunity for lower-division and community-college students. More parents are interested in opportunities for freshmen than for Ph.D. candidates; more voters are moved by a politician's defense of vocational education than by the pleas of the graduate faculty.

So the ancient rivalry between the few and the many is reincarnated as open admissions versus selective admissions, the accepted versus the ambitious, and the community colleges versus four-year colleges versus graduate schools, as academic executives compete in the knowledge society for higher education dollars now that the sky is no longer the limit.

At the other end of the Pushmi-Pullyu, the outsiders' expectations shift from equality to quality. They want the academic executives and professors to take an undifferentiated mass of students and arrange them according to intellectual achievement, ready for stacking in the hierarchical job market that awaits them off campus. Public policy is clear in the paradoxical way the Delphic oracle was clear: The policy is, in the admirably succinct phrase of James A. Perkins, former president of Cornell, "entry by egalitarian principles and exit by meritocratic standards."

A national system of postsecondary education to which more than two-thirds of our high-school students aspire will obviously serve multiple purposes: education as an investment (for the poor), education as a consumer good (for the affluent), education as a device for avoiding decisions about what to do next (for the unattached, the uncertain, and the unemployed). But whatever the individual purpose of "going to college," the social contract in American higher education is clear enough: Colleges and universities, and especially the public colleges and universities, are the egalitarian means for making an aristocracy of achievement acceptable in a democratic society. It is now part of our democratic ethos that if you apply the merit principle to a large enough body of students with a fair enough representation of previously disadvantaged kinds of people, the resulting discrimination is permissible. This double ethic suits the students fine: They want an equal chance to go to college, but they also want a job when they get out.

Of course no one is much good at forecasting the job market; the science of what people will be doing for a living is still an adolescent discipline. Most teachers have a hunch that the student is as likely to be the best forecaster of his or her life's work as a fluctuating job market or a government statistician would be.

The critics of higher education are judging by a simpler standard: If a job isn't awaiting the student as soon as she or he gets her or his credential, then the system of higher education is not working the way it should. Most educators, by contrast, think of themselves as helping students develop a capacity to learn what will be a continuing asset, and joy, to the student for decades to come. Our most important task, we think, is not to train for a meal ticket the week after graduation, but to educate for fifty years of self-fulfillment. Our egalitarian target is not an equal crack at a first job, but an equal chance at a full life.

In this longer time-perspective, the attempt to quantify human resource requirements is bound to produce nonsense. In a society of increasing information-richness, the content of many, perhaps most, jobs a generation hence is unknowable today—just as the children of yesteryear were unable, through the ignorance of their parents and guidance counselors, to aspire to service as astronauts, nuclear physicists, ecologists, computer programmers, television repairers, or managers of retrieval systems. (It was not until quite recently that the category of "guidance counselor" was added to the roster of our school systems.) Already a decade ago, the U.S. Department of Labor was guessing that by the year 2000, two-thirds of 1974's kindergarten students would be filling jobs that did not yet exist.

I have already set down my skepticism of the forecasting racket. Do not suspend your own skepticism as I now try, with an impressionist's broad brush, to project the kinds of work that are bound to be especially valued in a knowledge-rich society.

There will be more "information" and "service" work, and proportionately fewer "production" jobs, to be had. That is clear enough from the trends discussed in Chapter 2.

Machines will keep on eating up routine and repetitive tasks; the jobs left for people to do will require more and more brainwork and more skill in people-to-people relations, which machines are no good at.

"Computer literacy" will be part of knowing how to read, write, compute, and communicate. (That doesn't mean more than a rudimentary understanding of the architecture and electronics of microprocessing; it does mean understanding what computers, linked to telecommunications, can do for us—just as most of us understand an automobile's functions without being able to repair it.)

Despite tenure systems and retirement benefits, people will move around even more than they do now, from place to place, from function to function, from career to career.

Work, and therefore education for work, will become less competitive, more organized around cooperation.

There will be a growing market for education as a nonpolluting leisure-time "consumer good." Already some union contracts entitle workers to time off for education; Italian metalworkers, for example, are entitled by contract to 150 hours of education a year.

A growing proportion of the demand for higher education will be for *recurring education,* the 1980s' international in-word for what used to be called adult or continuing education.

Education for leadership in varying forms will be a growth industry, because the proportion of the population that performs some leadership functions will keep growing.

More and more people will work at the management of international interdependence—in the federal government, in multinational corporations, and in private voluntary agencies and international organizations both public and private (if you can tell the difference). International travel for work and for leisure and the expansion of global telecommunications will also keep spreading, and swelling the demand for people with training in crosscultural communication.

This is a vision of full and interesting employment. Will there be enough jobs to go around? No one knows. What Howard Bowen said in the 1970s still seems a good guess in the 1980s: that "two centuries of history have revealed no secular trend toward greater unemployment as technology advances." There is no finite amount of "work" to be divided up among a given number of "workers." Work, along with capital, expands with our capacity to use what is new in new ways for new purposes. The United States did not get to be a great nation by redoing in each generation what it used to do well in the one before, like making propeller aircraft or mechanical adding machines or oversized automobiles. It got there by constantly thinking up new things to do—like linking computers to telecommunications—before others did.

The fusion of computers and telecommunications and the developments in biotechnology are the basis for a legion of new activities, new things to do, new "jobs," on earth and in the oceans and in the atmosphere and outer space. The numbers and quality of "jobs" will be a function not of physical constraints but of the human imagination. Will we use our imagination to create full and fulfilling employment or, at the other extreme, to blow up the human experiment when it has hardly begun? We are back to Barbara Ward: "We do not know. We have the duty to hope."

But to two predictions I would assign a high probability value. People who do not educate themselves, and keep reeducating themselves, to participate in the new knowledge environment will be the peasants of the information society. And societies that do not give *all* their people a chance at a relevant education, and also periodic opportunities to tune up their knowledge and their insights, will be left in the jetstream of history by those that do.

Many of the most interesting dilemmas for the academic executive are the direct result of student choices that make nonsense of what the planners have planned for them. Part of the chronic crisis in vocational education is the difficulty of defining its role in an information society if both instructors and their industrial sponsors are hung up on the moral value of obsolescent forms of manual labor, while the students are searching not just for a meal ticket but for meaning. In the liberal arts, undergraduates have often created serious budgetary problems by flocking into courses on art and religion and ethnic studies in colleges that had planned for them to take biochemistry and political science. The growing preference for multipurpose graduate education (law, business, public affairs) betokens the students' search for a middle ground between trying to guess right about a shifting job market and investing too many years in an unmarketable academic joyride.

When college undergraduates vote with their feet by crowding into the lectures on "The Meaning of Life" and boycotting the courses in econometrics, they symbolize the second collision about what should be taught and what should be learned in higher education.

It is an open secret that the modern university is not well suited to the task of educating people for the get-it-all-together function. The university's self-image, its organization, and its reward systems all tilt against breadth.

The university as we know it developed as an expression of the scientific method and progressed to its prestigious role in society by dividing into separate compartments the different kinds of knowledge, and into separate disciplines the proven methods of inquiry. We still need the experts this kind of higher education is good at producing. We will need more of them, and nothing I am about to say should be taken as hostile to the primary function of academic departments and professional schools.

But in my judgment we have an even greater need for what the modern university, by and large, is *not* producing: analysts who can relate "hard" technologies to their "soft" impacts and implications; reflective practitioners who are concerned with human values; educators who can teach in widened perspective; managers who can bring their more specialized brothers and sisters into organizations to make things happen; legislators who can relate all the policies they make to each other; in a word, generalist leaders who can get it all together.

If complexity is growing faster than anything else in the United States, then the education of men and women to manage complexity should be the fastest-growing function in American higher education. It isn't, not yet.

Evidence that university education for leadership is lagging behind the demand curve for trained leaders is clear enough. Think tanks for policy analysis, systems analysis, strategic studies, futures research, integrative studies, humanistic studies, strategic management, public affairs, and other names for get-it-all-together thinking are proliferating as a new growth industry in themselves. In the second half of the 1970s, the same began to be true in Europe and Japan.

These think tanks have lured out of the research universities and graduate schools an impressive number of first-rate academics who feel stifled by the obstacles to and the absence of rewards for ranging beyond their own disciplines and teaming up with colleagues in other departments. Large corporations and government agencies, unable to find in universities the advanced, integrative, interdisciplinary, interprofessional, and international reeducation their specialty-trained midcareer executives both need and want, are commissioning independent institutes to fill the gap or creating very large educational and policy-analysis structures of their own, matching in size and overmatching in resources all but the major university graduate programs.

One trouble with this trend is that many of the freestanding think tanks exist to push particular points of view, and the industrial research establishments (with a few notable exceptions, such as Bell Labs) focus exclusively on research likely to be helpful to the corporations' own prosperity. The situation as a whole gets short shrift.

Another trouble is that neither the think tanks nor the industrial research labs do much teaching; some of them don't do any. And the executive training schools typically focus sharply on the skills and the psyche of the individual executive (a necessary but not sufficient emphasis) and on the policies and problems of their parent corporations. They are often not in close contact, as universities are, with the broader public and international context, or with the development of younger potential leaders. They may contribute useful ideas to the adults who are currently, in Paul Appleby's memorable phrase, trying "to make a mesh of things." But they are not helping to hone the fresh new integrative minds we are going to need to get through the 1990s into the twenty-first century.

What's needed is a university-based fusion of integrative policy analysis, midcareer education for leadership, and training of younger students for roles in the policy process—the students, the midcareer leaders, and the policy researchers working together on real world problems.

The academy's students, and its outside critics too, notice that the vertical academic disciplines, built around clusters of related research methods, are not in themselves very helpful in solving problems. No real-world problem can be fitted into the jurisdiction of any single academic department. As every urban resident knows, we know every specialized thing about the modern city, but we seldom "get it all together" to make the city livable, efficient, safe, and clean.

As they awaken to problem solving, students therefore gravitate to those of the academy's offerings that seem to promise an interdisciplinary approach. These offerings are sometimes disappointing. A course on environmental issues may be taught by an evangelist less eager to train analysts than to recruit zealots. A workshop on a "problem" may mask a research contract for a client (a government, a corporation, a wealthy donor) who knows the answer and is looking for ammunition and an academic seal of approval for a predetermined course of action.

When I managed a university system I noticed that we had many interdisciplinary courses listed in the catalogue. On inspection they turned out to be mostly team-taught, that favored academic device for avoiding interdisciplinary thought. Team teaching means that two or three or four professors share the task of teaching the same group of students. What too often happens is that each teacher teaches his or her own discipline. It is the students who are expected to be interdisciplinary.

I complained about this one day to a gather of deans and could see their tolerant smiles at this presidential naïveté. "Don't take it so hard," said Terry Rogers, the irreverent dean of Hawaii's medical school, "it's the same all over. In a modern urban hospital, the only generalist left is the patient."

The only truly interdisciplinary instrument is not a committee of experts but the synoptic view from a single integrative mind. In university education, what is too often lacking is an interdisciplinary role model up front by the blackboard. Even so, many students prefer offerings that promise to cut across the vertical structures of method and help them construct homemade ways of thinking about the situation as a whole.

The revolt against methodology is also powered by the quickening interest in ethics, which started even before Watergate. A growing number of students come to college after some life experience—in the army or on a job or in a commune. They are groping for purpose, for effective ways of asking "Why?" and "Where are we supposed to be going anyway?" Disciplines that seem neutral about purpose and modes of analysis that are equally usable to kill people or build low-cost housing make these students uncomfortable.

The students' intuition may not be wrong. Yet they face an impressive phalanx of opposition to their instinct that the vertical disciplines should be stirred together in problem-solving, purpose-related combinations. Access to academic journals, collegial admiration, and promotion and tenure are not achieved by having lunch with colleagues in other departments. And the external critics are for once on the professors' side: The division of knowledge into manageable compartments enabled the alumni to develop self-esteem and a decent living, so they don't understand why the curriculum has to be controversial.

But doesn't the new knowledge environment place a much greater premium on integrative thought? Won't we have to take a new look at higher education systems that award the highest credentials for wisdom to those who master the narrowest slices of knowledge?

I want to suggest a way out. But first, a word about the case for integrative thought.

The idea of *integrative thinking* is so central to my thesis, in this chapter and throughout this book, that I owe you an explanation of what I mean by it.

I have already suggested that we are born with naturally integrative minds. A newborn baby knows from the start, by instinct, that everything is related to everything else. Before a child is exposed to formal education, its curiosity is all-embracing. The child hasn't yet been told about the parts, so it is interested in the whole.

The more we learn, ironically, the less tied together is our learning. It's not situation-as-a-whole thinking, it's the separation of the specialized kinds of knowledge, that (like racial prejudice) "has to be carefully taught."

The holistic learning comes especially in grades K to 4; fourth-grade teachers are perhaps the premier generalists in our society. (Think of the variety of subjects on which they have to be able to answer the question "Why?") Farther up the ladder of formal schooling, we do manage to persuade most children that the really important questions start with "When?" and "Where?" and "How?" and especially "How much?" Fortunately for the nation and the world, some young citizens persist in asking "Why?"

Jasmina Wellinghoff, a Twin Cities scientist and writer, writes about her first-grader:

> When my six-year-old learns that we heat the house with forced air, she immediately wants to know who is forcing the air, where natural gas comes from, and how it got stuck underground. After I have done my best to explain all this, comes the next question: "If we didn't have natural gas, would we die in the winter?" There you have it. Geology, engineering, physics and biology, all together in a hierarchy of concepts and facts.
>
> However, a few years from now my daughter will be studying the structure of the earth's crust, combustion, hydraulics and the classification of living beings—all in different years and quarters, neatly separated, tested and graded.

In 1980 I edited, with scientist Alexander King, chairman of the International Federation of Institutes of Advanced Study, a book on *Bioresources for Development.* In our opening essay he and I tried to get into one paragraph what we meant by integrative thinking. It took rather a long paragraph, but we made it:

> The adjectives "holistic" and "integrative" are already bordering on the cliché, but they have a very special significance in the use and management of the bioresource. They mean, quite literally, that the problems of a nation, of a city, of a village are to be seen as interconnected and therefore to be tackled simultaneously and as a complex, not separately or sequentially. The community's future comprises economic, social, cultural and political as well as technical facets; these cannot be dealt with by the politician alone, or by the economist, the engineer, or the scientist in isolation. When it comes to the use of resources, it is necessary to consider them all: agricultural, forest, soil, water, microorganisms, plants, animals, men and women. In a particular development scheme, only an integrated approach can make the optimum use of the resources; consider food and energy requirements together; arrange for full use to be made of "wastes" and "residues"; include traditional agriculture in the community's planning; maintain soil fertility and humus content; explore food addition possibilities through fermentation and the use of plants not commonly consumed; use plant, animal, and human wastes to generate biogas for cooking, lighting, refrigeration and distillation; develop algal and fish culture; invent or adapt simple solar and windpower devices; and so on almost without end. An integrated plan will include a careful appreciation of the carrying capacity of the soil, so that its fertility can be maintained indefinitely, as well as of methods of augmenting it, for example by inoculation with nitrogen-fixing bacteria. It will consider the energy balance to ensure that the net energy balance is positive. And it will look to the preservation of the environment, locally and globally, in recognition of

the place of man in the ecosystem, living in mandatory symbiosis with all species of creation.

I cannot find a single individual who is against integrative thinking. Everyone seems to know that in the real world, all the problems are interdisciplinary and all the solutions are interdepartmental, interprofessional, interdependent, and international.

Yet our institutions start with a heavy bias against breadth. It has been a useful bias: The secret of success of the Scientific Revolution was not breadth but specialized depth. Chopping up the study of physical reality into vertically sliced puzzles, each to be separately deciphered by a different analytical chain of reasoning (*disipline*), made possible the division of specialization and of labor.

But one thing led to another, as E. B. White thought it would, and the resulting complexity now makes it imperative that these differing analytical systems be cross-related in *interdisciplinary* thinking and coordinated action. Those who would lead must therefore get used to thinking integratively.

This is difficult doctrine. Our whole educational system is geared more to categorizing and analyzing patches of knowledge than to sewing them together. Yet the experts obviously don't have the answers, and we are exposed to daily and dramatic demonstrations that the coordinators don't have the answers either.

Now the good news. Just in time, new instruments that can be used for thinking in breadth are coming to hand.

The computer, the complex simulations it makes possible, and its hookup to a worldwide network of electronic communications now make it possible for individuals and small groups to analyze enormously complex natural systems (global weather), economic markets (the international monetary system), technologies not yet deployed, decision "trees," models of voting behavior, and crisis management and conflict resolution. Tools such as these empower those who learn to use them to make complex judgments in the more mindful knowledge of alternative futures. Systems thinking has created new ways to help encompass in a single mind some approximation of "the situation as a whole," as it relates to the problem being studied.

Don't get me wrong. There are dangers in excessive dedication to systems analysis. Part of the body count in Vietnam is certainly traceable to quantifying the tactics of war while neglecting the impressionistic strategies of peace. Still, it is useful for decision makers to be able to count what can be counted, as long as they remember that just because it can't be counted doesn't mean it doesn't count.

The machines that are so useful in processing information are, of course, stupid beyond belief. Despite the attribution to them of intelligence (in the much misunderstood term *artificial intelligence*), they can still only count (almost lightning fast) from 0 to 1 and back again, and transmit the results (at nearly the speed of light, in large and increasing volume) from place to place around the world. People have to do all the rest: define the human needs and purposes, select and analyze the relevant data, fix the assumptions to be made, stir in the inferences and insights and imagination, form the organizations, make the decisions, issue or implement the instructions, and above all deal with other people.

The people to perform these functions will be mostly college men and women. What should they be learning, for this purpose, during the years they are students?

It would be nice if the dilemma were simple. But the ancient clashes between training and education, between vocational and general, between honing the mind and nourishing the soul, divide the outside critics, divide the professional educators, and divide the students too.

Just now our favorite way to resolve the dilemma is to delegate it to the individual student. We "maximize the student's options" by creating a bewildering proliferation of courses and programs of study, a cafeteria of the intellect, using what the food service people call the "scramble system." For the limited number of students who know just what they want and why, the new freedom doesn't work badly. But most students expect some guidance in creating an intellectually nutritious trayful of reading, discussion, writing, computing, and work experience.

My guess is that if U.S. colleges and universities continue to proliferate courses, external pressure groups and the state and federal governments will sooner or later impose social and economic and even political criteria for curriculum building in higher education. At the graduate level such coercion is already felt to some extent, as government bribes the universities with research funds to teach what political leaders think important and are certain is safe. At the undergraduate level, if our ultimate curricular principle is the cop-out called "maximum options," the outsiders will, in the end, tell the academics what to teach and the students what they can learn at the public's expense.

The answer, as usual, is not to settle the argument by choosing one or the other of the dilemma's horns. Honing the mind and nourishing the soul are both functional in the new knowledge environment. What we need now is a theory of general education that is clearly relevant to life and work in a context that is based more and more on the information resource—a rapidly changing scene in which uncertainty is the main planning factor. Perhaps, in the alternating current of general and job-oriented education, it is time for a new synthesis, a new "core curriculum"—something very different from Columbia University's "World Civilization," Syracuse University's "Responsible Citizenship," or the University of Chicago's "Great Books," yet still a central idea about what every educated person should know, and have, and try to be.

Such a core is not going to have much to do with learning facts. It is said that each half hour produces enough new knowledge to fill a twenty-four-volume edition of the *Encyclopaedia Britannica.* Our world of indiscriminate erudition turns out millions of new books and articles and pamphlets in a year's time. Most of the facts we learn in school are unlikely to be true for as long as we can remember them.

(The last time I took physics, in the mid-1930s, my instructor told me the atom couldn't be split. When I studied Keynesian economics with a young Oxford tutor named Harold Wilson, I learned that inflation and recession were periodic, but occurred at opposite ends of the business cycle; the idea that they might be fused in a persistent stagflation was not mentioned. This remembered learning has not been very useful to me, of late; it didn't seem to work very well for Prime Minister Wilson, either.)

If, however, we thought hard about the requirements of the new knowledge environment, and consulted the instincts and perceptions of our own future-oriented students, I think we could construct a new core curriculum from such elements as these:

- Education in *integrative brainwork*—the capacity to synthesize for the solution of real-world problems the analytical methods and insights of conventional academic disciplines. (Exposure to basic science and mathematics, to elementary systems analysis, and to what a computer can and cannot do are part, but only a part, of this education.)

- Education about *social goals, public purposes,* the *costs and benefits of openness,* and the *ethics of citizenship*—to enable each educated person to answer for himself or herself two questions: Apart from the fact that I am expected to do this, is this what I would expect myself to do? and Does the validity of this action depend on its secrecy?

- A capacity for *self-analysis*—through the study of ethnic heritage, religion and philosophy, art and literature, the achievement of some fluency in answering the question Who am I?

- Some *practice in real-world negotiation,* in the psychology of consultation, and in the nature of leadership in the knowledge environment.

- A *global perspective* and an attitude of personal responsibility for the general outcome—passports to citizenship in an interdependent world.

In 1980 I was invited to take on leadership of the University of Minnesota's Hubert H. Humphrey Institute of Public Affairs, which had just been created as a freestanding graduate college with a sizable endowment raised in honor and memory of the most gifted political leader in Minnesota history.

To set the tone for a new kind of university activity, I presented to the Board of Regents (on the day they appointed me) an ambitious description of the future terrain:

> "Public Affairs" is not one more discipline, to be defined by a particular method of analysis. It is not a new profession, either, in the tradition of medicine and business and the law. It is the *public action,* the *public responsibility* component of every discipline and every profession.
>
> "Public Affairs" focuses on how the general management of any society uses expert knowledge and specialized methods to make something happen. It is concerned with the politics of value and the values of politics. It does not mistake growth for progress, but asks "Growth for what? Growth for whom?"
>
> In "Public Affairs," research and analysis must above all be integrative. "Public Affairs" means learning to think integratively.
>
> The ladder to leadership in our society is always expert excellence. But the practice of leadership is a different line of work, requiring different insights, different intellectual tools, different values, and different personal relationships.
>
> If the central concern of an institute of "public affairs" is the reflective practice of leadership, the institute needs to work across the university with every discipline and profession, and outside the university with diverse local, national and international communities that are trying to clarify the purposes and develop the techniques for getting things done in the public interest.

The Humphrey Institute already offered graduate degrees in public affairs and planning, and we got to work on an agenda of policy research and analysis to make the institute also a university-based think tank in which students could participate. After a year of wide consultation, including some stimulating contributions by John Gardner, we created in 1981 a new program called Education for Reflective Leadership. The yearlong seminar, building toward another degree program for those who need the credential, is open to men and women in midcareer; we established no lower or upper age limits, but accepted applicants who had at least ten years of work experience, showed evidence of working through their specialties toward leadership roles, and (whatever their age) still thought their most exciting and productive years lay ahead of them.

We think of this program as a continual experiment, and we change the formula each year as we gain experience with it. We have found that a seminar with thirty to forty people is viable if there is enough small-group work in the curriculum. We have tried hard to get away from a classroom atmosphere; it's a "seminar," not a "course." Leadership cadres do not want to sit in rows like students, so we created a very large but informal Living Room, with table lamps and comfortable furniture, framed pictures on the wall, and a large world map and globe to stress the perspective they were invited to share. The members of the seminar are called *participants,* not *students*; the faculty (including a good many visitors from around the United States and abroad) is called *moderators,* not *teachers,* and we are indeed learning more than we teach. The seminar is as much of a roundtable as we can make it, though the danger is ever present that well-known visiting moderators will draw questions for them to answer rather than challenges for them to riposte.

The reflective leadership program is a mix of two kinds of experience. One is a focus on the leadership function itself, designed to help the participant think hard about his or her goals, ethical standards, maturity, and leadership style. The idea is to use psychological tests as a stimulant to self-analysis, without bordering on what one of our consultants (who had been through one) called "an embarrassingly touchy-feely experience."

In parallel with their effort to think about themselves as leaders, we challenge the participants to immerse themselves in the wider context: the changing character of governance in our mixed public-private economy; the post–New Deal thinking about social policy, including health and welfare issues, neighborhood politics, racial discrimination, and the changing status of women (in the United States and around the world); the social fallout of science and technology (inquiring, for example, how society is going to cope with nuclear fusion, genetic engineering, and space colonization); the impacts and implications of "information as a resource" (to which you have been exposed at some length in this book); nuclear weapons, military strategy, and arms control; and world security (including the kinds of nonmilitary threats and potentials that were sketched in Chapter 7).

As the program developed, we tried to fold in a most important insight from research on adult education: that adults learn best by action followed by reflection. Toward the end of the thirty-week seminar small groups of the participants themselves take the responsibility to organize a learning process on a policy issue the small group is free to choose, with a budget allotment to make it possible for them to import talent for the occasion.

In the 1980s new programs of education for leadership are springing up around the United States, and are being watched with interest from Europe and Japan. Some of them are more inclined to lean heavily on psychology-based self-analysis; others are strong on cognitive learning about selected topics. Our theory (the practice always falls short) is to engage midcareer leaders in working on problems, even world-scale problems such as nuclear arms control, as if *they* had to deal with them. Leadership is both knowing and doing something responsible as a consequence of knowledge. These are the two priceless ingredients in strategic management.

If there was ever a moment in history when a comprehensive strategic view was needed, not just by a few leaders in high (which is to say visible) office but by a large number of executives and other generalists in and out of government, this is certainly it. Meeting that need is what should be *higher* about higher education.

A few years ago the adult leaders of the Little League baseball organization announced that henceforth their "World Series" would be limited to American teams. They did not say why. But one sportswriter reported, deadpan, that teams from Taiwan and Japan had captured seven of the last eight world championships.

The American people, who have to make the policy before our leaders can carry it out, are merely grown-up schoolchildren and college students. If they don't grow up with an understanding of our international interdependence, our foreign policy decisions will be lacking in common sense and won't work. So a whole people needs to be educated in global perspective.

In the mid-1970s, the idea of global perspectives in education was so new it sounded radical. But change is so rapid in our society that by the mid-1980s, global perspectives had become the mainstream of a powerful reform movement in our public schools and was creeping into colleges and universities, too.

Let me try to make clear what is *not* meant by *global perspectives.* It doesn't mean stuffing more courses in international relations into already overcrowded school and college curricula. By global perspectives in education we will have to mean something more pervasive: that *every* subject in school or in higher education—biology and physics and mathematics, history and philosophy and English, economics and sociology and public affairs—is an occasion for introducing concepts that help young people understand that the world is round and fragile and fully packed.

Is this a practical idea, for real teachers in real classrooms with real students? I could bring out many witnesses for the defense, but I'll content myself with one. On a visit to Cape Cod, I happened to meet a third-grade teacher in the Barnstable public schools. To make conversation, I asked what she was doing to introduce her charges to a global perspective. I expected a defensive answer; what I got was a revelation.

"I discovered," she said, "that it isn't actually illegal in Massachusetts to make up your own problems for teaching a subject. One of the concepts you have to introduce in the third grade is arithmetic fractions, so I have constructed some problems using the fluctuations in international currency exchange rates to illustrate how to use fractions."

There you have it. This young woman was teaching the basics.

But in the process she was also smuggling into a roomful of nine-year-olds an introduction to the international monetary system. That's creative education, and it should be decriminalized in our schools. Shortly after my Cape Cod encounter I had occasion to address a convention of schoolteachers. To them I suggested an alternative to the slogan "Back to Basics," with which the public schools were then being flayed by their political opponents. The updated slogan I proposed was "Forward to Basics."

I am not saying that the elementary-school teacher, the very model of a modern generalist, should teach about everything at once. I'm not neurotic about global perspectives, merely insistent. But I do believe that young children can learn to think in *systems*. They live with interdependence every day—in families and homerooms and the local public park, a complex ecological system. The ambience of mutual dependence, the ambiguities of personal relations, the conflicting ambitions of groups are the stuff of socialization from our earliest years.

Once we learn that family and school and local government can be unfair, we are more ready to reckon with the global fairness revolution, the push for the satisfaction of basic human needs worldwide.

Once we know how to think about value questions in our everyday life and work (questions to which the answer is very often, "It all depends"), we are more than halfway to coping with value choices in that complexity of planetary puzzles called climate change, food production, energy use, population planning, development strategy, environmental protection, ocean law, trade, investment, and money.

Once, in short, the child can follow cause and effect around the corner, the child grown up should be able to follow cause and effect around the world. And with that kind of education for wisdom, we the policy-making people can tackle with less diffidence the Cheshire Cat's first question: "Where do you want to get to?"

In one of the consultations leading to the Minnesota experiment in Education for Reflective Leadership, journalist/author Perdita Huston proposed the word *glocal* for issues on which we are all going to have to think globally while we act locally. Is it unrealistic to suppose that millions of Americans can, over measurable time, learn to think and act in glocal perspective?

Of course it isn't.

Consider the rapidity with which we are all becoming aware of new limits: an *upper limit* to warfare that the weapons of frightfulness have brought about, an *outer limit* to the physical capacity of the biosphere to sustain human life, and a potential *time limit* on the life expectancy of the human race—we are the first generation to know that it is literally possible for our grandchildren or our great-grandchildren not to exist at all.

We can change our collective minds in a hurry when we need to. Who would have thought, in the 1950s, that changing attitudes toward population would bring U.S. population growth below the replacement level of fertility rates in the 1970s? Who would have predicted the charisma of the environmental movement? Who would have thought that a war could be stopped, not by winning it, but by a decision, starting at the grass roots, that it just didn't make sense?

Yet these rapid changes in personal philosophy and social action, partly the consequence of pressure from the young, have come about without much help from the leadership of our schools or colleges or universities, which discovered only belatedly the relevance to general education of family planning, the assessment of environmental impacts, and the analysis of conflict.

How much better could we do if most schools and colleges and universities were teaching, rather than running to catch up with, the global perspective that is now built into the future of the United States of America?

12

The Knowledge Seniors:
Commencement
at 65

I n the autumn of 1982 I was invited to speak at a bicentennial celebration of the Harvard Medical School, on the subject of longevity. The invitation was sufficiently puzzling to accept: I never went to medical school, let alone Harvard's, and I was not an expert on the length of life. On my way to the meeting, I figured out why they wanted me there. The program needed what is called, in the reductionist language of the profession, a piece of "clinical material."

For this role, I came close to qualifying. It was only a few months till my sixty-fifth birthday, which in an earlier time would have meant compulsory retirement on account of age. I was beginning to understand what some wag meant by saying of his aging human organs, "If it's working, it hurts. And if it doesn't hurt, it probably isn't working." And I had developed those little tricks that are a cover for forgetfulness: as Bruce Barton suggested, I knew that if the toothbrush was wet, I had already brushed my teeth; and if I was wearing one blue sock and one brown sock, I knew that there would be another pair just like it somewhere. But I like to believe that the reason older people forget more than younger people is that they have so much more stored in their random-access memories.

As I passed my nonretirement age, still on the job, it occurred to me to ponder why I would not have been ready to retire if the courts and Congress and the University of Minnesota's Board of Regents hadn't recently lengthened the work expectancy of professors. I can now present the fruits of a wholly unscientific inquiry: For me and perhaps for most people and almost certainly for our society as a whole, a public policy of retiring everybody at a given age just doesn't make sense anymore.

I do not mean, of course, that the older members of a corporation, law firm, medical center, university, nonprofit agency, government bureau, or other organized human activity should be like federal judges, with guaranteed tenure for life, at the judge's option. For many kinds of employment, it is important to move the older people along to leave room for the advancement of fresh blood. But this worthy principle of good management seems to have led by thoughtless reasoning to a premise that all retirees have tired blood, and must therefore be placed on the government payroll.

The social disease called retirement is really a subhead of a more pervasive malaise. That large trouble, just coming into view, can be miniaturized in three words: After affluence, what?

Just now, in a society with 6 to 10 percent of its workers officially unemployed, and some multiple of that number unofficially excluded from the labor force, it may seem quixotic to be worrying about what comes after affluence. Since the earliest human civilizations, most people in every society have been preoccupied with a common goal: to guarantee their own personal security, to achieve an assured and decent standard of life for themselves and their children. The bulk of humankind is still too busy making ends meet to worry much about the next goal after that.

Even in what we like to call the advanced societies, the semi-prosperity we achieve is deceptive. It is still very unfairly distributed: 12 to 20 percent of Americans are below somebody's definition of the poverty line, and a heavily disproportionate number of them are women and members of racial minority groups. Such prosperity as we have achieved is still too closely connected with the production of arms we hope not to use and wish we didn't have to sell abroad to improve our balance of payments. And our affluence results partly, as Robert Hutchins, the youthful president of the University of Chicago, once said, from "our patented way of getting rich, which is to buy things from one another that we do not want at prices we cannot pay on terms we cannot meet because of advertising we do not believe."

But suppose—just suppose—we can in this century achieve a durable prosperity and spread it around in a reasonably egalitarian fashion. What then?

The idea used to be that the purpose of making a living was to stop working when you had it made. According to this philosophy, you would retire as early as possible, pull up stakes, and head south to spend the Golden Years fishing in the sun, snoozing in a hammock, watching the surfers, playing cards in glorious idleness, and happily awaiting the Grim Reaper in bovine indifference to the world about you.

Or, if you were not really old enough to call it retirement, you could work limited hours, choosing the kind of work that avoids on-the-job excitement and thus averts overtime. Then you could spend long hours and long weekends fishing, snoozing, watching, and playing, for all the world as if you *were* retired. The invention of television, plus the lack of inventiveness in its prime-time offerings, has made it easier for all of us to do nothing, even if we have something to do, than it ever was before.

There have been, of course, more active forms of leisure. When only a few people were rich, they could get away from the others on a yacht, or at least drive into the empty countryside for a spin. They could go to the opera or ballet, hunt elephants, fish for marlin, play tennis, work on that golf stroke, splash in the surf themselves, or travel to museums and cathedrals and foreign restaurants and other broadening places. The object, in any case, was to achieve as much leisure time as possible, then crowd it with leisure-time activity.

But once a whole population decides to be prosperous, the traditional forms of leisure are somehow not so attractive anymore. The lakes and coastlines are crowded, the country lanes become four-lane death traps, the fishing streams get polluted. The need for television talent runs hopelessly ahead of the talent supply. The theaters and courts and courses and pools and beaches and restaurants are congested with people who have just as much right to be there as you do. Even the elephants and marlin have to be rationed. Only the cathedrals are still empty.

Because playtime is available to all, it comes back into perspective. As the by-product of a busy, productive, relevant life, leisure is a boon and a balm. As the purpose of life, it is a bust. (Every few months, some television interviewer is visibly astonished when the winner of several million dollars in a lottery says that she or he hopes to keep on working in the same occupation as before.)

What lies beyond affluence, for most people young and old, is not likely to be the use of their guaranteed income to finance their weekends and vacations. Young people will certainly want to use their economic security as a launching pad for adventure, for action. Young or old, most people will find their adventure not in their leisure time but in their working time. The fortunate ones will not be able to tell the difference.

It now seems quite possible that we shall be much better supplied with older people than the conventional wisdom dreams of. A poll of people who study population trends might still today reveal a consensus that there is a "natural" age limit for the human animal. One influential estimate, in the *New England Journal of Medicine,* sets it at about eighty-five years. A 1984 World Bank report assumes that no country's people will have an average life expectancy greater than eighty-two years in the year 2100, more than a century from now.

In thinking about population futures, as in other kinds of predictions, the original statistical sin has been to mistake current trends for human destiny. The experts call this "surprise-free" forecasting. Wouldn't it be surprising if there were no surprises?

For a start, we are already well into a demographic transition of historic proportions. We are accustomed to planning for and complaining about population growth. But in most of the industrial nations, plans and complaints will have to be directed more and more to the consequences of declining births, lengthening lives, more knowledgeable workers, as many working women as working men, more labor shortages and less unemployment—or, at least, less excuse for unemployment.

Among the developing, Third World populations, of course, the dramatic success in keeping infants and older people alive will continue for a couple of generations to offset the almost equally dramatic fall in birthrates nearly everywhere. It is these societies that will provide the labor that enables older-style production to grow, and will also furnish most of the refugees and migrants who will clamber over the crumbling walls of the more affluent (because more information-based) societies. But in the postindustrial societies themselves, longevity may give rise to the biggest social problems, and the greatest opportunities, beyond the year 2000.

We are already witness to the lengthening of life through better nutrition, less smoking, vitamins, regular exercise, and the widespread emphasis on "wellness." Add the now familiar medical miracles such as the coronary bypass, kidney dialysis, control of diabetes with insulin, early cancer detection, organ transplants, and prosthetic devices, and subtract, if you will, the rising tide of auto accidents and industrial explosions. The result is a relentless trend of progress against mortality, an accelerating trend that calls into question the assumption that we yet know where the curve of science's battle against death begins to round off and flatten out. And these strengthening defenses against dying at the proverbial threescore and ten or even in one's seventies are bound to produce a changing approach to old age among the elderly themselves. Many people think they have a sort of right to live as long as they want to live and to die when, in their own opinion, their time has come.

James Vaupel, a mathematician and systems analyst who has turned his attention to demography, presents a strong case for assuming a dramatic lengthening of active life in societies that work hard at biological research and genetic engineering. He calls the resulting puzzle "the challenge to Methuselah."

The biological sciences, he argues from a survey of the literature on aging, "may be poised to make major breakthroughs in extending life." He describes the prospect of cellular repair by DNA, and the possibility that, "if the expression and repression of certain genes at certain ages is responsible for aging," then "manipulation of the order of this expression and repression could extend life." He cites research that focuses on the harmful oxygen free radicals formed during natural metabolic processes, which damage cells and may play a part in such disorders as arthritis, immune deficiencies, digestive tract diseases, and aging in general. He quotes Gregory Buckley, professor of surgery at Johns Hopkins University, that "it will not be too surprising if we find that [the role of free radicals] is so central [that its early studies] will assume a level of importance comparable to that of the early studies of DNA."

Life expectancy, Vaupel continues, "might be greatly increased by modifying the immune system, which breaks down with age, rendering people more susceptible to weakening disease." If "scientists are now able to make copies of a gene and then insert the gene into an embryo, giving the new organism traits it did not inherit from its parents," would it be so surprising if the genes responsible for aging attracted the special attention of genetic engineers? He quotes biologist Robert A. Weinberg: "It is likely that major new pharmacological developments will allow the prevention of certain types of atherosclerosis," which would help prevent heart disease, still the number-one killer in the United States. And as for the number-two killer, the National Cancer Institute said in 1984 that its goal was to cut in half the "age-adjusted cancer mortality rate by the year 2000." And "work in neurobiology may lead to the prevention of senility and brain diseases which afflict the elderly."

Continuing progress against mortality would have such dramatic consequences, on the number of elderly and on the very definition of *old,* that it cannot be discounted as much as orthodox actuarial estimates still seem to discount it. Vaupel illustrates the statistical gap by calculating, on varying assumptions, the life expectancy of his own baby daughter, born in March 1984. The official estimate would give her a little more than 78 years to live. If progress against mortality continues at its 1970s rate, she would likely live to be 90. If progress should continue to accelerate as it did between 1950 and 1980, she would live to 94. And if progress in retarding death were to be as much as 2 percent a year (it's been well over 1 percent in recent decades), she would make it past the century mark to 102.

Surprises can affect the future in both directions, of course, the world is oversupplied with nuclear weapons and all manner of biological and chemical dangers, purposeful or accidental. The bowels of the earth and the thin layer of atmosphere that sustains life could backfire on the history of humankind. Huge disasters cannot be planned for. But what we humans do to our environment and to ourselves can be tracked and taken into account in family decisions, business strategies, and public policy decisions.

We may never come close to the tongue-in-cheek scenario with which Jim Vaupel catches our attention: professors tenured for 80 years, Edward Kennedy running for president at 92, a Politburo with members averaging 101. But the distinct possibility of a very large proportion of very old people in the world's knowledge-rich societies should be a planning factor in the strategic management of every enterprise, and every government, that expects to be around for a while.

Public policy about retirement is preoccupied with pensions: take-home pay for not working. There is indeed a problem. By providing a stipend for everyone in the population at a date certain, in a society where there are bound to be more older people and fewer younger people, the government has made sure that fewer and fewer people will be paying the taxes that have to fund more and more people.

How can the young folks afford to keep supporting the old folks? Some communities are already paying for two firefighting teams—the one that responds to fire alarms and the equal number of men who once did and perhaps wish they still could. By the end of the century, many local jurisdictions will have the equivalent of two retired fire departments for each active one.

If we ask how on earth the work economy can afford to support all those people who are officially doing nothing, the answer is bound to be some version of "You can't get there from here." But suppose we were to redefine *work* to include both young and old, each doing what he or she is best at? What if we didn't throw people on the ash heap at a given age, and organized the work to be done in such a way as to enable them to be workers—functional, relevant, engaged, complaining the way other workers do that they never have time to take a long enough vacation?

Viewed from this perspective, the retirement barrier is revealed as a man-made obstruction, a hazard produced not by God but by public policy, a cultural obstacle and not (for most) a physiological landmark. To be sure, the human body gradually wears out, though it is lasting, on the average, longer each year. With less frequency, the mind sometimes deteriorates with age, though I have known deteriorating minds at every age level.

Most physicians naturally spend a disproportionate amount of their time with the elderly and weak; so do pastors, nurses, and paramedical people. So we look to them as experts on aging. But what do they know about the much larger number of elderly and coping, perhaps as many as four out of five people over sixty-five? Most of these are not in the hospital or being comforted by clergy-people or being cared for (and occasionally kicked around) in nursing homes. They are active, they are more or less well, they are at home, and they are available.

After more than a half-century of New Deal philosophy and legislation, the notion of retirement as the end of active life is built deep into our collective politics and our individual psyches. The central idea is expressed in the word *entitlement,* which is frozen into public law and the federal budget as Social Security, medical benefits, veterans' benefits and hospitals, and indexed pensions for military service and public employment. By extension, the same principle has been built into organizational practices and collective bargaining agreements throughout the private sector as well.

The theory is that people deserve a chance to rest after thirty or forty years of work, which defines *work* as something people do when they would really rather do something else. But to provide a safety net for everyone who manages to live to sixty-five discriminates in favor of the already affluent and against those who enjoy their work. It also builds into our society a disincentive for the elderly to work, to remain active and relevant, to "keep up with the world."

Economist John Kenneth Galbraith makes a useful distinction "between those who retire to escape a physically or mentally debilitating effort, and those for whom retirement is an unwelcome divorce from what gives life interest and meaning." The notion of a fixed retirement age for both categories, Galbraith argues, "is barbaric. It selects the old for the denial of lifelong enjoyments."

Some form of money entitlement will doubtless continue to be needed for people who are incapable of adapting in later life to the skills required in a constantly changing labor force, or who are, even if working, still unable responsibly to provide a socially determined level of basic human needs for their families. But there is no reason for passing out drawing rights on federal, state, and local public treasuries to everyone who reaches a particular chronological age, regardless of need or circumstances.

The universal pension system has, to be sure, released an enormous flood of potential energy: men and women who don't need to "work for a living" because their living is provided and they can "do what they want to do." A few corporations and nonprofit agencies have creative programs to place their retirees as volunteers in community activities. For more than two decades the International Executive Service Corps has been placing retired executives overseas, mostly in developing countries, to help with the management of small businesses and development programs. But for the most part, our society assumes it has done its part by paying retirees for not doing what they used to do, leaving the retirees to answer for themselves such questions as "How do I get connected with my community?" "Where can I find a useful function?" and "What am I going to do for adventure?"

The affluent elderly do not need more income, yet are still entitled to the entitlements. The paid-out entitlements, however, are not by themselves enough to keep retirees without other resources in more than genteel poverty. Some sink into checker-playing dependence, but many also hustle other income, often by bartering their services in ways that escape the notice of the Internal Revenue Service. Indeed, the investment of retirement energies is now a rapidly growing part of the large "informal economy" not counted in the GNP, which also includes homemaking, teenagers supplementing their allowances if any, all sorts of counseling activities, and a wide assortment of crimes ranging from the sordid (prostitution, drug pushing) to the socially acceptable (cheating on one's income tax).

A central part of the entitlement idea is that government benefits should *not* be distributed according to need. More than 80 percent of federal entitlements for individuals are paid without a "means test"—that is, without taking account of need. Those payments now account for more than one-third of all federal spending. This pseudoegalitarian philosophy widens the gap between the poor and the rest of us; the payments are not tied to any of our society's wealth-creating functions (savings and investment, goods production, service delivery, knowledge creation and distribution), and the load they require younger people to bear can only grow as the demographic transition multiplies the ratio of retirees to members of the nation's working force.

Will there be jobs to go around if the senior citizens who want to work keep on working? The assumption that there is a fixed amount of "work" to be divided among the "workers" has been a staple of socialist doctrine for more than a century, and curiously still survives in capitalist thinking too, as a relic of the "things" era, the production-based economy. But with information now the dominant resource, the most important factor that limits the expansion of work is not land or raw materials or capital equipment or transportation, but the ultimate components of dynamism: science, technology, values, and social organization—in a word, the human imagination.

There were two main strands of social philosophy in the New Deal. One was the campaign for full employment and the other was a war against poverty. Neither struggle has been won. Somehow, the idea of universal entitlements distorted both of those original purposes. Maybe it's time to get back to basics.

Luckily, in the knowledge society there should be much more room for workaday adventure. As new machines, new kinds of energy, and fast computers take over the drudgery that men and women—and children—used to endure, what is left for people to do is the creative, planning, imagining, figuring-out part of each task. Our more complex, agile, and intuitive human brains have to feed the speedy but stupid computers. And the handling of relationships among people has to be a rapidly growing industry when nearly everyone becomes, through education, a sovereign thinker and communicator, and communications technology makes remoteness and isolation a matter of choice and not of geography or fate.

Now, who is likely to be best qualified for the kind of work that is heavy with personal relations, integrative thinking, and reflective action? Who are the most natural members of the get-it-all-together profession? Who are the people among us with the most experience in solving unprecedented problems, the people most likely to have seen more of the world, mastered or at least dabbled in more specialties, learned to distinguish the candor from the cant in corporate and bureaucratic life and in public affairs, the people with the most time for reflection and the most to reflect about? The answer leaps to the eye: They are, on the average, those who have lived longer.

Our increasingly desperate need for integrators and generalists happens to coincide with technological changes that enable people to work without *going* to work. The home computer will put work, including part-time work, within the reach of all who are willing to retrain their brains and use their imaginations.

Those of us in our sixties and beyond, therefore, will have less and less excuse for advocating a short day in a short week in a short year, and no excuse, short of serious illness or death, for "retirement" in the sense of dropping out of a socially useful working life. The tasks that machines make possible but cannot do themselves should be creative enough to lure older citizens into work schedules that may sometimes be shortened by the limits to elderly energy but may also be lengthened by the sheer excitement of what needs to be done.

In such a society, the people who seek the easy jobs and the earliest retirements will die of the most readily curable human diseases: absence of adventure, suffocation of the spirit, and boredom of the brain. The age at which they succumb to these avoidable maladies will hardly matter—"Died at forty, buried at eighty" will be their epitaph.

I don't know anything from experience about dying, and I don't pretend to know what comes after that. *Something* surely does; it would be plain ridiculous to do all this learning and growing and maturing and then have it lead to oblivion. But I think I know when each of us begins to die. It is when we come to feel that our most fruitful and fulfilling years are already behind us. For the knowledge executive, it's always too early for that.

Afterword

Each year, in each century, the management of conflict and cooperation seems to be somewhere near the center of the human experiment. Not long ago I sat down for a weekend and tried to figure out what I have learned, in four decades, about dissolving disagreements. What came out were fourteen aphorisms from experience. *The New York Times,* noting that the illustrations I used were from *international* experience, made room for thirteen of them ("All the news that fits, we print") under the title "Aphorisms for Diplomats."

I have since tried them out on executives in many settings, and find that they are widely applicable to the human condition—that is, to conflict resolution inside corporate bureaucracies and government bureaus, on university campuses, in troubled communities, and between public and private purposes. You will find these notes about process scattered through the chapters of this book, wherever this learning-on-the-hoof seems to apply. But they are presented here in capsule form, still illustrated mostly from what I have seen and heard in international affairs, and I leave it to you to judge how loudly they speak to your condition in other settings.

1. No conflict, negotiation, settlement, or bargain is merely two-sided. Much of our social life is squeezed into a two-sided frame, so it will fit into a courtroom, a television debate, a football field. But most real-world problems seem to have five or six sides. (For one week at the State Department I counted the active sides of every issue that came across my desk. The average number of sides that week was 5.3, which proves only that you can quantify any intuition if you try.) If you don't get all the sides involved in the solution, they become part of the problem.

2. A third party (it's really a sixth or seventh) **is usually indispensable and often lacking.** Conflict resolution requires some source of independent elucidation of the issues, someone able and willing to do catalytic policy analysis.

3. All real-world problems are interdisciplinary, interprofessional, and international. Policy analysis means combining the rigors of different disciplines, the insights from multiple professions, the workways of multiple cultures. But remember that a committee of narrow thinkers doesn't produce integrative outcomes. The best interdisciplinary instrument is still the individual human mind.

4. Courage is directly proportional to distance from the problem. Near neighbors have too many axes to grind. That is why, in the early 1960s, the UN's best peacekeeping troops in the Congo (now Zaire) came from India, Malaysia, and Scandinavia—far enough away to be uninvolved in African politics. It is also why, in the 1970s, the neighbor Africans had such a hard time bringing themselves to deal with Uganda's Idi Amin. Just as in domestic quarrels, the best counselor is usually not a member of the family.

5. Force by itself is not power. Mere muscle-flexing, as Harvard's Stanley Hoffmann once put it, can make us merely the biggest fly on the flypaper, or, as the Chinese would say, Big Noise on Stairs

Nobody Coming Down. In international politics, energy, money, trade, culture, education, data flows, and democratic values are all relevant forms of power.

Karl Deutsch, the patron saint of modern political science, puts it succinctly: "Prestige is to power as credit is to cash, and physical force is to power as gold is to paper money."

6. Creep up carefully on the use of force. Violence is easy to escalate, hard to de-escalate. It should never be used just to provide a release for the user's frustration. President Kennedy didn't understand this in 1961, when he approved the abortive invasion of Cuba at the Bay of Pigs. He learned fast from experience: Eighteen months later, reacting to the Soviet deployment of offensive missiles in Cuba, the president rejected advice to invade Cuba or bomb the missile sites and instead set up a naval blockade that required the Soviets to consider whether they wanted to start a war. They didn't. If we had started the violence, they wouldn't have had that choice.

7. Widen the community of the concerned. The world is polycentric; problems and their solutions are multilateral. In such a world, unilateral action both looks bad and works badly. The U.S. response in Korea in 1950 looked good and worked tolerably well because it was folded from the start into a United Nations operation. The U.S. response in Vietnam in the 1960s goes down in history as a unilateral failure, even though we actually had more foreign troops associated with us in Vietnam than in Korea.

8. Voting is an inferior means of conflict management; consensus procedure usually works better. Voting takes a snapshot of a disagreement, but doesn't often modify the behavior of the minority, who prefer their own rights to the majority's righteousness. The major breakthroughs in global cooperation (the triumphs in public health, the weather forecasting system, the Outer Space treaties, the Law of the Sea treaty) have been accomplished by consensus procedure.

9. Consensus is not the same as unanimous consent. In the Pacific islands to the west and south of Hawaii, the villagers do not have ready access to *Robert's Rules,* and they do not share our Western enthusiasm for dividing a meeting in two by voting. To plan an important operation, the villagers gather in a circle and the village elder solicits what we moderns would call *input* from all concerned. Gradually, those who are not much concerned about that particular decision edge their way to the perimeter, while those whose oxen might be gored press toward the center of the circle to make themselves felt.

When the talk and the talkers are thoroughly exhausted, the leader suggests a consensus; if he guesses wrong, the talk resumes until those really involved decide to compromise or silently acquiesce. At this point, in the participatory West, we would destroy the consensus by insisting the meeting end with a recorded vote—giving an equal voice to those who care less, dividing a many-sided complexity into a two-sided simplification, freezing the losing minority in its intransigence, molding the future by political arithmetic rather than human relations.

Everybody doesn't have to be in on everything. The world's work gets done by coalitions of the concerned. So consensus means moving by "no objection" procedure: the acquiescence of those who care about the decision, protected by the apathy of those who do not.

10. Openness has costs as well as benefits. In a closed society, openness works as a change agent. In an open society, openness is often a way of saying "no" to innovation. But usually, two heads are better than one, three heads are better than two, and so on for quite a number of heads before the nth addition to the circle of knowledge-based responsibility adds nothing more to wisdom.

11. Process is often the surrogate for substance. People will often clothe their substantive disagreements in procedural raiment: "Have you asked for a legal opinion?" "I didn't get a copy of your paper." "It's time for lunch." A feel for the role of process in arriving at negative or positive action is therefore an essential part of substantive expertise. Policy proponents, or opponents, cannot afford to think that procedure is beneath their notice.

12. Our standards are not universal standards. A viable purpose of American foreign policy is "to make the world safe for diversity" —the words of John F. Kennedy heard round the world, sometimes forgotten in the actions of his successors. That purpose is not served when, in Clarence Darrow's phrase, we judge others by their actions and ourselves by our intentions.

13. Resolving conflict is not always a Good Thing. Some tensions are promising: the global urge for fairness, insistence on human rights, competitive hustling, rising expectations. The problem is not just to keep the peace; it is to keep change peaceful.

14. People can agree on next steps to be taken together if they carefully avoid trying to agree on *why* they are agreeing. We could never have achieved a nuclear-test-ban treaty with the Soviet Union, or the Camp David peace between Egypt and Israel, or global rules about the exchange of weather data and the use of the frequency spectrum if we had tried first to get agreement on ultimate purposes, on ideology. In complex human affairs, don't practice "management by objectives." Try management despite diverse objectives.

Notes

SOME THANK-YOUS

This book has, in a way, been in preparation ever since my earlier book on leadership and management (*The Future Executive*) was published in 1972. Some of the ideas and formulations it contains have seen a print shop before, in articles and published speeches; it isn't plagiarism if you steal from yourself. But writing a book is something very different from stapling together a collection of essays. More than half the words between these covers are new writing, produced during a seven-week blitz in the late summer of 1984 at a cottage in Punalu'u overlooking the surf-covered, lava-rock southern coast of the Big Island of Hawaii. I have not listed here all the ephemeral writings that served as tryouts for some sections of this book, except as they provide fuller explanations to which the unusually diligent reader might want to refer.

My wife, Lois, and I have two special friends on the Big Island. Amiko and Reggie Pell have labored "beyond the call" to create a support system that makes our remote condominium cottage an efficient environment for creative work. There is no way to repay their kindness; the book's dedication is a token of our continuing gratitude. There is also, of course, no way to acknowledge in typeset print Lois's own forbearance; her supportive love has once more seen me through that curious mixture of pain and exhilaration that attends the birth of a full-length book.

Whatever useful insights are distilled in these pages are derived from literally thousands of executives and other generalist leaders with whom I have worked, or whom I have been privileged to watch from a ringside seat, in my forty-five years of working life so far. They are also derived from readings that have become part of my own thinking without my having had the patience to record, or in most cases the memory to retrieve, the original source.

Sometimes I wonder whether there is such a thing as an original source, so often do I discover that some blinding intuition I considered "mine" was better expressed by Aristotle or Lao Tse, or perhaps by others, even longer ago, whose wisdom was not captured by scribes in prescriptural times. But there are wise people in our own time, too; three of them played a special role in the rethinking that led to this book. The person who led me to take so seriously what he called "the changing information environment" was the late John McHale. John W. Gardner has deepened my insights into "leadership" as a serious object of study. And the probing, metaphorical mind of Donald Geesaman has helped me remember, as Einstein is supposed to have said, that "every proposition should be as simple as possible—but not one bit simpler."

I asked several friends to read the whole book in manuscript. The reactions from this "quality circle," a useful mix of encouragement and criticism, resulted in a good deal of rewriting. Their critique was an expression of friendship at its best. This informal editorial board included Stuart Gerry Brown, John Craven, Donald

Geesaman, Royce Hanson, Joseph Jaworski, Magda Cordell McHale, Vivian Jenkins Nelsen, Duane Scribner, Robert Terry, and, for assistance on special topics, Peter Ciborowski, John Firor, Sidney Hyman, Ted Kolderie, Barbara Nelson, Harry B. Price, and Walter Orr Roberts. The chapter on education is partly derived from discussions with James A. Perkins and the late Stephen K. Bailey. An especially valued critic was my son, Alan T. Cleveland, a public executive and urban planner in Fort Worth, Texas; his careful and perceptive reading showed how much more he has learned than I have been able to teach him. Colleagues in several parts of my working life helped me to recall more accurately incidents I have used as illustrations in the text.

One of the joys of life in a university is the chance to work closely with graduate students. Tim Marx and Mary Shallman participated in the earlier phases of an exploration that led me to conclude that thinking hard about "information as a resource" might lead to a new kind of common sense for the management of complexity. Sandra Braman helped in the semifinal editing, and in assembling these Notes.

Book writing is said to be a lonely task, and so it was perhaps when quill pens were the relevant technology. But when a book is produced on a computerized word processor by someone who also has a full-time executive job, his office staff has to be part of the conspiracy. Sally Menefee reconciled my deanship with my writing, screening out the world at crucial moments of creation; Marion Gorman developed the retrieval system for earlier writings; she and Jeanne Shupe, a self-made word-processing whiz, converted my words into electronic symbols the publisher's computer could swallow.

The aspiration that became this book owes much to the enthusiasm and perceptive reactions of Truman Talley, my editor and publisher, and of the late John Cushman, too briefly my literary agent, in New York. But for the finished product I must offer the customary absolution to all of the above. Congratulations may be addressed to the publisher; complaints will be gratefully received by the author as welcome evidence of close reading.

NOTES AND COMMENTS

E. B. White's words on complexity are from the title story in *Quo Vadimus, or the Case for the Bicycle* (New York: Harper & Bros., 1938), page 26. James Thurber's story "The Night the Bed Fell" is in *My Life and Hard Times* (New York: Harper & Bros., 1933).

"'Shut up,' my father explained" is a paraphrase of dialogue by Ring Lardner in *The Young Immigrants,* collected in *The Ring Lardner Reader,* ed. Maxwell Geismar (New York: Charles Scribner's Sons, 1963), page 426.

The paradoxical, and therefore memorable, sentence about fear and negotiation is from President John F. Kennedy's inaugural address, January 20, 1961.

1. THE GET-IT-ALL-TOGETHER PROFESSION

Thomas Jefferson's comment about an "insurrection . . . of science, talents and courage" is from his letter of October 28, 1813, to John Adams (Papers of Thomas Jefferson, Library of Congress).

The magazine I worked for in the 1950s, and for which I did a study of "opinion leaders," was *The Reporter,* a national "fortnightly of facts and ideas" that was published from 1949 to 1968.

My comments to the city managers may be found in full in "A Message for Messiahs," in *Public Administration Review* (January–February 1971).

Woodrow Wilson's description of leadership, and Sidney Hyman's comments on it, are from Professor Hyman's classic study, *The American Presidency* (New York: Harper & Row, 1954).

The thoughts of John W. Gardner scattered throughout this book were expressed in his lecture to the University of Minnesota's Hubert H. Humphrey Institute of Public Affairs on October 29, 1980, and in other writings collected in *Leadership: A Sampler of the Wisdom of John Gardner* (Minneapolis: University of Minnesota, Hubert H. Humphrey Institute, 1981).

I am indebted to Joseph E. Slater, president of the Aspen Institute for Humanistic Studies, for passing along Isaac Stern's wise comment about "the intervals between the notes."

Charles Olson's advice comes from *A Bibliography on America for Ed Dorn* (San Francisco: Four Seasons Foundation, 1964). Olson, considered by some to be the most important American poet of the twentieth century, has been influential in cutting a path through the bushes for other American (and European) poets and prose writers.

The English translation of Liu Shao's work was reprinted in 1966 by the Kraus Reprint Company of New York under the title *The Study of Human Abilities.* It is the oldest known book in the field that used to be called personnel administration, transmuted now to *human services management.*

Alfred North Whitehead's description of the structure of ideas comes from *The Aims of Education* (New York: The Macmillan Company, 1929).

Jean Monnet's *Memoirs* can be found in English with an introduction by George W. Ball (New York: Doubleday, 1978).

The best biography of Hubert Humphrey so far is Carl Solberg's *Hubert Humphrey: A Biography* (New York: W.W. Norton, 1984). Jim Callaghan's comment on Humphrey is from *The Political Leader* (Minneapolis: University of Minnesota, Hubert H. Humphrey Institute of Public Affairs, 1982).

Barbara Ward's feel for the present as the "hinge of history" is expressed in her draft version of what appeared in printed form, co-authored by René Dubos, as *Only One Earth* (New York: W. W. Norton, 1972), page 12.

The Peter Drucker quote regarding the commonweal is from *Managing in Turbulent Times* (New York: Harper & Row, 1980), page 208. John Gardner's "The War of the Parts Against the Whole" is included in *Leadership.* The "first birds off the wire" metaphor is also his.

2. THE KNOWLEDGE DYNAMIC

Daniel Bell introduced the concept of the postindustrial society in his book *The Coming of Post-Industrial Society* (New York: Basic Books, 1973). The note he struck has resonated into a chord that now includes postmodern society, postliterate society, post–New Deal social policy, post-Keynesian economics, and other efforts to describe the present by mentioning what went before.

The possibly apocryphal story about Martin Luther and the pope was passed to historian Sidney Hyman, on a Christmas Eve decorated by falling bombs in Italy during World War II, by now Professor Emeritus and Pulitzer Prize–winner Richard Warrington Baldwin Lewis of Yale University.

Among the most important contributors to the development of the concept of information as a resource are Harold Innis, *The Bias of Communication* (Toronto: University of Toronto Press, 1951); Peter F. Drucker, *The Age of Discontinuity* (New York: Harper & Row, 1968); Kenneth Arrow, *Information and Economic Behavior* (Stockholm: Federation of Swedish Industries, 1973); John McHale, *The Changing Information Environment* (U.K.: 1972; Boulder, Colo.: Westview Press, 1975); Hans Peter Gassmann, ed., *Information, Computer and Communications Policies for the 80s* (Amsterdam: North Holland, 1981); Herbert Schiller, *Who Knows: Information in the Age of the Fortune 500* (Norwood, N.J.: Ablex, 1981); Joan Edelman Spero, "Information: The Policy Void," *Foreign Policy* (Autumn 1982): 139–56; *Information, Economics and Power,* ed. Rita Cruise O'Brien (London: Hodder & Stoughton, 1983); and Colin Cherry, *A Second Industrial Revolution?,* to be published in 1985. It is evident from this list that the idea arose almost independently in the fields of economics, sociology, communications, management science, and political science. See also Harlan Cleveland, "Information as a Resource," *The Futurist* (December 1982), and "King Canute and the Information Resource," *Technology Review* (January 1984).

The reluctance to acknowledge that information is a critical resource, in *The Limits to Growth,* maintained the traditional economic view of resources as physical goods only, excluding services and information. This first report to the Club of Rome, which sold more than 3 million copies in many languages, is available in book form as *The Limits to Growth,* by Donella H. Meadows, et al. (New York: Universe Books, 1972).

T. S. Eliot explores the nature of knowledge at length in his poem "The Rock." See *The Waste Land and Other Poems* (New York: Harcourt, Brace & World, 1955), page 81. This piece has stimulated many of those who are trying to relate new ideas about information to traditional concepts of knowledge. See, for example, Henryk Skolimowski's piece "Freedom, Responsibility and the Information Society: A Time of Philosopher-Kings Is Coming," *Vital Speeches of the Day* 50, no. 16 (June 1, 1984): 493–97.

The metaphor of data as ore and information as the product of the refiner's fire originates with Professor John Craven at the University of Hawaii.

Yi-fu Tuan discussed the information/knowledge/wisdom hierarchy in a personal communication with the author.

The classic work of Claude E. Shannon and Warren Weaver, *The Mathematical Theory of Communication* (Urbana: University of Illinois Press, 1949), is fundamental to current work in information science.

Klaus Krippendorff's paper, presented in San Francisco to the 1984 International Communication Association Conference on Communication in Transition, May 24–28, 1984, was titled "Information, Information Society and Some Marxian Propositions."

Kenneth Boulding explores the question of the nature of knowledge and its relationship to economics in "The Economics of Knowledge and the Knowledge of Economics," *American Economic Review* (May 1966): 1–13; this work falls within a context he spelled out in *Ecodynamics: A New Theory of Societal Evolution* (Beverly Hills: Sage, 1978). The quote included here is from page 122 of that book. His notion of the *noösphere* is derived from Pierre Teilhard de Chardin's *The Phenomenon of Man* (New York: Harper & Bros., 1959).

Lewis Branscomb's article "Information: The Ultimate Frontier," *Science* (January 12, 1979): 143–47, tries to predict what will happen to information technology in the next hundred years.

In his book manuscript titled *A Second Industrial Revolution?* Colin Cherry explained the "sharing" nature of messages, while making clear that *meaning* is not necessarily or even usually shared. The discussion here is based on that manuscript and on talks with Professor Cherry about his draft in Aspen, Colorado, in the summer of 1979.

The expression "the informatization of society" was used by Simon Nora and Alain Minc in their influential examination of the impacts of the new communication and computer technologies, *L'Informatisation de la Société*. Originally produced as a commissioned report by two civil servants to President Giscard d'Estaing, it quickly became a best-seller in France and influenced the thinking of Giscard's successor, President François Mitterand. The book was eventually translated into English as *The Computerization of Society* (Cambridge: The MIT Press, 1981), with an introduction by Daniel Bell. The English version of the title misses the point that Nora and Minc were making in their book, which is that the marriage of computer *and* telecommunication technologies is the new dimension of society.

The statistics on the redistribution, between 1880 and 2000, of the U.S. work force were culled from the research of G. Molitor, Public Policy Forecasting, Inc., by Henry M. Boettinger, who headed AT&T's corporate planning before he joined E. F. Hutton as head of its Office of Information Strategy and Technology. "Information Industry Challenges to Management and Economics," *New Jersey Bell Journal* 7, no. 1 (Spring 1984): 12–21. Mr. Boettinger's own comment on the trend toward information work is worth repeating: "With these statistics in mind, we can hold up politicians as examples of leaders who cling to fast-fading but once pervasive realities. Politicians who make their major appeal to once all-powerful farming and manufacturing interests, either out of nostalgia or ignorance, ultimately will find success elusive. In Scotland, for example, there are three times as many workers in Silicon Glen electronics firms as there are in shipbuilding and mining. Yet out-of-date politicians eagerly leap for headlines in disputes affecting those crumbling fortresses of the Industrial Revolution and little is heard from them of the new activity that is establishing the region's economic future. Cries of 'not one more pit will close' or 'we will restore our world leadership in shipbuilding' only add to waste and, more seriously, to disappointment." I don't know why he singles out politicians for special mention here. A similar mind-set can be observed in executive suites, trade union offices, government departments, legislative committees, and university faculties—and not only in Scotland.

The growing awareness of information or knowledge as the dominant resource in the U.S. economy owes much to the early work of Daniel Bell (see, for example, *The Coming of Post-Industrial Society* and "The Social Framework of the Information Society," in Tom Forester, ed., *The Microelectronics Revolution* [Oxford: Basil Blackwell, 1980], pages 500–70) and Fritz Machlup (summed up in *Knowledge: Its Creation, Distribution, and Economic Significance, Volume 1: Knowledge and Knowledge Production* [Princeton, N.J.: Princeton University Press, 1980]).

The methodology widely used in the 1970s and early 1980s for comparing an "information sector" to other sectors of an economy is traceable to the durable Ph.D. thesis of Marc Porat, *The Information Economy* (Ann Arbor, Mich.: University Microfilms, 1976).

Porat defined information as "that bundle of activities that produce, process, and distribute symbols as opposed to things" (pp. 2–3). To measure the significance of information on the U.S. Gross National Product in 1967 Porat distinguished between "primary" and "secondary" information sectors. The primary sector consisted of economic activity that produces information machines, sells information services, or sells information directly, such as advertising, education, and accounting. This primary information sector accounted for 25.1 percent of GNP in 1967. The "secondary" sector, information work that contributes to the production of things, accounted for 21.1 percent of 1967's GNP. So the total information component of GNP in 1967 was 46.2 percent.

Also in 1967, 46 percent of the U.S. labor force were information workers. These workers accounted for 53 percent of total employee compensation. The discrepancy between the 46 percent and the 53 percent is explained by the fact that information workers, on the average, make more money than noninformation workers.

Categorizing information workers as all of those "primarily involved with information work" (which he admitted involved some arbitrary categorization), Porat projected that information workers would constitute 51.3 percent of the labor force by 1980. He estimated that the growth in the information sector work would taper off. But the burgeoning opportunities in the information sector, brought about by recent advances in technology (especially the pervasive application of microprocessors and their combination with electronic telecommunications in systems throughout the economy), seem likely to cause the information sector to grow, as Molitor's figures suggest, to as much as two-thirds of the labor force in the most "advanced" economies.

University of Minnesota economist Vernon Ruttan adds a cautionary note: "It has been conventional, or perhaps merely convenient, to assume that the impact of new knowledge or new information is subject to constant or increasing rather than decreasing returns. But as the knowledge sector expands relative to the total economy may we not face diminishing returns to advance in knowledge or information? While I am still willing to assume that we are still in the increasing returns stage, the question deserves serious consideration."

The OECD report *Information Activities, Electronics and Telecommunications Technologies: Impact on Employment, Growth and Trade* (Paris: OECD, 1981) was one of a series of reports OECD has conducted as it tries to trace the impact of the information age on, and its implications for, member countries.

Philosopher of human management Peter Drucker was already discussing knowledge as capital in the 1960s: *The Age of Discontinuity: Guidelines to Our Changing Society* (New York: Harper & Row, 1969), see for example page 264.

G. Edward Schuh's comments were made in a personal communication to the author.

The Nora and Minc judgment about the obsolescence of both

"liberal and Marxist approaches" is found in *The Computerization of Society,* page 133.

According to the *Statistical Abstract of the US* (Washington, D.C.: Bureau of the Census, 1984), page 440, there are currently 22,811,000 members of major trade unions in the United States. Membership in the older "smokestack industries" has been declining but membership in public employee and other service-oriented unions has grown. Overall, the labor movement remains a powerful element of American society.

John McHale's book *The Changing Information Environment* covers the changes in communications, resource use, education, business and management, and political process that derive from the impact of information upon society.

Anne Branscomb's characterization of information as "a synergistic resource" is from a personal communication to the author.

Gary Hart emphasized the importance of the labor force in an information society in "Investing in People for the Information Age," *The Futurist* (February 1983): 10–14.

Dieter Altenpohl discussed the role of materials development and their social, economic, and ecological impacts (thus illuminating the role information plays in materials substitution) in his book *Materials in World Perspective* (Heidelberg, GFR: Springer-Verlag, 1980). His chart relating the weight of materials to their degree of sophistication can be found on page 201.

The erosion of hierarchies as a consequence of the informatization of society was the theme of a paper I prepared for a National Academy of Engineering symposium on information technology held in Washington, D.C., in September 1984 and an international workshop on Pacific Communications in Singapore in December 1984. The paper was published as "The Twilight of Hierarchy," *Public Administration Review* (January–February 1985). Most of the material for that writing was taken from an early draft of this book.

3. CONTROL: THE TWILIGHT OF HIERARCHY

Magnus Magnusson in *The Vikings* (London: Bodley Head, 1980) explains what King Canute (Knut) thought he was doing when he commanded the tides to stand still.

Chester Barnard's theory of executive process is spelled out in *The Functions of the Executive* (Cambridge: Harvard University Press, 1938).

The environment being described here seems a natural outgrowth of the observations and forecasts in an earlier book of mine, *The Future Executive: Guide for Tomorrow's Managers.* The trends then projected have been accelerated by the informatization of society, but the *direction* of change seems still to be from more vertical to more horizontal modes of getting things done.

Apropos Alexander Haig's "I am in control here": Although Haig in his memoir (*CAVEAT: Realism, Reagan and Foreign Policy* [New York: The Macmillan Company, 1984]) does not defend his choice of words, he discredits the television press with editing and editorializing to make the comment look worse than its intent. Ted Koppel of ABC, he says, spread the word that Haig had gotten the presidential succession wrong. But Haig wasn't making a declaration on presidential succession. The secretary of state knew perfectly well that he was the fifth, not third, in line; that's the sort of information a presidential appointee is not likely to forget. Within the executive branch, for the management of a crisis, Haig had it right: With the president incapacitated and the vice-president away from Washington, the secretary of state was the senior officer present.

CBS's editing also contributed to Haig's trouble—on purpose, he told me. Haig had said that he was "in control . . . pending the return of the vice-president." On Dan Rather's evening newscast, Haig says, the softening latter part of the sentence was snipped off.

With openness, policy widens out to become something like what Paul Appleby, that farseeing philosopher of public administration, called it a generation ago: "Policy," he said, "is the decisions that are made at your level and higher" (*Policy and Administration* [Tuscaloosa: University of Alabama Press, 1949], p. 21). But note that the vertical process implied by Appleby's definition is already obsolescent.

Russell Baker's column, "The Ship of Followers," appeared in *The New York Times* (November 13, 1979), page A23.

Walter Lippmann's extreme expression of cynicism about the notion that the people govern is found in *The Phantom Public* (New York: Harcourt, Brace & Co., 1925), pp. 61–62.

The comments on Moses were provided in personal communication with Professor Sidney Hyman of the University of Illinois, an adjunct faculty member of the University of Minnesota's Hubert H. Humphrey Institute of Public Affairs. The biblical citations are Exodus 32:15–19 and 34:1–4. Moses also learned the hard way about delegation of authority: He tried at first to give all the orders and settle all the disputes himself. His father-in-law, Jethro, told Moses that he was "wearing out yourself and the people as well," and persuaded him to find some able and honest men "and appoint them leaders of thousands, of hundreds, of fifties and of tens." After that things evidently worked better, and Moses certainly stayed healthy: When he died at age 120, "his eye was not dimmed, nor was his vigour abated" (Exod. 18:17–26, Deut. 34:7).

Mao Tse-tung would not be overjoyed at the recent turn of events in China, where the contents of his book *The Thoughts of Chairman Mao* (London: Gibbs, 1969) are no longer treated with biblical respect.

Chester Barnard's comments about the importance of interaction between leaders and followers are found in *The Functions of the Executive,* page 180.

The Minneapolis-based INFACT organization accumulated information to demonstrate that Nestlé's infant formula destroyed more Third World infants' lives than it helped. Because the formula must be mixed with whatever water is available to be usable, infants are exposed to pathogens from which they would be protected were they drinking their mother's milk. INFACT then brought this information to international attention and through political action such as lobbying and boycotts eventually forced Nestlé to sign a commitment that Third World marketing of this product would be stopped.

4. SECRECY: COSTS AND BENEFITS OF OPENNESS

Stuart Gerry Brown and I turned our paper for the Senate Watergate Committee into an article, "The Limits of Obsession: Fencing in the 'National Security' Claim," which was published in the Bicentennial issue of *Administrative Law Review* (Summer 1976): 327–46.

A chief executive's-eye view of events at the University of Hawaii during its period of campus turbulence in 1969 and 1970 was presented in my "Campus Dissent and Disruption," *The Honolulu Advertiser* (November 19, 20, and 21, 1970).

The discussion of sunshine laws here is based on a commissioned study, "The Costs and Benefits of Openness: Sunshine Laws and Higher Education," published by the Association of Governing Boards, Washington, D.C., in April 1985. This study developed a fifty-state spectrum of comparative openness and analyzed the impact of openness on the governance of higher education in the United States. The field research was done by Sandra Braman, but the responsibility for its interpretation is mine.

Thomas Jefferson believed so strongly that a democratic republic would not survive unless its people were thoroughly informed that, if given a choice between a government without a newspaper or a newspaper without a government, he said he would prefer the latter. After his presidency Jefferson worked mostly on the diffusion of knowledge; his resulting philosophy became the basis for the University of Virginia.

The purpose clause of California's Bagley-Keene Open Meeting Law can be found in Article 9 of the California Government Code, Section 11120.

Charles Lindblom's book *The Intelligence of Democracy* (New York: Free Press, 1965) introduced the concept of *mutual adjustment* in the management of both public and private organizations and institutions. He updated his thoughts in a lecture at the University of Minnesota's Center for Strategic Management Research, "Incremental Strategy: Still Muddling Through," on May 13, 1983.

The French government has placed such a high priority on the development of telecommunications for France that it is planning eventually to put a very large public investment into wiring the entire country for broad-band digitized information transmission, and ensuring that the entire citizenry will have the hardware and software needed to access the system. At the end of 1984, however, the experiment was operational in only two communities.

The results of the National Institute of Education study of tenure were discussed in "Learn to Weed Out Bad Teachers, Study Tells Schools," *The Sunday Star-Bulletin and Advertiser* (Honolulu) (August 12, 1984), page A13.

The comments and quote from David Riesman in this section come from my extensive correspondence with him in 1983–84 on the subject of openness in university governance.

The Fourth Judicial District Court, Hennepin County, State of Minnesota, issued its order #84-9639 on June 25, 1984, demanding that the Regents of the University of Minnesota file with the court statements narrating their recall of the meetings they held with the consultant on the ten-year evaluation of President C. Peter Magrath of the University of Minnesota.

5. OWNERSHIP: KNOWLEDGE AS A SHARED RESOURCE

Colin Cherry discussed the importance of *sharing* to our understanding of information in his book *On Human Communication,* which was first published in 1957 and by 1977 had reached its third edition (Cambridge: The MIT Press). Cherry further explored these concepts in "On the Political Nature of World Telecommunication," presented to the International Telecommunications Union at its Telecommunications Forum, October 5, 1975, in Geneva; and in "Communication: Some Contradictions, Dilemmas and Dangers," in *Proceedings of the Conference on Cost Conscious Communications,* Institute of Administrative Management, Beckenham, Kent, U.K., November 24, 1975. The quotation, however, is from his unfinished manuscript, *A Second Industrial Revolution?,* referred to above.

The settlement between the Association of American Publishers and New York University over the issue of copyright infringement by professors who distributed multiple copies of photocopied works to their students is described in "Settle Between NYU and AAP," *The New York Times* (April 15, 1983), sec. 2, page 4. Columbia Broadcasting System's suit against Vanderbilt University, which was distributing videotapes of CBS News for study by journalism students, is described in "They Think They Can 'Own' History," *LA Daily Journal* (November 29, 1983), page 4.

John Cirace explored the consequences of attempting to distinguish fair use from unfair use when copying copyrighted material, in "When Does Complete Copy of Copyrighted Works for Purposes Other than Profit Constitute Fair Use?" 28 *St. Louis University Law Journal* (June 1984): 647–82. As examples, Cirace discusses *Universal City Studios* v. *Sony Corporation of America,* 104 A. Ct. 774 (1984), as well as the earlier case of *Williams & Wilkins Co.* v. *US,* 530 UD 376 (1975).

The courts are not, of course, the only policy-making bodies that are tied to obsolete, technologically defined categories by which to understand the communication process. Quasi-judicial bodies such as the Federal Communications Commission and state public utilities commissions also find their attempts to regulate the new technologies tripping over outdated distinctions among print, broadcast, and common carrier means of information transport, as do Congress, scholars, and almost everyone else.

The blurring of categories (between public and private or, in Chapter 7, between domestic and international) is a characteristic of contemporary life not limited to the social sphere. Anthropologist Clifford Geertz widens our perspective: "This genre blurring is more than just a matter of Harry Houdini or Richard Nixon turning up as characters in novels or of midwestern murder sprees described as though a gothic romancer had imagined them. It is philosophical inquiries looking like literary criticism (think of Stanley Cavell on Beckett or Thoreau, Sartre on Flaubert), scientific discussion looking like belles lettres *morceaux* (Lewis Thomas, Loren Eiseley), baroque fantasies presented as deadpan empirical observations (Borges, Barthelme), histories that consist of equations and tables or law-court testimony (Fogel and Engerman, Le Roi Ladurie), documentaries that read like true confessions (Mailer), parables posing as ethnographies (Castaneda), theoretical treatises set out as travelogues (Lévi-Strauss), ideological arguments cast as historical inquiries (Edward Said), methodological polemics got up as personal memoirs (James Watson). Nabokov's *Pale Fire,* that impossible object made of poetry and fiction, footnotes and images from the clinic, seems very much of the time; one waits only for quantum theory in verse or biography in algebra." Clifford Geertz, "Blurred Genres: The Refiguration of Social Thought," *American Scholar* (Spring 1980): 165–66.

Ted Kolderie's ideas in "Many Providers, Many Producers: A New View of the Public Service Industry" (Minneapolis: University of Minnesota, Hubert H. Humphrey Institute of Public Affairs, 1982) have served as the stimulus for dozens of explorations into just how private institutions could take responsibility for what have previously been defined as public functions.

The comments on the role of nongovernments are taken from an earlier analysis in Harlan Cleveland and Thomas W. Wilson, Jr., *Humangrowth: An Essay on Growth, Values, and the Quality of Life* (New York: Aspen Institute for Humanistic Studies, 1978), page 39.

The extraterritoriality issue—the attempt by one nation to extend its legal sanctions to the territory of another nation—has been heated to the boiling point by U.S. policy. It has conveyed to U.S. customers that the movement of IBM equipment requires U.S. State Department approval not just to move a mainframe computer from one city to another but also to move an IBM PC Jr. from one office to the room next door. Some British reaction to this move can be judged from "IBM's Role in Europe," *Financial Times* (January 19, 1984). For a summary of the defense arguments offered to support such actions, see "Computer Exporters Play War Games with America's Generals," *The Economist* (February 25, 1984): 61.

6. PRIVILEGE: THE FAIRNESS REVOLUTION

The notion of differing "up" and "down" perspectives on the need to ensure greater fairness within a society is based on work by Robert W. Terry, Senior Fellow at the University of Minnesota's Hubert H. Humphrey Institute of Public Affairs.

Quantitative differences in earning between men and women can be found in Earl F. Mellor's article "Investigating the Differences in Weekly Earnings of Men and Women," *Monthly Labor Review* (June 1984). Several recent governmental publications also provide details of the progress women have made in employment and in education, including *American Women: Three Decades of Change* (Bureau of the Census), *Children of Working Mothers* and *Women at Work: A Chartbook* (Bureau of Labor Statistics), *Work and Women in the 1980's* (Congressional Caucus for Women's Issues), and *A Growing Crisis: Disadvantaged Women and Their Children* (U.S. Commission on Civil Rights).

Some of the information about higher education for the black minority is drawn from Richard F. Koubek, "The State of Black America," which was published by *Newsweek* magazine's Education Department in 1984. Bayard Rustin's comments quoted therein come from his article "Civil Rights: 20 Years Later," *Newsweek* (August 29, 1983).

The comparative figures on college graduates and doctoral degrees come from an editorial by Clifton R. Wharton, Jr., "The Minority Student Challenge," *Science* (June 1984), which discussed a National Research Council survey, and from a keynote address by Chancellor Wharton delivered to the Albany National Association for the Advancement of Colored People in Albany, New York, on May 20, 1984, titled "30 Years After Topeka: Education and the Right to Aspire," from which the direct quotation is drawn.

Many commentators have noted the critical role that new information media, primarily the photocopy machine and cassette tapes, played in making the Iranian revolution possible—a particularly clear example of a case where changes in the use of information brought about a shift in the power structure.

The effects of the new information environment on relationships between developing and developed nations are analyzed in *Information, Economics and Power: The North-South Dimension,* ed. Rita Cruise O'Brien (London: Hodder & Stoughton, 1983).

Ivan Illich argued that computers are doing to communication what fences did to pastures in "Silence Is a Commons," *The CoEvolution Quarterly* (Winter 1983): 5–9.

7. GEOPOLITICS: THE PASSING OF REMOTENESS

For a fuller discussion of the Founding Fathers' understanding of their international interdependence 200 years ago, see Harlan Cleveland, *The Third Try at World Order: U.S. Policy for an Interdependent World* (New York: Aspen Institute for Humanistic Studies, 1977), pages 19–23. That passage was based on the work of Ralph Ketcham, professor of history at the Maxwell Graduate School of Citizenship and Public Affairs, Syracuse University.

The increasingly ubiquitous refugee problem is thoroughly documented in *Staff Report of the Select Commission on Immigration and Refugee Policy* (University Publications of America, 1983).

The quotation by the French journalist-philosopher Raymond Aron is from his background paper "Thirty Years After—Two Centuries Later," prepared for a Berlin Conference on "The Future of European-U.S. Relations" in November 1975. The paper is published in *Report from Aspen Institute Berlin* (Berlin: Aspen Institute for Humanistic Studies, 1976), pages 31–46.

Admiral Noel Gayler has frequently spoken out on the unusability of nuclear weapons since leaving his post as commander-in-chief of the U.S. Pacific Theater (CINCPAC). Robert McNamara voiced similar sentiments at an Aspen Institute arms-control seminar in 1982, adding that under no conceivable circumstances would either of the presidents (John F. Kennedy and Lyndon B. Johnson) he served as secretary of defense have given the order to fire a nuclear missile first. See also John M. Lee (Vice Admiral, U.S.N., retired), *The Use of Nuclear Weapons* (Minneapolis: University of Minnesota, Hubert H. Humphrey Institute of Public Affairs, 1984).

Comparative figures on defense spending are tracked from year to year in the annual reports by Ruth L. Sivard, *World Military and Social Expenditures* (Leesburg, Va.: WMSE Publications). Contemporary wars are tracked by Admiral Gene LaRocque's Center for

Defense Information in Washington, D.C., and, as compiled, the information is released through the center's newsletter, *The Defense Monitor*.

In characterizing the Soviet Union's poor economic performance, I have used the formulation of Teng Hsaio-ping, China's deputy premier, whose caustic criticism of the leading "centrally planned economy" is recorded in my *China Diary* (Washington, D.C.: Center for Strategic and International Studies, Georgetown University, 1976), the log of a 1975 visit to the People's Republic of China.

The world population figures are from the United Nations Fund for Population Activities. The quote from the World Food Council was taken from *World Development Forum* 2, no. 16 (September 15, 1984).

The interactions of transnational science and national politics are discussed in *Regimes for the Ocean, Outer Space, and Weather* by Seyom Brown, et al. (Washington, D.C.: Brookings Institution, 1977). International problems that have arisen from the technological breakthrough of remote sensing from space were discussed in depth in *Remote Sensing from Space: Prospects for Developing Countries,* a report by the Ad Hoc Committee on Remote Sensing for Development of the National Resource Council (Washington, D.C.: National Academy of Sciences, 1977).

The text of Henry Steele Commager's "Declaration of Interdependence" and Philadelphia's Bicentennial project based on it are part of the story told in *The Third Try at World Order.*

The blurred line between *domestic* and *international* is discussed in detail in "The Internationalization of Domestic Affairs," my contribution to the volume on "The Human Dimension of Foreign Policy: An American Perspective," *The Annals of the American Academy of Political and Social Science* (March 1979).

The Adam Yarmolinsky quote is from his *Organizing for Interdependence: The Role of Government* (Princeton, N.J.: Aspen Institute for Humanistic Studies, 1976), p. 6.

8. THE SOCIAL FALLOUT OF KNOWLEDGE

9. A HARNESS FOR TECHNOLOGY

The argument in these two chapters draws on a paper I prepared for a seminar in the Office of Technology Assessment in 1979, subsequently edited and published as "The Worm Has Turned: Reflections on the Social Assessment of Technology," *New Jersey Bell Journal* 3, no. 1 (Spring 1980): 1–10.

Walt Kelly's "enemy is us" philosophy can be found in *Impollutable Pogo* (New York: Simon & Schuster, 1970), page 128.

The discussion of comparative "dynamism," among nations across the centuries, is based on the joint work of Dr. Ibrahim H. Abdel Rahman and myself, written as the concept paper for the United Nations Conference on Science and Technology for Development, held in Vienna in 1979. The paper was published as UN Document A/Conf. 81/5 Add 1/. An edited but quite full version of that paper was published under the title "Dynamism and Development" in *World Development* 8, no. 4 (April 1980): 275–90. It also appeared in a book of selected conference papers titled *Social Innovations for Development,* ed. C. G. Heden and Alexander King, International Federation of Institutes for Advanced Study (IFIAS), Paris (Oxford: Pergamon Press, Ltd., 1984), pages 129–50. Dr. Abdel Rahman is a former minister of planning in the government of Egypt, and was the founding Executive Director of the UN Industrial Development Organization (UNIDO), with headquarters in Vienna.

The Seabees' slogan is often diluted as "The difficult we do at once; the impossible takes a little longer." But I am assured by an officer of one of the Navy's World War II construction battalions that the unexpurgated version is the one that appears in the text.

The comments on the U.S. Navy's Polaris program are based on discussions with Dr. John Craven, former chief scientist of that project, author of *Ocean Engineering Systems* (comp. and ed. T. Gray Curtis [Cambridge: The MIT Press, 1971]), and director of the International Law of the Sea Institute based at the University of Hawaii.

My recollections of the development of the World Weather

Watch have been checked for technical accuracy and content with several of the key participants, including Dr. Robert M. White, then chief of the U.S. Weather Bureau and now president of the National Academy of Engineering. I should in honesty report that Dr. White does not recall the luncheon conversation as such, which only shows that on that occasion I was learning more from him than he was from me. But he confirms the attitudes we developed during that creative moment in the development of science policy; and he helped me get the chronology straight.

A comprehensive assessment of up-to-date findings about the greenhouse effect may be found in "The Greenhouse Problem from the Perspective of Risk and Public Policy," in Peter Ciborowski and Dean Abrahamson, eds., *Greenhouse Climate Change: Policy Alternatives,* Proceedings of the Symposium on Policy Responses to the Greenhouse Problem (Minneapolis: Center for Urban and Regional Affairs, 1985). The remarkable tonnage of the world's termite population comes from research at the National Center for Atmospheric Research.

I am indebted to Professor Richard Caldecott, former dean of the University of Minnesota's College of Biological Sciences, and Dr. N. L. Gault, former dean of that university's Medical School, for helpful insights on the social fallout of genetic engineering and biomedical science. Especially helpful also was the rapporteur's report by Martin Klein on "Critical Questions in Genetic Medicine" (New York: Aspen Institute for Humanistic Studies, 1982).

During the writing of this book, I was also conducting by computer teleconference a seminar on leadership with business and public executives around the country. One of them was former Apollo astronaut Rusty Schweickart, as Energy Commissioner for the state of California I sent him an electronic message asking whether it was true that NASA did sperm counts on him and his fellow astronauts. His irreverent reply, quoted with permission: "I vaguely recall something about sampling sperm on some of the lunar missions. . . . The general rule seemed to be, 'if it's there, poke it, probe it, stick something into it or up it,' whichever applied. It appeared that what got done was whatever we let happen since almost anything was fair game. My recollection is that the sperm count didn't make it past the rebellion test. . . . "

My comment about "a widespread ethic of prudence" is an abbreviated version of a picture I tried to draw in the 1970s of the "sevenfold limits" that seemed to constitute an emerging "ethic of ecology," the maturing stage of the environmental movement in the industrial world. The fuller argument may be found in *The Third Try at World Order*, pages 25–31.

The pioneering work of John and Magda McHale, which called early attention to the prospect that affluent societies would *not* be more and more resource-hungry, is reflected in many writings. The basic text is John McHale, *The Changing Information Environment.*

Ralf Dahrendorf discusses the consequences of the development of industrial society in his book *Class and Class Conflict in Industrial Society* (Stanford, Calif.: Stanford University Press, 1958).

10. THE GENERALIST MIND-SET

One chapter, "A Style for Complexity," of my book *The Future Executive* explores in some detail the elements of management style for the generalist executive who lives with complexity and ambiguity.

The Carnegie study on the careers of Americans who have gone abroad was published as *The Overseas Americans* (New York: McGraw-Hill, 1960). My co-authors were Gerard J. Mangone and John Clarke Adams.

The revealing comments of novelist Ray Bradbury are from his article "Management from Within," *New Management* 1, no. 4 (September–December 1984).

Warren Bennis's comments in this chapter come from his lecture, "The Making of a Superleader," delivered on September 7, 1983, at the Spring Hill Center in Wayzata, Minnesota.

The boast of the retiring British researcher comes from Thomas P. Hughes, once head of Research and Intelligence for the U.S. State Department and now president of the Carnegie Endowment for International Peace in Washington, D.C.

The First Global Conference on the Future was held in

stantially Increase Life Expectancy" (Laxenburg, Austria: IIASA, December 12, 1984).

John Kenneth Galbraith's speculations on nonretirement are from an article in the anniversary issue of *Modern Maturity* (April 1984). The magazine is published by the American Association of Retired Persons.

A very full treatment of the issues involved in employment of the elderly is contained in *Developments in Aging: 1983 Volume 1*, Report of the U.S. Senate's Special Committee on Aging (Washington, D.C.: U.S. Government Printing Office, 1984), especially Chapter 6, "Employment," pages 268–93. This Senate report sums up the basic dilemma in one sentence: "Older workers are caught between the traditional employment and retirement policies of the previous two decades urging them to get out of the work force early, and the economic insecurities and desire to stay productive driving them to continue working."

AFTERWORD

Karl Deutsch's succinct analysis of power and its relationship to communications is from his classic *Nerves of Government* (New York: Free Press, 1966), page 124.

Index

251

HARLAN CLEVELAND, political scientist and public executive, is dean of the University of Minnesota's Hubert H. Humphrey Institute of Public Affairs, and professor of public affairs and planning.

A Princeton University graduate, he was a Rhodes Scholar at Oxford University in the late 1930s; an economic warfare specialist (in Washington, D.C.) and United Nations relief administrator (in Italy and China) in the 1940s; a foreign aid manager (the Marshall Plan), magazine editor and publisher (*The Reporter*), and graduate school dean (The Maxwell School of Citizenship and Public Affairs at Syracuse University) in the 1950s. He was a New York delegate to the 1960 Democratic National Convention.

During the 1960s Harlan Cleveland served as assistant secretary of state for international organization affairs in the administration of President John F. Kennedy, and as U.S. ambassador to NATO under President Lyndon B. Johnson. From 1969 to 1974 he was the president of the University of Hawaii. From 1974 to 1980 he was director of the Program in International Affairs of the Aspen Institute for Humanistic Studies, with headquarters in Princeton, New Jersey. During 1977–78 he was also chairman of the U.S. Weather Modification Advisory Board, and in 1979 he was appointed for one semester as the Distinguished Visiting Tom Slick Professor of World Peace at the Lyndon B. Johnson School of Public Affairs, University of Texas at Austin. In 1980 he was appointed to his present position at the University of Minnesota.

Mr. Cleveland is a past president of the American Society for Public Administration, and a long-time member of the American Political Science Association. Among numerous board memberships, he serves as vice-chairman of the Atlantic Council and of Global Perspectives in Education, Inc.; as trustee-at-large of the University Corporation for Atmospheric Research; as director of the Institute for the Future; and as director of two foundations, the Joyce Mertz-Gilmore Foundation in New York City and the General Service Foundation in St. Paul, Minnesota. He is the recipient of nineteen honorary degrees, Princeton University's Woodrow Wilson Award, and the U.S. Medal of Freedom, and was the 1981 co-winner of the Prix de Talloires, a Swiss-based international award for "accomplished generalists." His books are listed at the front of this volume.